For more information, contact:

Caitlin O'Hara
University of California Press
2120 Berkeley Way
Berkeley, CA 94704-1012
tel. 510.643-3467
fax 510.642.9737
caitlin.ohara@ucpress.edu

Surfing about Music

ROTH FAMILY FOUNDATION

Music in America Imprint

Michael P. Roth

and Sukey Garcetti

have endowed this

imprint to honor the

memory of their parents,

Julia and Harry Roth,

whose deep love of music

they wish to share

with others.

Surfing about Music

Timothy J. Cooley

UNIVERSITY OF CALIFORNIA PRESS
Berkeley · Los Angeles · London

University of California Press, one of the most
distinguished university presses in the United States,
enriches lives around the world by advancing scholarship
in the humanities, social sciences, and natural sciences. Its
activities are supported by the UC Press Foundation and
by philanthropic contributions from individuals and
institutions. For more information, visit www.ucpress.edu.

University of California Press
Berkeley and Los Angeles, California

University of California Press, Ltd.
London, England

Library of Congress Cataloging-in-Publication Data

Surname, Firstname, birthdate–.
    Title : subtitle / Author.
        p.   cm.
    Includes bibliographical references and index.
    ISBN 978-0-520-27663-5 (cloth : alk. paper) —
ISBN 978-0-520-27664-2 (pbk. : alk. paper) —
ISBN 978-0-520-95721-3 (ebook)
    1. Subject—Subsubject.   2. Subject—Subsubject.
3. Subject—Subsubject.   4. Subject—Subsubject.
I. Title.
    ClassifNumber   PubDate
    DeweyNumber'—dc23   CatalogNumber

Manufactured in the United States of America

23   22   21   20   19   18   17   16   15   14
10   9   8   7   6   5   4   3   2   1

In keeping with a commitment to support
environmentally responsible and sustainable printing
practices, UC Press has printed this book on Rolland
Enviro100, a 100 percent postconsumer fiber paper that
is FSC certified, deinked, processed chlorine-free, and
manufactured with renewable biogas energy. It is
acid-free and EcoLogo certified.

Contents

Figures

Online Examples

The audio and video examples discussed in this book are available at www.ucpress.edu/go/surfing.

4. "Pirati," music and lyrics by Gian Maria Vaglietti, performed by Ex Presidenti and released on their album *Pirati,* Surfer Girl Records, 2005 (www.expresidenti.com). Used by permission of Vaglietti.

5. "The Wolves," lyrics and music by Ben Howard. From *These Waters* (EP 2009). www.benhowardmusic.co.uk. Used by permission of Owain Davies.

6. "H2O," music and lyrics by Kelli Heath, performed by the Girlas and released on their album *Now or Never*, Kototama Productions, 2006, (www.myspace.com/thegirlas). Used by permission of Heath.

7. "Little Brown Gal" (1935, by Don McDiarmid, Lee Wood, and Johnny Noble). Performed by the Manhattan Beach Crew (Mike Goodin, Gene Lyon, Al Lee, and Laurie Armer). Field recording by the author, 2 December 2006. Used with the permission of the performers.

8. "Makaha," by Troy Fernandez, performed by the Kaʻau Crater Boys (Troy Fernandez and Ernie Cruz Jr.) from their *Making Waves* album. Use courtesy of Roy Sakuma Productions, Inc. ℗ 1996 (http://roysakuma.net/).

9. "Golden Orb Weaver," from the *Life Like Liquid* soundtrack, written and performed by Low Pressure Sound System, 2006. www.lowpressureproductions.com. Used with permission.

VIDEO

1. *Slippery When Wet*, Bruce Brown, 1958. Opening scene and credits with music by Bud Shank. 2:58. Courtesy of Bruce Brown Films, LLC (www.BruceBrownFilms.com).

2. *The Endless Summer*, Bruce Brown, 1964. Opening credits with the "Endless Summer Theme" by the Sandals. 2:14. Courtesy of Bruce Brown Films, LLC (www.BruceBrownFilms.com).

3. *The Innermost Limits of Pure Fun*, George Greenough, 1969. The "Coming of the Dawn" excerpt. Music by Farm. 0:59. Used by permission of Greenough, Dennis Dragon, and Denny Aaberg.

4. *Storm Riders*, David Lourie, Dick Hoole, and Jack McCoy, 1981. Segment about pro surfer Marc Richards, accompanied by "Big City Talk," by Marc Hunter, Polygram Records. 2:39. Used by permission of Jack McCoy.

5. *Momentum*, Taylor Steel, 1992. Segment featuring Kelly Slater surfing and "God Song," by Bad Religion. 1:32. Used by permission of Steel and Graffin.

6. *Blue Crush:* Surfing in Mexico, featuring Amel Larrieux singing Towa Tei's "Time after Time." 2:04. Used by permission of Ballard.

7. *Litmus:* Opening scenes from the film, with an original composition, "Rain," by the Val Dusty Experiment. 4:37. Used by permission of Kidman.

8. *The September Sessions:* Segment accompanied by Jack Johnson's "F-Stop Blues." 2:56. Used by permission of Johnson.

Acknowledgments

This book is a collaborative effort, and I own many individuals and institutions a debt of gratitude. I am especially grateful to the individuals who took the time and effort to read and comment on drafts of parts of this book. Jane Schmauss, staff historian at the California Surf Museum, read early versions of several chapters and offered insights based on her years of activity in Southern California's surfing community. Then she dipped into her deep well of contacts when I was struggling to find a few key individuals to request their permissions for illustrations and examples. Ricardo D. Trimillos, Professor Emeritus in Asian Studies and Ethnomusicology, University of Hawai'i at Mānoa, read several versions of the introduction, and chapters 1, 3, 4, and 7 (over half the book), and then fielded frequent questions throughout my writing and revision process. Patrick Moser and C.D. Ka'ala Carmack read chapter 1 concerning historical Hawaiian surfing. Ka'ala continued to entertain my many questions about Hawaiian music throughout the book. My colleague David Novak read and engaged me in a fruitful conversation about chapter 2 on California Surf Music. A special thanks to Lauren Davies, the writer for several recent films about surfing, who selflessly provided valuable comments about my chapter on surf movies even though I do not profile her films. Finally, my wife and fellow academic, Ruth Hellier-Tinoco, read the entire book, some parts multiple times. Though I cannot claim to have been successful in satisfying all of their concerns, nevertheless the comments, corrections, and criticisms from these generous readers made this book much better that it would have been had I been left on my own.

While researching and writing this book, I was very fortunate to have opportunities to present my ongoing work to groups of keen students and faculty in several states and countries, some with strong surfing communities such as in Ireland and Portugal, but others for whom surfing is somewhat exotic, like Germany and the Netherlands. Without fail, however, students and faculty provided valuable perspectives on my work. Campuses where I presented my work include the University of California, Riverside, where Deborah Wong provided especially helpful comments and critiques. I also aired early versions of my work at the University of California, San Diego; San Diego State University; and UCLA. Sonia Seeman and Veit Erlmann provided critiques and encouragement when I presented my work at the University of Texas, Austin. At the University of Hawaiʻi, Mānoa, professors Ricardo Trimillos, Fred Lau, Jane Freeman Moulin, Jay Junker, Victoria Holt Takamine, and Barbara B. Smith were especially helpful with their knowledge of Hawaiian cultural practices and history. I am grateful to Jonathan M. Dueck, who invited me to present a virtual lecture to the Franklin Humanities Institute Faculty Working Group on Sports at Duke University. Jonathan also organized several paper panels on music and sports at for the Society for Ethnomusicology's annual meetings in which I was privileged to take part. Presenting my work at my alma matter, Brown University, in the company of some of my faculty mentors, Rose Subotnik and Jeff Todd Titon, was a distinct honor.

In continental Europe I was invited to present my research at the Ethnography Museum of Neuchâtel, Switzerland; Groningen University and Utrecht University, the Netherlands; Universidade Nova de Lisboa, Portugal; and at the Hochschule für Musik und Theater, Rostock, Germany. I am especially grateful for the encouragement and helpful suggestions of Yann Laville in Switzerland, Barbara Titus and Kristin McGee in the Netherlands, Frederick J. Moehn and Salwa Castelo-Branco in Portugal, and Britta Sweers in Germany. In the United Kingdom, I presented my work at Oxford University; Sheffield University; Goldsmiths, University of London; City University, London; and Queens University, Belfast. At these universities, my key interlocutors were Martin Stokes, Anna Stirr, Jonathan Stock, Barley Norton, Stephen Cottrell, Keith Negus, Laudan Nooshin, and Suzel Ana Reily. The Republic of Ireland has a lively and growing surfing community, and I had the pleasure of presenting my work there on three different occasions: at University College, Cork; at the main campus of the University of Limerick; and later, as the keynote speaker for the International Council for Traditional Music, Ireland, held at Mary Immaculate College, University of Limerick. I benefited from the comments and observations of several keen surfers on these Irish campuses, as well as faculty colleagues Juniper Hill, Colin Quigley, Helen Phelan, and Tony Langlois. All of these scholars and their students added depth to—and helped me identify the limits of—my understanding of surfers as an emerging global affinity group.

My home institution, the University of California, Santa Barbara, granted me a sabbatical to work on this book, which I took in England. This may seem like an odd move for someone researching and writing about surfing, but have a good look at a map. The United Kingdom encompasses several islands that are washed by north Atlantic swells. There I had the great pleasure of meeting Brian Page and "Turbo" Tim, who showed me the surf spots in southern England, and Scotty and Aaran Williams, who taught me about surfing on the Isle of Wight. In Cornwall I had the pleasure of interviewing British surfing musicians Ben Howard and Neil Halstead, as well as Roger Mansfield, author of *The Surfing Tribe: A History of Surfing in Britain*. My spirit benefited from the camaraderie that I experienced in these British surfing scenes.

At the University of California, Santa Barbara, I am very grateful to Dean David Marshall for supporting my sabbatical leave, and for providing research funds. The Interdisciplinary Humanities Center on campus provided the first forum for me to present my early research on the topic, and subsequently granted me release time from teaching so that I could focus on research and writing. The Academic Senate also generously provided me with travel funds for several fieldwork trips. This project would not have happened with their support. Here at my home campus I also received sustaining intellectual support from my departmental colleagues, notably Stefanie Tcharos, who help me theorize notions of genre. I also wish to acknowledge Dick Hebdidge and Holly E. Unruh, former director and associate director, respectively, of the Interdisciplinary Humanities Center, who offered support and insightful comments about popular music in California; and sociologist Jon Cruz, who was a sounding board for ideas throughout the process. Finally at UCSB was a "posse" of surfing professors, staff, and graduate students who formed a core group with which to share ideas: Kip Fulbeck, Hank Pitcher, Stuart Sweeney, Michael Petracca, Judy Bauerlein, Ali Bjerke, John Lee, and Malcolm Guart-

Williams. Thanks to you all for creating an intellectually stimulating and supportive community.

Other institutions that became important locations in my research include the Surfing Heritage Foundation and Museum, San Clemente, California, which welcomed me to their well-stocked library and archives. Barry Haun, Curator and Creative Director, was particularly helpful. The Bishop Museum Archives in Honolulu is a key source for any project involving surfing culture and history. I have already mentioned the California Surf Museum, Oceanside, especially Jane Schmauss. The International Surfing Museum, Huntington Beach, California, was always a welcoming site; I am especially grateful to JoAnn Beasley, who up until her death welcomed me and thousands of others into the museum every year. Goldsmiths, University of London, became my research home when in England.

I am very pleased that the editors and Editorial Board of the University of California Press saw some merit in this project and agreed to publish it. I am especially thankful for the editorial guidance of Kim Robinson, the Regional Editor, who first provided substantial comments on my book proposal; Mary C. Francis, the Executive Editor of Music and Cinema Studies, who took the book on; Kim Hogeland, the Editorial Coordinator, who was both efficient and personable; Rose Vekony, the project editor, who appears to have read every word of the book; and Carl Walesa, a freelance copyeditor who took a close look at every word. Editors put up with a lot, and rarely get the credit due them. I feel very blessed to have had such an excellent editorial team. I am also grateful for the anonymous peer-review and Editorial Board readers for UC Press, who provided challenging and ultimately supportive comments on the book manuscript.

I wish to acknowledge a core group of individuals who were invaluable links to significant communities of people. I thank David Weisenthal, for introducing me key members of the San Onofre Surfing Club, including Craig Ephraim, three-time president of the club. Both David and Craig helped me sort out who was who in various photos, and they did their best to keep my facts in order. I also thank Bob "Jake" Jacobs, "Honeybaby" Gwen Waters, and Fred Thomas, who each sat with me for long interviews about the history of the San Onofre scene. Dennis Dragon, member of Farm, a band discussed in chapter 3, as well as the infamous Southern California band Surf Punks, has been for years now an affable correspondent fielding many questions, and even guest-lecturing in one of my university classes—much to the delight of my students. Gaston Georis of the Sandals met with me several times to talk about his music since the early 1960s and also graced my university classes. Zach Gill facilitated a number of key introductions, fielded countless questions about some of today's most popular surfing musicians, and gave generously to me and my students with several guest visits to my classes. Andrew Kidman and Andrew Crockett became essential links to surfing communities in Australia. Finally, Aaron J. Salā, Assistant Professor of Hawaiian Music and Ethnomusicology at the University of Hawai'i at Mānoa, generously organized audio recordings of Hawaiian mele for this book that illustrate key themes in chapter 1.

Finally I wish to acknowledge individuals who contributed to this project by allowing me to interview them formally, or informally, on the beach, in the surfing lineup waiting for waves, or wherever we may have exchanged ideas, but whom I have not for various reasons named in this book. It is indeed unfair that so many people made this book possible, but that my name alone is found on the cover. Thank you, co-researchers, named and unnamed. All that is good in this book is due to your efforts, while the mistakes and misconceptions remain solely my own.

Introduction

Riding a wave—surfing—is a cultural practice. Surfing is a deeply experiential act of playing with the power of wind that has been transferred to water to form ocean swells. Sliding down the face of a moving aqueous mound that is forced upward as it approaches shore, a surfer engages with the forces of gravity and water tension. Using techniques handed down through countless generations of coastal dwellers, the surfer harnesses the wave's energy to move over water in a dance across that liminal zone between open ocean and wave-lapped land. Surfing is a balancing act on a watery tightrope stretched between a silently rising swell and a thundering breaking wave. Yet no matter how much skill, strength, and grace the surfer displays, no matter how small or large the wave that propels the surfer, in the end surfing leaves no trace on the water's surface. Wave riding creates no lasting product save a memory, a kinesthetic impression.

In this way surfing is like music, for sound waves vanish the instant they are heard. Both surfing and musicking[1] are ephemeral cultural practices that have no quantifiable results or functions other than the feelings they may engender, and the meanings given to them by people. Surfing and musicking require much more time and energy than is reasonable if their purpose is to achieve basic material needs. We clearly engage in them for other reasons. Yet even if we believe passionately that surfing and music are imbued with great meaning, we may not always be able to articulate what that meaning is. Let's sing another song . . . I'm going to catch one more wave . . .

This book is about surfers and the types of music that they create and associate with surfing. But I need to be clear about which surfers I am attempting to interpret and represent. Surfers form a global affinity group, but as with any group of people, no statement or claim can be true for every individual in that group. We could conceive of surfers forming any number of distinct affinity groups globally. The stories I tell here are illustrative of surfing communities that I have access to: primarily cosmopolitan surfers from California, Hawai'i, Australia, Italy, and the United Kingdom, with much more limited input by surfers from other points on the globe. These surfers are global—collectively they have surfed at the best surfing beaches around the world—but they still represent relatively affluent cosmopolitanism from North America and Europe more than the cultural sphere on any given beach in Indonesia, for example. To put it another way, dozens of surfers—some of them very influential in my posited global surfing affinity group—have contributed to this book, but that still leaves millions of surfers worldwide whose voices are not represented here.

This is a deeply personal book. I have aspired to ride waves and to make music since I was a child, and being a surfer and a musician has been an important part of my self-identity since my early teen years. Therefore, readers will notice that my authorial voice changes from time to time from that of writer-scholar to that of surfer-musician. In particular, I shift to the first-person plural pronouns *we* and *us* occasionally and talk to the in-group tribe of surfers—a community I invite you to join if only for a moment. Come in . . . the water is nice.

The critical scholar in me knows that the "I" and "we" here have very limited experience in the context of globalized surfing. I grew up surfing in Virginia and Florida before moving to California. I also spent about a decade living in Illinois, where I would surf in the chilly waters of Lake Michigan. Once I encountered another surfer at my local Chicago-area break, but only once. Beyond the mainland United States, I have had the pleasure of surfing in Mexico, Hawai'i, Australia, and the United Kingdom. Yet my experience with surfing—and with musicking—is individual. My experience is also highly mediated. As with every surfer-musician I interviewed for this book, my experiences are influenced by commercial interests. By this I mean that even the private pleasure of riding a wave is not pure and unaffected by the entertainment industry and other commercial concerns that use surfing as a marketing tool. For example, I am told what I should feel when catching a wave by an old Beach Boys song, just as I am reminded by the latest issue of *Surfer* magazine that I would look much better in a new pair of boardshorts.

This book asks two interrelated questions: First and foremost, how is music used to mediate the experience of surfing? And second, how does surfing, and changing notions of what a surfing lifestyle might be, affect surfers' musical practices? Through my interviews and analysis, I find that music is necessary for making sense of surfing, for communicating important information about surfing, and for creating a collective space where surfers communicate together something of the experience of surfing. All of these uses of music by surfers help to form and define surfers as an affinity group.

WHAT DOES MUSIC HAVE TO DO WITH SURFING?

In a feature story in *Surfer* magazine, Brendon Thomas wrote, "The connection between music and surfing is undeniable," and *Surfgirl Magazine* editor Louise Searle described how "[s]urfing and music go hand in hand: like Fred Astaire and Ginger Rogers, strawberries and cream, and vodka and tonic—they're all better together."[2] Surfing has even been (incorrectly) called the first sport with its own music.[3] The notion that music and surfing somehow naturally go together seems to be gaining traction.

Four recent films offer very interesting takes on the topic of surfing and musicking.[4] The first is *Pounding Surf! A Drummer's Guide to Surf Music,* produced in 2006 by musicians Bob Caldwell, Paul Johnson, and others. Though this film was first envisioned as a primer on playing drums for instrumental rock, it evolved into an elaborate filmic history of early 1960s California surf music and its ties to Southern California surfing culture. Also released in 2006 was Australian surfer Dave Rastovich's *Life Like Liquid,* consisting entirely of footage of surfers improvising music together, interspersed with clips of the same people surfing and musing about the relationship between musicking and surfing. In 2008 two additional films were released on the subject. *Live: A Music and Surfing Experience,* produced by California-based surfing film maker David Parsa, is a wide-ranging look at music and surfing that contains brief comments by leading professional surfers, surfing industry icons, and popular musicians. The fourth film, *Musica Surfica,* by Australian surfer and filmmaker Mick Sowry, is a curious and at times perplexing meditation on Australian Chamber Orchestra director Richard Tognetti's genre-expanding violin playing interspersed with Derek

Hynd's quiver-expanding challenge to design and ride finless surfboards. Taken together, these four films spin an intriguing tale about the interweaving of the human performative practices of surfing and music-making. The first sticks close to the named genre Surf Music and captures a key moment in the history of surfing's reinvention in the twentieth century. (I capitalize the term *Surf Music* to indicate that I am referring to a specific genre and not all music associated with surfing.) The second is an extended experiment to see what would happen if one cloistered surfing musicians together for some days. The third is an expansive survey of music performed and endorsed by influential modern surfers. The fourth reminds us that both surfing and music-making cannot be limited to the narrow practices celebrated in surfing contests and by popular media.

Music and surfing are mixed and matched in many other ways. Festivals that combine some aspect of surfing and music are popping up around the world in obvious locations like Hawai'i and California, but also in places such as the United Kingdom, Portugal, France, Italy, and Slovenia. Surfing magazines routinely list professional surfers' favorite music, review music CDs, promote concerts and music festivals, and publish feature articles on surfing musicians.[5] Surfing brands such as Quiksilver promote musicians, include music-related products in their lines, or, in the case of clothing company Rhythm, imply music in their brand name. Much of this is business as usual. Rare is the festival without music, and commercial industries long ago figured out that music was a compelling way to boost and sometimes define their brand images. While this phenomenon is not unique to surfing, the use of music by the surfing industry tells us something about how the industry interacts with and manipulates surfing communities.

More striking, however, is the surprising number of former and even current professional surfers who have second careers as popular musicians. This includes, most notably, the eight-time platinum-album-selling surfer-musician Jack Johnson, from Hawai'i; three-time world surfing champion Tom Curren, from California; two-time world longboard champion Beau Young, from Australia; two-time women's world longboard champion Daize Shayne, from Hawai'i; free surfer Donavon Frankenreiter, from California (fig. 1); and other surfer-musicians featured in chapter 5 of this book. There are also professional musicians of all sorts who are passionate about and draw inspiration from surfing, including popular musicians Eddie Vedder, Jackson Browne, Tristan Prettyman, Ben Harper, Chris Isaak, Brandon Boyd of Incubus, and Metallica's Kirk Hammett and Robert Trujillo.

FIGURE 1. Surfwear company Billabong's "Only a Surfer Knows the Feeling" ad, featuring surfer-musician Donavon Frankenreiter, that appeared in the Fall 2010 issue of the *Surfer's Journal*. Reprinted with the permission of Burleigh Point, Ltd. dba Billabong USA.

But is there anything inherently musical about surfing? Is the relationship between music and surfing—taken for granted and celebrated by insider surfing media and films—real and meaningful, or is it a myth propagated by that periodically revived genre labeled Surf Music from the early 1960s (the Beach Boys: but more to the point, that "King of the Surf Guitar" Dick Dale)? Or are these the wrong questions?

They are the wrong questions. Rather than asking if the connection made by some musical surfers between musicking and surfing is real or mythical, it is more satisfying (not to mention ethnographically appropriate and productive) to accept those connections as meaningful cultural constructions that must be taken seriously. Surfing is a cultural practice; its development, style, and, ultimately, meaning are all expressions of human creativity. Making and listening to music are also cultural practices that, like surfing, are expressive of the human condition. Yes, listening to music is an expressive practice; it is an activity not that far removed from making musical sounds oneself. In many ways music is in the listening. The same sound may be heard by one person as music and by a second as noise. Choosing what music we listen to, get into, dance to, worship to, compose, and share with our friends is one of the ways we create who we are as individuals and as groups. The decision to play in the water, to lie, kneel, or stand on a surfboard, the riding styles we imagine and achieve are also part of who we are as individuals and groups. We can spin this out indefinitely: the size and shape of the surfboard you choose suggest something about your style and skills (or aspirations), as do the color and cut of your boardshorts or bikini. Likewise, the instrument you play and the outfit you wear when performing suggest ideas about the sounds you intend to make even before you begin making musical sounds.

Let's stick to surfing and music generally for the moment. Any individual's and group's ideas about meaningful relationships between these cultural practices and others form part of that individual's and that group's cultural identity. It is part of who they are and the identities that they create for themselves. When an individual proclaims that he or she makes music this or that way because of religious beliefs or ethnic heritage, we tend to take that seriously. Surfing may or may not hold similar cultural weight for any given wave rider, but we owe it to surfers to take seriously the connections they make between their musicking and surfing. The music that surfers associate with surfing is key to what surfing is, or rather the many things that surfing is, as well as to who surfers are and aspire to be. This is what this book is about. This is why making music about surfing and surfing about music is serious business.

AFFINITY, COMMUNITY, AND THE SURFING LIFESTYLE

Since the essence of surfing is one person dancing with the power of an ocean (and occasionally smaller bodies of water), the sport lends itself to individualization. Yet while a modern trope is that the surfer would just as soon surf alone, surfers (like all other humans) seek communities of like-minded people. Sometimes in some societies this may begin by surfers saying what they are not. As Belinda Wheaton notes in the introduction to her book *Understanding Lifestyle Sports,* surfers and participants in other lifestyle sports may deliberately seek to challenge existing orders by being transgressive.[6] Yet even transgression seeks company. Challenging and transgressive behaviors soon form the basis for a new identity group and even a community of sorts.

Surfing did not start out as transgressive behavior; it originated with seafaring islanders who probably first enjoyed the boost from waves when they returned to shore with a vessel full of fish. Before Europeans and North Americans sailed to Hawai'i, surfing was practiced and celebrated by all segments of Hawaiian society. In the early nineteenth century, Calvinist missionaries to Hawai'i instilled the still-prevalent view that surfing was unproductive and a waste of time, necessitated nudity, and was thus sinful. Much less common in Hawai'i at the turn of the nineteenth into the twentieth century than it was a century earlier, surfing quietly took root in California and then spread around the world, but it carried with it some of the taint of transgression given it by missionaries in Hawai'i. Of course that hint of danger and rebellion suited some midcentury surfers, and later became an attractive (to some) quality of skateboarding and snowboarding, both descendent board-sports first developed by California surfers. Globalized surfing today continues to cultivate the image of danger, independence, and subcultural edginess.

Embraced by some but resisted by others, a term frequently used by surfers today to refer to a surfing community is *tribe*.[7] The term captures some of the tensions between individualism and a desire or even need for community. *Tribe* sounds a bit out of place in many modern societies, and suggests a collective that is somehow different from—and slightly threatening to—any given mass society. A tribe is only slightly more respectable than a gang in popular usage. Yet *tribe* also suggests desirable qualities. A tribe is inclusive (women, men, and children of all ages are welcome and needed in a tribe), has some sense of heritage and history, and of course has rituals. An e-mail message I recently received from the California Surf Museum promised such a tribal ritual. It began: "Join the tribe—come celebrate *Surfer* magazine's 50 years . . . " The celebration would be a gathering of the tribal leaders, yet even lowly villagers like me were invited. By attending the celebration, one could ritually reaffirm one's own membership in the surfing affinity group—the tribe—and at the same time distinguish oneself for a moment from the rest of society.

Surfing is all about balance. Navigating the inherent individuality of surfing itself and the human need to form communities requires balance. Any discussion of surfing communities must seek to balance the contradictions and contrasts that make them what they are. In his book *Dancing the Wave*, Jean-Étienne Poirier writes with poetic power of these contradictions: "Surfing is the center of a sphere where some values evolve in one direction while others move in the opposite: sometimes the image of surfing is gentle and romantic, with a setting sun and surfers with magnificent smiles; sometimes it is war-like and violent, with illustrations of titanic waves that leave no room for refinement and delicate dance moves. . . . Because opposing forces together create gravity, surfing remains in motion."[8] Surfing communities need the solitary surfer seeking empty waves,[9] as well as the local surfer who surfs the same spot whenever the waves are up with the same group of friends, and even the surfer who rarely gets wet but who dreams of the perfect ride. All are part of a surfing tribe; the internal contrasts and oppositions are part of what keeps that community vital.

Frankly, I also need there to be some sort of vital community for this book to make any sense. To approach music as an ethnomusicologist, I need a group of people making and consuming music. As the prefix *ethno-* suggests, the discipline of ethnomusicology is very concerned with group identities, often defined as *ethnicities*. My study of music and surfing is in part a critique of my discipline's obsession with the increasingly problematic divisions of individuals into politically defined ethnic categories.[10] The posited global affinity group of surfers that I am writing about here challenges the sorts of subjects that make up the stock-in-trade of ethnomusicology: groups that form around shared heritage, religion, regions, occupations, and so forth. Here I find more useful recent theories of elective communities—from "cultural cohorts" to "affinity groups" and "lifestyle sports."[11]

Surfing is arguably the prototypical lifestyle sport—a sport that can be distinguished from what are called in sports studies "achievement sports." Achievement sports are those typically taught in institutions (for example, football, rugby, baseball, track, and wrestling), and they emphasize teamwork and competition. Lifestyle sports are also called many things, including "alternative sports," "new sports,"[12] and, especially in the United States, "extreme sports," as promoted in ESPN's X Games.[13] Windsurfer and sports scholar Belinda Wheaton prefers the term *lifestyle sport* because in her ethnographic research she found that this is the term that participants themselves used and that they actively "sought a lifestyle that was distinctive, often alternative, and that gave them a particular and exclusive social *identity*."[14] My ethnographic work with surfers agrees with Wheaton's—play (playing music, sports play, and so forth) and lifestyle choices are ultimately about core issues of identity. For example, surfing musician Brandon Boyd of the band Incubus does not like to consider surfing a sport but rather a lifestyle.[15] Similar debates about whether surfing is a sport or an art have been going on since at least the 1950s.

To take on a surfing lifestyle is a voluntary proposition; it is to enter an *affinity group*. Affinity groups form around volunteer participation in cultural practices rather than through the genetic, heritage, or location ties (sometimes called "involuntary affiliations") that drive most discourses on ethnicity. In some cases, affinity groups may become ethnicities over time; for example, certain religious groups tend toward this progression. Other affinity groups briefly burn brightly and then disappear or move into a subcultural scene. Individuals may move into affinity groups at will, perhaps lingering for some time and then moving away, reframing their identity with other affinity groups, or even as former members of an earlier group: "I used to be a surfer . . ." Surfing is demanding, however, in that a reasonably high level of fitness must be maintained if one is to participate. As Wheaton notes, with most lifestyle sports active participation is key. Still, even deep involvement in a sport may be just a part of any individual's multiple identities. This is an important quality of what I am calling affinity groups. An individual may move in and out of several affinity groups, even daily. For example, seeking job security, I hid my identity as a surfer from my colleagues in the music department during my first years as a professor at the University of California, Santa Barbara, but then would surreptitiously shift into my role as a surfer as I walked the few hundred feet from my office to Campus Point to go surfing. As we all do in our everyday lives, I performed different versions of myself—or foregrounded certain identities—depending on the demands of the moment.[16]

There are three primary characteristics of *affinity groups* as I am using the term. First, a cultural practice draws the group together: a particular type of musical practice, a penchant for dog shows, a love of gardening, or a singular dedication to participating in a sport. Second, the most salient feature of an affinity group is that the individuals in the group are connected by desire--not by obligation born of family ties, religion, place of origin, shared history, or anything else. Yet more often than not such groups invent histories, origin myths, family ties, and even a sense of spiritual connection that approaches religion. Third, since participation is driven by desire, it is also voluntary and often temporary, as already noted: members may leave the group at some stage, or move in and out of the group. One can imagine cases where desire leads to voluntary participation that then becomes involuntary through the compulsion of addiction or even economic necessity. Thus even affinity must be seen as a sliding, fluid notion, perhaps a point on a continuum somewhere between attraction and obligation or addiction.

THE FEELING OF SURFING: ONLY A SURFER KNOWS

It is an article of faith among many surfers that only a surfer knows the feeling of, well, surfing. The phrase "only a surfer knows the feeling" has been used as a successful advertisement slogan by the Billabong surfwear company, and is uttered by surfers regularly (much to the delight of Billabong; see fig. 1).[17] Both my conversations with surfers and items written by surfers reveal that the meaning of the phrase goes beyond the tautology that only surfers know what it feels like to surf. Surfers describe feelings of euphoria from surfing, and this feeling is often spoken of in mystical terms: they speak of its healing power, and some find surfing spiritually redemptive. Steven Kotler takes a long look at the feelings of euphoria and spiritual awareness that surfing generates in his book *West of Jesus: Surfing, Science and the Origin of Belief*.[18] He discovered that similar feelings of euphoria and spiritual awareness were generated by a range of extreme experiences, not just by surfing, but he starts and ends with surfing, as I do here.

The feeling of surfing is summarized by some surfers with two related but distinct terms: *stoke* and *flow*. According to Matt Warshaw's *Encyclopedia of Surfing*, the term *stoke* comes to English from the seventeenth-century Dutch word *stok*, meaning to rearrange logs on a fire or add fuel to increase the heat. Surfers adopted the term in California in the 1950s. As its derivation suggests, it means "to be fired up, excited, happy, full of passion." As a description of emotional experience, *stoke* is complemented by another term, *flow*, suggesting an obvious kinesthetic play of moving bodies—the movement of water and the movement of the surfer through or over water. But flow goes beyond the obvious and into the realm of optimal experience, as theorized by Mihaly Csikszentmihalyi in his book *Flow: The Psychology of Optimal Experience*.[19] As Csikszentmihalyi explains, the mental state of flow is achieved through intense focus and concentration so that distractions disappear and one feels in harmony with one's surroundings and oneself. One can experience flow when doing any number of things (including the antithesis of surfing for most surfers: working). However, I suggest that three definitive qualities of surfing create flow, and the interrelated feelings of stoke. These qualities help explain why so many surfers try to express or even replicate that surfing feeling (emotional and embodied) with music. These qualities are risk-taking, waiting, and submission.

The first definitive quality of surfing is risk-taking. The cultural act of surfing takes place in the highly volatile liminal zone between open ocean and dry land (see fig. 2). One rides a wave along a thin line of transition between a harmless swell and the dangerous impact zone of a crashing wave; the zone of bliss is balanced between safety and despair.

FIGURE 2. The liminal zone of surfing. Photograph by Chris Burkard (burkardphoto.com).

In that zone, one generally does not make music; even conversation is minimal. Instead, it is a place of waiting and watching for the choice swell that will become the crashing wave of a surfer's desire. Once a surfer has caught the wave and is up and riding it, she or he often compounds the risks. Experience-enhancing maneuvers, such as seeking speed in the steepest sections of a braking wave, or even stalling to place oneself in the volatile barrel of a wave that pitches its breaking lip out over the surfer, puts the surfer at risk of a violent wipeout. It is much safer, if less exhilarating, to ride well ahead of the breaking whitewater, and to kick-out (exit) the wave early. And many surfers seek ever-larger waves that occasionally prove deadly for even the most experienced.

Waiting is a second quality that defines surfing, and perhaps surfers. Surfers must wait for swells, preferably generated several thousands of miles away so that the strong winds that created them are not present when the waves reach the surfers' beach. No beach offers waves on demand. In his book *Dancing the Wave,* Jean-Étienne Poirier wrote that "[t]he sea has no schedule; it must be taken when it offers itself. It has its moods, and it is the surfer who must yield and accommodate them."[20] Thus, like a coy lover, the sea plays with its surfer courtiers, withholding favors or offering them at awkward times that demand sacrifice. No wonder some surfers will cancel appointments, miss work, and skip classes when the waves are good—a tendency celebrated in surfing brand Protest's "Drop-It-All" ad campaign (fig. 3). In my own experience, surfers struggle to balance school, jobs, relationships, families, and domestic duties with their love for the fickle ocean. Still, there is some truth in the stereotypes of surfers who are unreliable when the waves are good. The unpredictability of surfable waves does distinguish surfing from many other sports where one might schedule an outing unless the unpredictable happens (we will ride bikes Friday afternoon, unless it rains . . .). Instead, the surfer waits for the unpredictable, the unusual—for most places—weather conditions that produce good waves;. The surfer waits.[21]

When the waves are good, the surfer waits again. Only the inexperienced surfer rushes into the ocean upon arrival. The seasoned surfer knows to wait—wait and watch. Read the pattern of waves and wait for the optimal time to enter the water and to paddle out through the dangerous impact zone to the spot where you anticipate catching a wave. Once outside, wait for a good *set* (a group of waves; ocean swells usually arrive in sets of three to five waves). Rarely is the first wave of a set the best. Less experienced surfers will scramble for the first wave,

FIGURE 3. "Drop-It-All Sessions" ad campaign by surfing brand Protest that appeared in *Huck* 3, no. 15 (2009).

FIGURE 4. Surfers in Lake Superior waiting for the right wave. Photograph by Shawn Malone, LakeSuperiorPhoto.com.

clearing the *lineup* (a group of surfers in position to catch a wave) for those who wait. When other surfers are out, one might need to wait one's turn in the complexly negotiated lineup. If you don't find your place in this set of waves, wait for the next. There's always another wave for those who wait (fig. 4).

A third quality in surfing is submission. The ocean is the surfer's mistress/master and teacher. The wise surfer asks for permission to surf and never makes demands. Legendary Hawaiian surfer Paul Strauch says that he always pauses by the ocean before entering the water as he seeks permission to surf. Even if the waves are very good, if he does not sense that permission is granted, he turns around and leaves.[22] Generally, however, when the waves are good, the surfer submits to the call of the ocean and, once in the water, submits again to its unbounded power. As mentioned above, a surfer must put himself or herself in harm's way in order to catch and ride the wave. One must submit to the wave's power, then work with—play with—that power to achieve the optimal ride or flow. The same is true when one falls while surfing— when one wipes out—especially in large waves that can twist and turn a surfer, holding her or him down for long periods. Every experienced surfer knows that there is no sense in fighting the ocean. When it is ready, the ocean will release you, and you will float or swim to the surface for air. The best survival technique is to submit, relax, and wait.

Perhaps for these reasons, surfing leads some to become contemplative—waiting for signs, listening to nature, thinking about and submitting to mysterious forces. In return, many surfers seem to find healing and even redemptive qualities in surfing, both physical and psychological. This is a common (though hardly universal) theme in surfing literature.[23] The contemplative quality of surfing also leads many to talk about surfing in spiritual terms. The first decade of the twenty-first century saw an impressive output of books on surfing and spirituality.[24] Comments and even feature articles about surfing and spirituality also regularly crop up in surfing magazines, such as the article in *Surfer,* titled "Is God a Goofyfoot," in which Brad Melekian asks a Catholic priest, a Christian pastor, a Jewish rabbi, and a Buddhist monk if surfing itself might be a religion. (His conclusion is that it is not, but that it can be a powerful spiritual and meditative practice.)[25]

In my experience as a surfer, and in talking with other surfers, I've concluded that those who keep at it for some years tend to find the practice of riding waves to be a deeply but inexplicably satisfying experience. Personally, surfing adjusts my attitude, removes anxiety, and provides a level perspective on dry-land problems and pleasures. A Christian myself, I have a practice of surfing after church Sunday mornings, a tradition I only half-jokingly call the sacred ritual of the post-Communion surf. Sometimes this sacred ritual is more spiritually satisfying than Mass itself. (I hope my priest never reads this.)

The contemplative possibilities of surfing may also lead some surfers, though not all, to seek musical expression. Other surfers are more focused on the adrenaline boost surfing can provide, and this inspires their musicking (something that Dick Dale claims, as I will show in chapter 2). There are many reasons and ways that surfing might encourage musicking among some, but in most cases, surfing and musicking are enacted in different spaces/places/locations. On dry land—even on damp, wave-swept beaches—there is only memory of the adrenaline rush, the search for oneness, the healing power, the spiritual redemption, and so forth that motivates the surfer. There on the beach surfers try to recapture some of the feeling of being in the water, surfing. They swap stories about their best rides, tell lies, exchange knowledge, reenact their moves, and, as we shall see, make music. Therefore, the place of musicking is a place of removal, away from the place of surfing itself. Connections between surfing and musicking must always be tenuous, changing, fluid.

SURFING AND MUSIC: APPROACHES TAKEN IN THIS BOOK

A key ethnomusicological tenet is that musicality is an integral part of group imagination and invention. Though the affinity group *surfers* is fluid and as fickle as the surf during a rapidly changing tide, its individual members do share the core experience of riding waves. Water may be the universal solvent, but it also binds us all. In my look at the musical practices of surfers in locations around the world, I keep returning to this shared experience that binds surfers. And where I may theorize the global, I also keep it real by grounding my interpretation in the real-life stories of individual members of this community. This book presents a series of case studies that explore different ways that surfers—and sometimes nonsurfers—associate the cultural practices of surfing and musicking. Along the way, I also hope to expand ethnomusicological thinking about the many ways musical practices may be integral to human socializing, and perhaps to being human in the first place.

The first three chapters are historical and move chronologically, with some overlap. I start with the earliest known music associated with surfing—Hawaiian chant—and continue through Hawaiian popular music during the first half of the twentieth century. I then move to the named genre Surf Music. Third, I analyze the music used in surf movies to see what they can tell us about surfing and musicking from the mid–twentieth century to the present.

Chapter 1, "Trouble in Paradise: The History and Reinvention of Surfing," considers the origins of surfing and music about surfing in Hawai'i. The passage of time does not enable me to speak directly with pre-revival-era surfers, so I rely on Hawaiian legends and myths, early written accounts of surfing (most by Europeans and North Americans, but some by Hawaiians), and, most significantly for my work, Hawaiian *mele* (chants). A number of mele about surfing from the eighteenth and early nineteenth centuries are the earliest examples of surfing music. Through these voices from the past, we see that surfing was ubiquitous in pre-revival Hawaiian society, practiced by women and men, girls and boys, and though we know more about royal surfers since it is their surfing mele that survive, we also know that common folk surfed, too.

Thus it is not surprising that there were chants and dances, rituals, and even temples associated with surfing in Hawai'i.

Popular Hawaiian songs from the first half of the twentieth century reveal a changing role for surfing, especially as tourists began to visit Hawai'i and to learn to surf themselves. Surfing spread from Hawai'i to the rest of the coastal world, and at least during the first half of the twentieth century, emerging surfing affinity groups tended to look to Hawai'i for appropriate cultural practices, such as music and dance, to express community. *Hula* (dance or visual poetry) and *hapa haole* (half-foreign) songs from Hawai'i were and still are practiced by surfers on California's beaches, for example. Yet surfing also changed as more and more people traveled to Hawai'i, and as surfing was exported from the islands. The first stop for globalizing surfing was California, and I show how the interaction between Hawai'i and California led to the reinvention of surfing in the twentieth century. No longer the ubiquitous cultural practice of pre-revival Hawai'i, what I call *New Surfing* became hypermasculine, and would be increasingly driven by commercial interests.

Chapter 2, "'Surf Music' and the California Surfing Boom: New Surfing Gets a Sound," picks up the story in California, the first stop for globalized New Surfing. Most conversations that pair the words *surf* and *music* are focused on two related genres of music that came to be called *Surf Music:* instrumental rock à la Dick Dale and the Del-Tones, and songs about surfing à la the Beach Boys. Both genres emerged in the early 1960s, and they do capture something of the history of surfing, especially in California at that time. What Surf Music captures is the mass popularization of surfing that resulted from new technologies of mass-producing lighter boards, not unlike the mass production of electric guitars by Fender, a Southern California company that became the preferred brand of surf rock bands. Surf Music encouraged the global spread of surfing itself and engendered enduring myths about Southern California and a newly white, youthful, and masculine surfing lifestyle. However, naming a popular genre of music *surf* was a problem for some surfers at the time, and became a problem for many who desired to make music about surfing subsequently. This second issue has only recently been resolved with the popularity of a number of surfing musicians.

If music on the beaches of Hawai'i and Southern California is a good index of surfing trends in the first half of the twentieth century, the music used for surf movies is an even better index for the second half of that century. In chapter 3, "Music in Surf Movies," I survey the music used in a selection of surf movies that were particularly influential in shaping the musical practices of significant groups of surfers. I begin in the 1950s with the first surf movies for which we have the original musical soundtracks and then move through the formative boom years of the 1960s, to the VHS era, and then on to the present-day digital formats. With these movies I show what music was popular among at least some surfers before the named genre Surf Music existed, how some surfers responded to that genre, and the musical directions surfers have taken since the 1960s. The music used in surfing movies illustrates some of the diversity of musicking among surfers, but it also reveals distinct trends. For example, I show that surf-movie production emerged out of New Surfing's new cultural centers: California and Australia. Surf movies, made by surfers for surfers, were a powerful tool for spreading ideas about surfing culture, especially music, to a growing and globalizing number of surfers.

The next three chapters are focused on the present or near present, and draw from my ethnographic work with living surfing musicians. Chapter 4, "Two Festivals and Three Genres of Music," is a comparative study of two festivals, one celebrating a genre of music and the other featuring a surfing contest with an attached music festival. Both festivals took place in the summer of 2009 in Europe, and each represented very different approaches to music and surfing. The first festival took place in Italy and centered on the named genre Surf Music. However, there I discovered that the musicians most engaged with surfing were not playing Surf Music but were covering Jack Johnson songs or writing new songs about surfing in a punk rock style. The second festival was in Newquay, "the capital of British surfing," located 260 miles southwest of London on the wave-grabbing coast of the Cornish peninsula. The music at this festival, which started as a professional surfing contest, tended toward two poles described to me as "mellow and surfy" on the one hand and "heavy and punky" on the other. The two festivals nicely frame three broad genres or styles of music that have emerged as key to my project: Surf Music, punk rock, and generally acoustic singer-songwriter music favored by an influential group of prominent surfers.

Chapter 5, "The Pro Surfer Sings," asks how it is that some of the most influential and competitive surfers have managed second careers as musicians. It may be, as some surfer-musicians have suggested, an extension of their efforts at expression. Whereas for many of us just catching and riding a wave is an accomplishment (perhaps similar to getting through a piano étude without too many mistakes), the truly skilled surfer is able to move beyond the mechanics of the sport and use the ocean as a canvas for expression. It may also be that, since at least the mid–twentieth century, there has been a myth that surfing is a musical sport--a myth that first led me to this project. This chapter shows that musicking can be an effective way for professional surfers to expand their personal brand. Clearly the surfing body is a desirable commodity in the entertainment industry, and has been since the original Beachboys—the Waikīkī Beachboys, from Waikīkī, Hawai'i— appeared in the first half of the twentieth century.

Chapter 6, "The Soul Surfer Sings," returns to a persistent ideal introduced in chapter 3: the surfer who attaches great meaning to surfing before and beyond any professional opportunities it may offer. The category *soul surfer* does not exclude professional surfers or musicians, though I do attempt to balance the emphasis given to professional surfers and professional musicians in the previous chapter. Chapters 5 and 6 may appear to construct a dichotomy between the pro surfer and the soul surfer, but as with so many things core to surfing, the boundaries are fluid: all the action is in the liminal zone. Chapter 6 includes ethnographies of surfing musicians primarily from California and in Hawai'i. In these locations we find similar ideas about music and surfing, but some distinctions as well. Some Hawaiian surfers focus in their music on Hawaiian issues of significance to them personally. Some California soul surfers also sing about Hawai'i and reference ideas from Hawai'i. But I propose that the role Hawai'i plays in this musicking should be interpreted differently. Taken as a whole, the voices I present in this chapter find surfing profoundly meaningful, even necessary for the maintenance of their souls, and they express some of this through music.

The final chapter, chapter 7, "Playing Together and Solitary Play: Why Surfers Need Music," draws some conclusions about surfing and music-making as interlinked human practices. Looking again at individuals and groups of surfers who play music together, I draw out two recurring themes: *homologies* (surfing and musicking can be viewed as the same phenomena or, at the very least, as analogous) and *community sharing* (musicking allows surfers to form community in ways that surfing alone does not). Key to both of these themes is the belief among some surfers that both musicking and surfing create similar affective feelings or experiences, and that music provides a venue for exploring those feelings and experiences. I conclude with a well-worn and well-worth-rehearsing ethnomusicological finding: musicking is vital in creating community.

CHAPTER I

Trouble in Paradise

The History and Reinvention of Surfing

Na Kane i heʻe nalu Oʻahu
He puni Maui no Piʻilani
Ua heʻe a papa kea i papa enaena
Ua lilo lanakila ke poʻo o ka papa
Ua nāhāhā Kaʻuiki

Kane surfed at Oʻahu,
And all around Maui, Island of Piʻilani,
He surfed through the white foam, the raging waves,
The top of his surfboard in triumph rose on the crest
As waves crashed against Kaʻuiki.[1]

These are the opening lines of the third part of an extensive nineteenth-century *mele* (Hawaiian chant) catalogued in Honolulu's Bishop Museum as "He inoa no Naihe (Name Chant for Naihe)," which also bears the evocative titles "Deification of Canoe for Naihe" and "A Surfing Song" (audio example 1). Naihe was a chief associated with the Hawaiian royalty, and an accomplished surfer. He was born toward the end of the eighteenth century and died in 1831. Thus this is a late-eighteenth- or, more likely, early-nineteenth-century mele. The mele was later adopted for King Kalākaua,[2] the last reigning Hawaiian king, who died in 1891. He was nicknamed "the Merrie Monarch" because of his appreciation of and support for some of Hawaii's traditional arts, including surfing, mele, and *hula,* the latter popularly known as a Hawaiian dance style but better understood as visual poetry. The following fragment from the mele that I quoted above celebrates King Kalākaua's own surfing prowess (audio example 1):

Kaili Kalākaua i ka nalu,
Pau ka nalu lilo ia ia,
Ka hemolele a ke akamai,
Heʻe a ka lani i ka nalu.

Kalākaua rode the waves,
He rode on every wave deftly and skillfully.
The chief rode on the waves,
On the swirling waves.[3]

Much of what we know about pre-revival surfing comes to us from Hawaiian legends and mele—the original surfing music. Since at least the surviving mele tend to focus on Hawaiian nobility, they skew our picture of surfing history a bit. However, Hawaiian legends and early accounts by Hawaiians and non-Hawaiians leave no doubt that just about everyone surfed—royal and commoner; men, women, and children.[4] Yet the fact that nobility routinely surfed is a powerful reminder of the establishment role of surfing in pre-contact Hawaiian society.

By *pre-revival* surfing I mean surfing by Hawaiians up to the end of the nineteenth century. As the nineteenth century turned into the twentieth, many commentators claimed that surfing was on the verge of extinction. Recent research has shown that this was not the case at all but rather a myth propagated by non-Hawaiians, first out of ignorance and later in a deliberate effort to encourage tourists to visit Hawai'i: by suggesting that Hawaiians had abandoned surfing, it cleared the way for tourists to colonize the sport.[5] Even though surfing was never abandoned by Hawaiians and never died out in Hawai'i, it was "revived" in the sense that it was given new life in the first half of the twentieth century by tourists and white settlers in Hawai'i, and also by its spread to other coastal areas around the world. With this revival came great changes, changes so great that I believe surfing was also reinvented in the twentieth century. I use the term *New Surfing* to refer to what surfing became in the twentieth century as it was redefined and resignified by new surfers—in Hawai'i, more overtly in California, and then quickly around the world. The act of riding waves while standing on boards remains fundamentally unchanged; that is not what I mean by New Surfing. My interest here is in surfing as a cultural practice with accompanying rituals, habits, conceptions about who surfs and why, and of course musical ideas and practices.

Just as ancient mele tell us much about pre-revival surfing, changing music associated with surfing in the first half of the twentieth century informs us about the reinvention of surfing. Using musicking about surfing as my guide, in this chapter I retell the history of surfing, beginning with pre-contact surfing in Hawai'i, followed by the reinvention of surfing during the first half of the twentieth century. Where possible, the story is told through music associated with surfing, beginning with Hawaiian mele, then Hawaiian popular music during the first half of the twentieth century, up to a genre called Surf Music, which is the focus of the next chapter. There are some pages in the middle of this chapter where I don't write about music but instead present a history of the rumored demise of surfing, followed by its reinvention as it was globalized. The balance of the chapter and of the book, however, does address musicking among surfers.

HAWAIIAN SURFING: THE SPORT OF KINGS AND QUEENS (AND EVERYBODY ELSE)

Ka nalu nui, a kū ka nalu mai Kona,
Ka malo a ka māhiehie.
Ka 'onaulu loa, a lele ka'u malo.
O kaka'i malo hoaka,
O ka malo kai, malo o ke ali'i.
K kū, e hume a pa'a i ka malo.

E ka 'ika'i ka lā i ka papa 'o Halepō
A pae 'o Halepō i ka nalu.
Hō'e'e ka nalu mai Kahiki,
He nalu Wākea, nalu ho'ohu'a,
Haki 'ōpu'u ka nalu, haki kuapā.

The big wave, the billow rolling from Kona,
Makes a loincloth fit for a champion among chiefs.
Far-reaching roller, my loincloth speeds with the waves.
Waves in parade, foam-crested waves of the loin-covering sea,
Make the *malo* of the man, the high chief.
Stand, gird fast the loincloth!

Let the sun ride on ahead guiding the board named Halepō
Until Halepō glides on the swell.
Let Halepō mount the surf rolling in from Kahiki,
Waves worthy of Wākea's people,
Waves that build, break, dash against our shore.
(He Inoa no Naihe [A Name Chant for Naihe])[6]

Seafaring people around the world have found pleasure from the boost of speed provided by an ocean swell as they returned from the open seas to shore.[7] Heading into the water for the sole purpose of enjoying wave riding, most commonly practiced by children, was historically widespread throughout Polynesia. Ben Finney and James D. Houston, in their book *Surfing: A History of the Ancient Hawaiian Sport,* note that in most islands of East Polynesia, all ages, male and female, also took pleasure in wave riding, usually riding prone on short wooden boards. In Tahiti and Hawai'i, surfers took it a step further. There they developed longer boards, six feet or more in length, and rode them while standing.[8] Stand-up surfing was most highly developed in Hawai'i, where it was thoroughly integrated into society. Surfing was rich with rituals associated with everything from the making of surfboards to the act of surfing itself, and with taboos about who could surf where, when, and with whom. Legends and mele tell of elaborate surfing contests with associated activities from gambling to courtship. And of course there were chants about surfing and surfers.[9] Even if surfing did not necessarily originate there, Hawai'i remains the mythical font of surfing, and it is certainly the place from which stand-up surfing spread around the world during the twentieth century.

And surfing mele show us that Hawaiians knew that surfing came to them from elsewhere—that they had some sense of global surfing before anyone was using the term *globalization.* The extract of the mele at the beginning of this section refers to Kahiki as the origin of a particular surfing swell (audio example 1). Kahiki could mean Tahiti specifically, though in this context it probably refers to any distant place beyond Hawai'i.[10] The Hawaiian Islands were most likely first settled by Marquesans around 300 C.E. but were then conquered and resettled by Tahitians around 100 C.E.[11] Whether or not the particular swell celebrated in this and other mele literally originated in the waters around Tahiti is not the point. The mele can be interpreted as paying homage to an earlier homeland for these seafarers from whence Hawaiian people and cultural practices came—cultural practices including surfing.

The description in Naihe's name chant, excerpted above, of waves as "worthy of Wākea's people" is also a key to Hawaiian myths of surfing. Wākea and his wife, Papa, are the legendary ancestors of all Hawaiian genealogies, especially the chiefly clans.[12] Beyond the fragment reproduced above, the mele goes on to mention other notable ancestors and notable surfing spots, such as Kahalu'u, on the Big Island, Hawai'i, a surfing beach looked over by Ku'emanu, a large surfing *heiau* (temple) built by Hawaiians long ago. Such temples were used by nobility to pray for good surfing swells, and they typically also provided a favorable vantage point from which to watch surfing contests.[13] Thus in this mele, as well as in others, surfing is clearly associated with Hawaiian nobility and rituals that reaffirmed the power of the royalty, as well as with the geography of the Hawaiian Islands and beyond. Surfing was clearly integral to Hawaiians' self- and social conceptions, and to their sense of place both geographically and socially.

Today New Surfing is strikingly male dominated, despite the increasing numbers of female surfers during the first decade of the twenty-first century.[14] This is doubly striking and troubling when we realize that ancient Hawaiian mele concur with other sources to show conclusively that women, too, surfed (and were sometimes praised for surfing better than men). These few lines from the surfing mele for Queen Emma, the queen consort of King Kamehameha IV during the latter half of the nineteenth century, reveal several interesting images of Hawaiian surfing at that time (audio example 2):

> He Nalu ka hōlua no Waiakanonoula,
> He Nalu ka lio me ke kaa i uka o ka aina,
> He Nalu ke olaʻi naueue ka honua
> He nalu ke anuenue me ka punohu i ka moana,
> He nalu ka awa kau a ka manu iluna o ka laau
> He nalu ka popolo me ka laulele,
> E kaha ana ke kane me ka wahine,
> E hee ana ka luahine me ka elemakule,
> Pae aku, pae i ka nalu o Mauliola.

The hōlua sledding is the surfing of Waiakanonoula
The horse and buggy are surfing upon the land
The earthquake is surfing that shakes the earth
The rainbow is surfing and so is the low-lying rainbow on the ocean,
The awa planted by the birds on a tree is a "surf,"
The popolo and the laulele weeds are "surfs,"
Upon which men and women glide,
The old women and old men surf,
And land on the surf of Mauliola.[15]

I selected this fragment from the long mele in honor of Queen Emma because it starts with a mention of a *hōlua,* a wooden sled used for sliding down the sides of volcanoes, reaching speeds upward of fifty miles per hour.[16] The passage continues with other metaphors of surfing on land that provide insight into the modernizing Hawaiʻi of the mid–nineteenth century; horses had been introduced to the islands only in the first years of that century. The mele then extends the metaphors of surfing to create an atmospheric image of Hawai'i—earthquakes, rainbows, foliage, and fowl—before returning to the liquid waves we usually associate with surfing. There we are reminded that women did surf, even old women who "land on the surf of Mauliola"—literally, "the breath of life" or "life and healing." Queen Emma's mele shows us that, among many other things, at least some nineteenth-century Hawaiians understood the health benefits of surfing, and they considered it integral to many aspects of their ancient and modernizing lives—perhaps even a metaphor for life and movement itself.[17]

Queen Emma's mele illustrates another key quality of surfing mele: the naming of places, especially prime surfing locations. Mele effectively create poetic maps of the Hawaiian Islands. Queen Emma's surf mele begins on the island of Hawai'i, mentioning in line 6 "beautiful Waipio, whose surf is ridden by visiting chiefs. . . ." Waipio is on the northern shore of Hawai'i Island and contains an ancient surfing spot.[18] In the passage reproduced above, sledding on Waiakanonoula, not far from Waipio, is compared with surfing. Later in the mele, places like Kapohakau (now the name of a mountain summit on Kaua'i, but possibly the name of a surf beach in the past), Wahinekapu (a bluff near Kīlauea, Hawai'i, the taboo residence of a god), Puaenaena (probably Pua'ena, an ancient surfing area on O'ahu),[19] and many, many other significant locations are named. As mentioned above, Naihe's name chant mentions the surfing spot Kahalu'u, which is overlooked by a surfing temple, and his chant includes other named locations. Finney and Houston note that there are more named spots for surfing on the Hawaiian Islands mentioned in old Hawaiian stories and mele than were commonly surfed in the mid-1960s.[20] We do not know if surfers today yet appreciate all the potential surfing breaks that Hawaiians enjoyed on the islands centuries ago.

Extending place naming beyond the Hawaiian Islands, relatively modern mele, such as Queen Emma's surfing mele, remind us that Hawai'i was part of the globalizing world. These lines are heard near the end of Queen Emma's surf chant (audio example 2):

He kulana he'e nalu o Farani,
He hu'a o ka nalu o Maleka,
He ika no ka nalu o Rusini,
He paena na ka nalu o Beretane

A place to surf is at France,
The last of the "surfs" is America,

The force that carries the "surfs" along is Russia,
The place where the surf lands is England[21]

During Queen Emma's lifetime, none of these places were surfing destinations, though they all are now, including most recently Russia.[22] All were also empires with aspirations to colonize Hawai'i. Rather than being literally about surfing, these lines remind us that, as the wife of King Kamehameha IV, Queen Emma was a player on the world stage.

Close readings of surfing mele also show us that pre-revival Hawaiians rode waves in ways that many surfers in the New Surfing era thought were possible only with recent advances in surfboard technologies. For example, riding obliquely across the face of a wave just ahead of the break where the top of the wave pitches over or topples down to form what surfers call "whitewater" is the skill foundation of modern surfing. It was assumed that without fins or skegs on their surfboards, ancient Hawaiian surfers would have had very limited directional control of their boards, and would have typically ridden more or less straight in with the direction of the swell—certainly not obliquely, nearly parallel to the swell itself. Fins were added to surfboards in the early twentieth century, and there is no evidence that pre-contact surfboards ever had fins. However, these lines from a pre-revival mele, "He inoa no Naihe," reveal that Hawaiian surfers were able to ride across a wave obliquely (audio example 1):

Lala a kou ka malu a pae I O'ahu
'Au'au I ka Waiuli, Wailena

Ride in obliquely till you land at O'ahu
To bathe in the living waters, the waters of life.[23]

Royalty generally used long, narrow, thick, heavy boards called *papa olo* (fig. 5). They ranged from fourteen to sixteen feet, or even longer. Commoners used the more typical *papa alaia* (fig. 6), ranging from six to nine feet, flat on the deck and bottom, and much lighter.[24] This mele was for a surfer of the Hawaiian chiefly class, so it is assumed that he was riding a board fit for his class—a long, narrow, heavy *olo* board, which would be much easier to catch waves with, but much more difficult to hold in an oblique angle across a wave's face.

While it is likely that modern surfers have come up with moves that are new, it is also presumptuous to assume that surfing is fundamentally more advanced today than it was in pre-contact Hawai'i. After compiling and translating the earliest references to surfing by Hawaiians,

FIGURE 5. Engraving from 1825 depicting a domestic scene in Hawai'i, with a *papa olo* surfboard thirteen to fifteen feet long prominently displayed. Iles Sandwich: Maison de Kraimoku, Premier Ministre du Roi; Fabrication des Etoffes. By Villeroy, after A. Pellion. Image courtesy of the Bishop Museum, Honolulu, O'ahu, Hawai'i (www. bishopmuseum.org).

FIGURE 6. Man holding a *papa alaia* surfboard at Waikīkī Beach, with Diamond Head in the background, ca. 1890. Photographer unknown. Image courtesy of the Bishop Museum, Honolulu, O'ahu, Hawai'i (www.bishopmuseum.org).

Hawaiian surfer and historian John Clark concluded that "traditional Hawaiians surfers were as at home in the ocean and as skilled in riding waves as any surfer today. While they rode solid wood boards without fins, boards that limited the extent of their maneuvers, they still did all the basics that surfers do now."[25] This included riding inside barreling hollow waves, and riding very large waves. Surfers today do not know or fully appreciate the full extent of pre-revival Hawaiian surfing skills, but mele contain hints that ancient Hawaiian surfers were far better than we have imagined.

THE DEMISE OF SURFING?

The surfing mele referenced above span the late eighteenth century to the late nineteenth century—a period of increasing contact with Europeans and North Americans, as well as with sailors and explorers from the rest of the world. This was a time of rapid change in Hawai'i, and of a corresponding decline of surfing. I include a question mark in the subheading for this section because the decline of surfing tends to be both exaggerated and misattributed in surfing histories. In an article that he titled "The Rumors of Surfing's Demise Have Been Greatly Exaggerated," Patrick Moser traces the often repeated notion that surfing was on the verge of dying out to a 1854 article by one George Washington Bates, whose words are then repeated in histories of surfing up through the twentieth century and still now in the twenty-first.[26] Careful not to cast blame, and recognizing his own European heritage, Moser tactfully points out that the reports of surfing's demise are all by Europeans and Anglo-Americans, or what Hawaiians call collectively *haole* ("foreigner," usually implying white). Many Hawaiians in touch with their own surfing heritage know better; the rest of us just have not been listening.

Hawaiian surfer and historian Isaiah Helekunihi Walker hopes to set the record straight. Drawing from hitherto inaccessible or ignored Hawaiian-language newspapers published in the nineteenth and twentieth centuries and from his ethnographic research among Hawaiian surfers, Walker shows that surfing did not die out among Hawaiians, despite all odds.[27] Surfing—along with everything else Hawaiian—did, however, go through a tough patch in the nineteenth century. Missionaries had dramatic intended and unintended impact on Hawaiian society beginning in the 1820s. Some of them discouraged and disparaged surfing, usually for its associations with gambling, sex, and, perhaps worst of all, inutility,[28] but missionaries never directly legislated against surfing as is sometimes claimed. They didn't need to. The establishment of labor-hungry plantations on the islands and a shift by the royalty toward European signifiers of status (instead of traditional Hawaiian signifiers of status such as surfing prowess), together with new ideas about gods introduced by missionaries, destabilized just about everything in Hawaiian society.[29] Added to this social, spiritual, and economic upheaval was the decimating effect of disease on the formerly isolated islanders. The population of the Hawaiian Islands was estimated to be between five and eight hundred thousand when Captain Cook arrived in 1778, but disease introduced by Cook and his men and subsequent visitors reduced the population of native Hawaiians to 134,925 at the 1823 census,[30] and their numbers continued to diminish to the end of the century. By the 1890s Hawaiians were a minority people on the Hawaiian Islands.[31] Of course there were fewer Hawaiians surfing by the end of the century: there were fewer Hawaiians, period.

The impact on surfing of social upheaval and decline in the native Hawaiian population was most noticeable at centers of colonial influence, such as Honolulu—especially that former hotbed of surfing, Waikīkī. Yet if one moved away from the centers of foreign influence, it became much more likely that one would encounter substantial groups of surfers out on a good day. Such was the firsthand account of traveler Samuel S. Hill, who in 1849 visited the remote village of Keauhua, Hawai'i, only to find it empty of people. When his party finally encountered a few women, they were informed that everyone else from the village was down at a nearby bay surfing.[32] Hawaiians never gave up on surfing despite their hardships, but as more and more haoles began to learn surfing themselves in the twentieth century, they may have needed new myths that presented themselves as the inheritors of Hawaii's favorite pastime.

NEW SURFING: THE REINVENTION OF *HE'E NALU*

Tensions between the Hawaiian monarchy's and foreign industry's control of Hawaiian resources came to a head in 1893, and with the support of the U.S. Marines, Queen Lili'uokalani was deposed, Hawai'i was made a republic, and then it was illegally annexed as a U.S. territory in 1898.[33] Haoles were taking over Hawai'i; why not surfing?

With U.S. business and military interests effectively in control of Hawai'i, in the first half of the twentieth century many material and cultural aspects of the islands were transformed to accommodate the growing capitalist demands of the United States. *He'e nalu,* or what was increasingly referred to by the English-language term *surfing,* was not excluded. Walker's convincing argument that surfing remained essentially and defiantly Hawaiian—that the surf zone was the one area where Hawaiian men were able to resist colonial control (though as he notes, the prominence of women surfing in the twentieth century declined)[34]—is a crucial counterpoint to the story of reinvention that I tell here. Surfing was and is not one thing. While on the one hand the surf zone remained an arena where Hawaiian men strove to preserve agency beyond the reach of colonial domination, on the other hand the practice of surfing was simultaneously being reinvented to suit the purposes of non-Hawaiian practitioners both in Hawai'i and abroad. This reinvented, reinterpreted, revalued surfing is what I call *New Surfing.*

Alexander Hume Ford and Jack London were key figures in the reinvention of what became New Surfing. Ford was a wealthy world traveler who in 1907 moved to Waikīkī and adopted it as his home. He took to surfing with a passion and founded the Outrigger Canoe Club in 1908 in Waikīkī with the express intention of encouraging wave riding on boards as well as in canoes. The membership was almost exclusively white, and women were not admitted until 1926. The exclusion of Hawaiians was not written into the club's charter, but the idea of their inclusion did not mesh with Ford's greater agenda: the promotion of tourism and development in Hawai'i.[35] The Outrigger Canoe Club was for Honolulu's elite men, who at that time were predominantly white.

One of Ford's early converts to surfing was Jack London, who sailed to Hawai'i in 1907 with his wife, Charmian, shortly after Ford settled there. Where Ford was a wheeler-dealer man of action, London was a man of words. Through his writerly pen we see the transformation of surfing into a hypermasculine "royal sport for the natural kings of the earth."[36] A Hawaiian surfer whom London witnesses becomes: "[A] Mercury—a black Mercury. His heels are winged, and in them is the swiftness of the sea. . . . [H]e is a man, a natural king, a member of the kingly species that has mastered matter and the brutes and lorded it over creation."[37] Here, in the first years of surfing's reinvention, London introduces the notion of man's mastery over nature—strikingly different from earlier Hawaiian approaches that suggested working with natural forces for sustenance and pleasure. In an unintentionally backhanded way, linking surfing to Hawaiian royalty also made the sport attractive to wealthy haole men. All were acutely aware that just a few years earlier Hawaiian royalty had been deposed, clearing the way for the new champions of the universe—wealthy Western men—to enjoy the spoils of a bygone era.

While surfing remained a vital link to Hawaiian heritage for many, this is not the story that non-Hawaiian surfing historians have been telling. Instead, today surfing origin myths, after acknowledging that Hawaiians (emphasizing Hawaiian royalty) surfed long ago, tend to place the beginning of the modern sport squarely in white men's hands in the first years of the twentieth century. Patrick Moser points out how the myth of surfing's demise in the hands of Hawaiians plays into white histories of surfing—that surfing was rescued from obscurity by white industrial enterprise.[38] Walker makes a similar point but from a Hawaiian perspective: haole interests in Hawai'i needed to emasculate the strong Hawaiian male and emphasize instead the (tourism-industry sponsored) aloha of the Hawaiian hula girl.[39] A new genre of Hawaiian music emerged that helped this process along.

HAPA HAOLE MUSIC, TOURISM, AND THE EXPORT OF SURFING

I love a pretty little Honolulu hula hula girl
She's the candy kid to wriggle, hula girl
She will surely make you giggle, hula girl
With her naughty little wiggle
—Chorus of "My Honolulu Hula Girl,"
by Sonny Cunha, 1909 (audio example 3)

Annexed by the United States, Hawai'i quickly became the tourist destination of choice for those with the means to get there. Tourism is always a two-way street. The primary objective may be to bring paying customers to the tourist destination, but to do this the industry must first export inviting ideas about that destination. One genre of music that did this better than any other was *hapa haole* (half-foreign or half-white) songs. This genre combined English texts with some Hawaiian words or phrases, and Hawaiian musical aesthetic with then-popular mainland styles such as ragtime, jazz, blues, and so forth.[40] Hapa haole music, like surfing itself, became one of the greatest exports for Hawai'i globally, and during the first half of the twentieth century it was one of the most successful products of the mainland music industry as it changed its focus from selling sheet music and instruments to selling records. Up to the Great Depression of the 1930s, hapa haole was the best-selling genre for leading recording companies.[41] Music did much to shape the world's image of Hawai'i and Hawaiians.

Exports of cultural practices like surfing and musicking require the export of practitioners as well. Many leading Hawaiian musicians from the early twentieth century had their careers on the mainland, especially in California's port cities such as Los Angeles. A few Hawaiian surfers also personally introduced surfing to key coastal areas around the world.

Here I focus on the early exchange of personnel and ideas between coastal California and Hawai'i. Though Hawai'i remained the ideal surfing destination, and while Californian surfers emulated many Hawaiian cultural practices in addition to surfing, including hapa haole music and hula, the cultural center of surfing eventually shifted from Hawai'i to California. Over time, surfing was remade, reimagined, reinvented to reflect mainland U.S. and global cosmopolitan social and cultural norms of male dominance, competition, and commercialization. Music, too, reflected and sometimes participated in these changes.

This story is not without irony: Hawaiians themselves introduced surfing to the mainland United States and to Australia at the very time when some accounts were declaring Hawaiian surfing to be extinct. The first recorded surfing in California was accomplished by three Hawaiian princes, brothers Jonah Kūhiō Kalaniana'ole, David Pi'ikoi Kupio Kawananakoa, and Edward Kawananakoa. Natives of the island of Kaua'i, they were attending St. Matthew's Military School in San Mateo when, in 1885, they made their own boards with California redwood and surfed off the shore of Santa Cruz.[42] These royal surfers were succeeded by George Freeth, a hapa haole born in Hawai'i to a Hawaiian mother and Irish-immigrant father. In 1907 he moved to the Los Angeles area, where he was hired to promote tourism to the Hotel Redondo, in Redondo Beach, California, by demonstrating surfing, teaching surfing and swimming, and serving as a lifeguard.[43]

The greatest global surfing ambassador was the multimedaling Olympic swimmer Duke Paoa Kahanamoku, who introduced surfing to the U.S. East Coast in 1912 and to Australia and New Zealand in 1914 and 1915, respectively. He also spent time surfing in Southern California in 1915. Yet his international influence began earlier, at Waikīkī, where many tourists from around the world saw him surf, and even learned how to surf from him. Kahanamoku was also part of the loosely affiliated Waikīkī Beachboys—Hawaiian men who taught surfing, served as lifeguards, and provided all sorts of other services to tourists at Waikīkī, including playing music and singing (hapa haole songs as well as other

© Graham Peake

FIGURE 7. E. J. Oshier (left) and George "Peanuts" Larson, San Onofre, 1937. Photograph by Don James. From *Surfing San Onofre to Point Dume, 1936–1942: Photographs by Don James* (San Francisco: Chronicle Books, 1996), 41. Reproduced with permission of Graham Peake.

genres).[44] Thus at the very moment Ford and London were suggesting that Hawaiians had effectively abandoned surfing, Hawaiians were actually teaching them and the world how to surf.

During the first half of the twentieth century—the heyday of hapa haole music—surfing was still considered inherently Hawaiian, and this was confirmed by the musicking associated with early-twentieth-century surfing in Hawaiʻi and also in California, the first stop for globalizing surfing.

Noted early Californian surfer E. J. Oshier was active playing music on the beaches of Southern California from the 1920s until his death in 2007. The photograph in figure 7 was taken in 1937 by Don James at San Onofre, a beach between Los Angeles and San Diego that has been a popular surfing spot since the 1930s. The man playing ukulele with Oshier, George "Peanuts" Larson, was another early California surfer. Figure 8, also taken by Don James at San Onofre but two years later, includes friends of Oshier's playing ukuleles and guitars while Eleanor Roach does a hula dance.

© Graham Peake

FIGURE 8. San Onofre music and hula session, 1939. Eleanor Roach (dancing), Barney Wilkes, Katie Dunbar, and Bruce Duncan. Photograph by Don James. From *Surfing San Onofre to Point Dume, 1936–1942: Photographs by Don James* (San Francisco: Chronicle Books, 1996), 50. Reproduced with permission of Graham Peake.

In an interview, Oshier told me that before World War II, the music at San Onofre was 98 to 99 percent Hawaiian. According to Oshier, everything Hawaiian was paradise to the San Onofre crew, and they actively cultivated Hawaiian-language songs, and also learned how to dance a little hula.[45] Thus, even while haoles were appropriating Hawaiian cultural practices including music, dance, and surfing, the San Onofre group still conceived of those practices as Hawaiian. (I return to San Onofre and consider the present-day musicking and surfing scene there in chapter 6.)

The sense I get from my interactions with surfers who engage the hapa haole repertoire is that it is an icon of Hawai'i and surfing.[46] Few of the songs are about surfing. That is not the point. They are perceived as Hawaiian, and thus are appropriate for a surfing lifestyle. But hapa haole songs are also about post-contact, post-monarchy Hawai'i, and they carry messages about the reinvention of surfing in the twentieth century. Hapa haole songs do not feature the powerful surfing queens and kings of Hawai'i but instead present a romanticized image of

Hawai'i and especially Hawaiian women, who are forever small, soft, brown skinned, skilled at tourist-style hula, and always welcoming. This corresponds to a simultaneous regendering of surfing as the nearly exclusive domain of men, including white men, who take on surfing as a sign of appropriating Hawai'i, its women, and its lands. Hawaiian men are largely absent from the lyrics of English-language hapa haole songs, except for the few references of their surfing and canoe-paddling prowess.

HAWAIIAN SONGS, 1900–1950

Hawaiian songs from the first half of the twentieth century illustrate the new gendered roles for Hawaiian women and men, and occasionally their engagement in surfing. Here I survey Hawaiian songs from this period as found in four key sources. The first three sources are song collections published by eminent composers in Hawai'i who included in their songbooks some of their own compositions, as well as traditional pieces and songs composed by others. The first is the seminal *Famous Hawaiian Songs*, published by A.R. "Sonny" Cunha in 1914 and containing 45 songs. Cunha is often described as "the Father of Hapa Haole Songs." The second collection is Charles E. King's 1948 edition of *King's Book of Hawaiian Melodies*, which includes 101 songs, many of them also in the first edition of the collection, which was published in 1916. A contemporary of Cunha's, King emphasized more traditional Hawaiian music. The third songbook was published by Johnny Noble, a younger composer and publisher in the hapa haole genre who sometimes collaborated with Cunha. *Johnny Noble's Book of Famous Hawaiian Melodies* was published in 1935 and contains 32 songs. The fourth source considered here is the Web site *Hapa Haole Songs*, which contained about 560 songs when I analyzed its content in the fall of 2012.[47] All told, I searched over 700 songs and versions of songs for references to surfing. Many of these songs fall within the broad hapa haole genre, but the collections by Cunha, King, and Noble also contain traditional hula and other songs popular in Hawai'i. Here I give particular weight to the print collections since they are dated and each one represents especially influential collections of its era: the 1910s (Cunha and King), the 1930s (Noble), and the late 1940s (King). In these songs I searched for references to surf riding in both Hawaiian and English. In particular I looked for the term *surf* or the Hawaiian terms *he'e* (to surf) and *nalu* (wave or surf break). I generally did not mark songs that mention the ocean or waves without a surf rider, such as the many references to the surf washing up on the beach.

In Cunha's seminal 1914 collection, there is only one song that mentions surfing, "Ku'u ipo i ka he'e pu'e one," by Princess Miriam Kapili Kekāuluohi Likelike (1851–87). Composed in the later nineteenth century, this song remained popular in the twentieth. The opening line is the same as the title, and is translated in Cunha's collection as "Proudly riding on the crest of the ocean," though a more literal translation is "My sweetheart who surfs over the sand bar." In this song by one of the sisters of the two last ruling Hawaiian monarchs, we have a glimpse of pre-reinvented surfing that is integral to Hawaiian society.

There are no other direct references to surfing that I find in Cunha's book, though there are several references to canoe paddling. One is Cunha's own composition "My Tropical Hula Girl," and it stands in contrast to Likelike's Hawaiian-language song from a generation earlier. Cunha's song is set in a moonlit night at Waikīkī:

Where the breakers they are rolling in high . . .
All the hula girlies in reach,
Will be prancing up and down the beach,
Up and down the beach, they've nothing to do,
But to paddle in their little canoe,
In their little canoeoo,
In their little canoe.

At least in this early hapa haole song, copyright 1909, the Waikīkī "hula girlies" are depicted as being capable of paddling out in their canoe on a moonlit night with high breakers: they were capable water women. However, the rest of the song is about a visitor to Waikīkī courting a hula girl, spooning, looking into her eyes; and when the hula ends, "[y]ou'll be feeling kind of welakahao and raving for more." *Welakahao* is not a Hawaiian word, but if we break it up as *wela ka hao,* we have three Hawaiian words with a possible translation of "hot or lustful in the horn or iron." Cunha knew his audience well, including knowing when to switch to Hawaiian for his mainland audience. At any rate, the song is not about women's canoe surfing skills, and we are left wondering what hula girlies paddling their little canoe is really about. If this early hapa haole song from the father of the genre carries anything from earlier Hawaiian poetic traditions, it may be double entendre and innuendo.

Noble's 1935 collection, *Johnny Noble's Book of Famous Hawaiian Melodies,* reads as a musical siren call to Hawai'i. The first song is

"Hawaii across the Sea," in which the wanderer is called to return to " . . . Fair Hawaii, To these Sunny Isles across the sea." The very next page is a "descriptive novelty tone poem" called "The Surfboard Rider," with the subtitle "As He Is Seen from the Beach at Waikīkī Any Day in the Year." Composed by Noble, this tone poem is a somewhat breathless "musical lecture spoken and partially sung" (as described in the book) over a frenetic piano accompaniment. The narrator-singer tracks a surfer as he paddles out, catches a wave, builds speed, stands, falls, and paddles out for another wave. The only sung portion is: "Over the waves, oh see him surf. Over the waves . . . Over the waves, oh see him surf, over the waves he surfs along."

Turning the page of Noble's songbook, we find a two-column, six-photograph essay, "How to Ride a Surfboard: A Correspondence Course in the Hawaiian 'Sport of Kings,'" by Harold Coffin (fig. 9). The essay claims that "Waikiki is about the only place in the world where successful surfboarding has been practiced to any great extent," a falsehood introduced by Alexander Hume Ford two decades earlier. Overtly promoting tourism to Hawai'i, the essay recommends that the visitor wishing to learn to surf "supplement this correspondence course with several weeks (at least) of actual practice in the hands of an expert Hawaiian instructor in Honolulu." We should not be surprised to find printed in large font at the bottom of the page: "Used by Permission of the Hawaii Tourist Bureau," an organization supported by Honolulu businesses that early on saw the advantages of using both music and surfing to advertise Hawai'i.[48]

Singing through the songbook, our initiation into a Hawaiian lifestyle continues with the next song, "Kamaaina" ("The Old Timer" is the title translation provided by Noble, but kama'aina literally means "child of the land" or "native born"). This song is in the voice of a man who has come to Honolulu, finds it paradise, and wants to become a native. The very next song in Noble's collection completes the transformation: "I'm Not a Malihini Anymore." A malihini is one from somewhere else, a foreigner. In the song, the singer claims, "I've learned to eat fish and poi, and swim like a real beach boy," and concludes, at the end of the song, "I'm not a malihini any more I'm telling you, I'm just a Kamaaina now."

Our singing protagonist may have gone native, but if hapa haole songs are our guide, he and his ilk stick close to Honolulu, especially the Waikīkī neighborhood, including named tourist hotels such as the Royal Hawaiian—at least in the English-language songs.[49] In Noble's

How To Ride A Surfboard

A Correspondence Course in the Hawaiian "Sport of Kings"

BY HAROLD COFFIN

A SURFBOARD is best described as an overgrown ironing board that has gone native. The boards are usually about 10 feet long, wide enough to lie down on, and weigh about 50 pounds. Redwood and similar woods are used, the tendency being to make the boards lighter than the early implements that were fashioned from native woods.

With the help of these wooden water wings it is possible to walk on the waves of Waikiki. In fact Waikiki is about the only place in the world where successful surfboarding has been practiced to any great extent. The reason for this is that the contour of the ocean bottom at Waikiki, coupled with the location of the protecting coral reefs, is such that it supplies just the right kind of continuous surf crests to propel the boards for as far as two miles shoreward on one wave.

Surfboarding is the most thrilling of all water sports if you know how, and that is a big IF, because conquering the magic board is no small job. Many Hawaiians, especially the beach boys, are skilled surfriders, sitting down, standing up, balancing on their heads, carrying passengers on their shoulders and stunting in other ways.

The Hawaiian "sport of kings" can be explained in a few paragraphs because surfriding on a typewriter is comparatively simple, but would-be wave walkers are advised to supplement this correspondence course with several weeks (at least) of actual practice in the hands of an expert Hawaiian instructor in Honolulu.

The first problem is to paddle your way out from the beach to a point where the waves are breaking. In assuming position "A" you lie face down on the board. Use a perpendicular stroke through the water with your arms — not a breaststroke. Your feet are crossed on the board. To turn to the right, drag the right foot in the water. (Experienced paddlers guide the boards by shifting the weight of the body, and do not have to use their feet for rudders.)

Pick your wave — a single wave, because the double waves are good only for

canoe surfing. Watch for the steepest section of the surf. With your board facing to shore, paddle ahead of the wave as fast as possible. As the surf catches you, it is necessary to give an extra spurt of paddling and shift your weight slightly toward the rear of the board to keep the nose of the surfboard from diving.

The trick is then one of balancing properly and quickly. If the wave is exceptionally steep, ride more to the stern of the board. Then, after you "catch" the wave head the board at an angle with the surf This enables you to "slide" with the wave.

Now you are racing over the water at lightning speed. By getting to your knees and watching your balance carefully, you can sit up, stand up, and (maybe) stand on your head.

Tourists and other uninitiated surf-riders frequently find that it is far easier, however, to stand on somebody else's head, or at least to ride on the instructor's shoulders. Double-decker surfing such as this is achieved by riding tandem on one board and letting your surf-wise teacher do all the work.

There are several different surfing fields in the huge swimming area that is Waikiki.

The most popular wave line, directly in front of the Moana Hotel, is known as the Canoe Surf. In front of this, closer to the beach, is the Wahine Surf —"for women only." Next to these is the Cornucopia Surf off the beach in front of the Royal Hawaiian Hotel. The Cornucopia waves are choppier, but frequently are best for speed-burning and trick riding.

Fastest of all the surfing areas (but also short) is the famous Queen's Surf in front of Waikiki Tavern. Farther down the beach toward Diamond Head, opposite the Elks' Club, is the Castle Surf. Experts only venture into the giant waves of the Castle Surf.

At the opposite end of the beach between the Royal Hawaiian and Gray's Beach is Malihini Surf, where Malihinis are invited to try these directions.

"Used by Permission of the Hawaii Tourist Bureau"

FIGURE 9. "How to Ride a Surfboard," by Harold Coffin. Published in *Johnny Noble's Book of Famous Hawaiian Melodies* (New York: Miller Music, 1935), 8.

book, we have a cosmopolitan view of at least Honolulu as a nice place to visit, maybe even settle down. Surfing is one of the many attractions of Hawai'i, along with local women, stunning scenery, and temperate weather.

The third songbook considered here was compiled by Charles E. King. Eminent Hawaiian ethnomusicologist and performer Amy Ku'uleialoha Stillman refers to Charles E. King's songbooks as "bibles" of Hawaiian music that "could be found in many a piano bench across the islands."[50] One-quarter Hawaiian, King was fluent in the Hawaiian language and was close to the royal family. Queen Emma was his godmother, and Queen Lili'uokalani was one of his music teachers.[51] Though a contemporary of Sonny Cunha's, he represented a more conservative approach to Hawaiian music—one that reflected the aesthetics of the last quarter of the nineteenth century, when the monarchy was still in place, rather than the first half of the twentieth century, when the mainland consolidated its influence over the islands. While critical of hapa haole songs, King included some in his later compilations,[52] including one of his most popular compositions, "The Pidgin English Hula" (first copyright 1934). Thus King's attitudes toward Hawaiian music provide a counterpoint to those of Cunha and Noble, though there are some structural similarities to the way he presented his song collections.

The first edition of *King's Book of Hawaiian Melodies* was published in 1916.[53] Though I am using the 1948 and final edition of this collection of 101 songs and mele, it has much in common with the original edition and can be read as a history of popular Hawaiian songs from the first half of the twentieth century. I find only two songs that mention surfing. The first is "Kaimana Hila" (Diamond Head), by King (copyright 1916), where in the last verse the singer proclaims:

We all went to the Seaside Hotel
And looked with wonder at all the riders of the surf
Gliding swiftly.

The second, "Honolulu Maids," is also attributed to King and again has an original copyright date of 1916. This song is "after an old style of hula," though the protagonist is depicted as a visitor to Honolulu, and indeed the style and content could easily be heard as hapa haole.[54] It contains six short verses in which the protagonist is beguiled by the maids of Honolulu and, in the last three verses, learns how to surf and has an exchange with one maid in particular:

With those charming beautiful maids of Honolulula,
I learned to ride the surf like a kamaaina la.

I said to one beautiful maid of Honolulula,
"May, oh may I ride on life's ocean with you la?"

Oh that charming beautiful maid of Honolulula,
Gazed at me and said, "Aole hike la."

I take the proposition to "ride on life's ocean with you" to be a marriage proposal, and I find rather nice the reference to surfing used as a metaphor for sharing life together. I also imagine the beautiful Honolulu maid smiling warmly as she gazed at her suitor and replied in Hawaiian, a language he did not understand: "*Aole hike la*" (No, never can do, la). Poor haole. He never knew what hit him. That Honolulu maid probably gets a proposal every weekend. Leaving our haole's heartbreak aside, I note that in this song, it was the Honolulu maids who taught the tourist how to surf, not their male counterparts, the famous Waikīkī Beachboys.

Like Noble's book, King's overtly promotes tourism to Hawai'i in song and in photographic inserts that celebrate Hawaii's attractions. These include a two-page spread featuring a map of the Hawaiian islands, labeled "The Paradise of the Pacific, Territory of Hawaii, USA," that shows shipping routes to Vancouver, Seattle, San Francisco, Los Angeles, the Panama Canal, South America, the Antipodes, and "the Orient"—all radiating out from prominently marked Honolulu and Waikīkī Beach. On two corners of the spread are photographs of swimmers at "Waikiki in January" and "Surf-riders at Waikiki." Even more interesting for our purposes is the photograph on page 101 featuring, in the center, Duke Kahanamoku, flanked by two bits of text (fig. 10). On the left side:

You may travel the world over but you can find no sport so exhilarating and intensely exciting as surfing. The Hawaiians are children of the sea and they love to play with the waves as they sweep towards the shore by riding majestically on them with surf board or canoe. Waikiki beach affords the sojourner in Hawaii the best opportunity for enjoying this harmless pastime of the natives.

And on the right:

Duke Kahanamoku, Hawaii's favorite son and the champion swimmer of the world, is here depicted with his winning smile and reliable surfboard. He is ready for a plunge into the waters of Waikiki.[55]

With surfing's greatest ambassador in the center, two now familiar tropes of Hawaiian surfing are rehearsed: Hawaiians are amphibious

You may travel the world over but you can find no sport so exhilarating and intensely exciting as surfing. The Hawaiians are children of the sea and they love to play with the waves as they sweep towards the shore by riding majestically on them with surf board or canoe. Waikiki beach affords the sojourner in Hawaii the best opportunity for enjoying this harmless pastime of the natives.

Duke Kahanamoku, Hawaii's favorite son and the champion swimmer of the world, is here depicted with his winning smile and reliable surfboard. He is ready for a plunge into the waters of Waikiki.

FIGURE 10. Duke Kahanamoku featured in *King's Book of Hawaiian Melodies* (Honolulu: Charles E. King, 1948), 101.

"children of the sea"; and Waikīkī is the best place in the world to learn to surf.

The last collection of songs I consider here, the online source *Hapa Haole Songs,* rendered proportionately about the same number of references to surfing as the three publications considered above. Of the approximately 560 songs featured, only seven mention surfing (or *he'e nalu*); a few others feature canoeing. Four of the songs mentioning surfing are dated after 1960, and represent a different era for surfing—one that I discuss in the next chapter. This leaves a scant three songs that reference surfing. These include a song from about 1930 by Paul Summers called "I've Gone Native Now," which, like Noble's "I'm Not a Malihini Anymore," includes surfing as one of the marks of going native:

> I go surfing every day
> Way outside, catch a big wave
> Riding kahakai 'a 'ole kapakahi
> I've gone native now.

As any surfer today understands, it is not enough to know how to ride a wave. One must also know a bit of surfer lingo: *kahakai 'a 'ole kapakahi* (riding beachward without turning around, or straight in).

One particularly interesting if late song from the era is Jack Pitman and Bob Magoon's 1952 "My Waikiki Girl." The third verse paints this impressive picture:

> And when the sea is dark and stormy,
> Out in the surf you'll find her there.
> She rides the breakers on a surfboard
> With a hibiscus in her hair.

This song is notable for breaking the general rule of New Surfing that surfers are male. Furthermore, in this song the "Waikiki Girl" is depicted as surfing when the sea is dark and stormy, suggesting large, rough seas. She was an accomplished surfer.

THE NEW IMAGE OF SURFING

Hapa haole and Hawaiian songs such as these were a major global export for Hawai'i, and many of these songs are still popular among the dozens if not hundreds of ukulele clubs that thrive around the world. During at least the first half of the twentieth century, they constituted the core repertoire of the earliest active musicking about surfing among surfers outside Hawai'i. These songs were considered Hawaiian. And even though some hapa haole hits were written in New York by Tin Pan Alley composers, key influential sources of this genre were, as I have shown, composed by musicians from Hawai'i or working in Hawai'i, even if they were not all ethnically Hawaiian. While popular in Hawai'i, these songs were also promoted to and popular in the mainland United States, the United Kingdom, Japan,[56] and wherever else there was a market for potential tourists to Hawai'i. The songs broadcast world-wide images of Hawai'i and the emerging New Surfing.

New Surfing in hapa haole songs is decontextualized. No longer is surfing richly woven through chant into Hawaii's system of hierarchy, taboo, ritual, and geography. The only named surfing spot in these twentieth-century Hawaiian popular songs is Waikīkī; lost is the mapping of countless surfing beaches as found in mele. New Surfing also loses social context—with the exception of King's "Honolulu Maids," in which surfing is part of the protagonist's courtship of a Hawaiian woman. In the other songs, surfing is depicted as something to be marveled at, or to learn as an individual who wishes to go native. Though that is very interesting in and of itself, there is no suggestion in these songs that certain individuals should ride only certain types of boards, at certain locations, in the company of certain people. Surfing is reduced to a flat (a nasty word in modern surfing parlance, meaning "no waves") achievement, at best a way of demonstrating one's attachment to Waikīkī. Lost are the elaborate descriptions of named surfers, of named surfboards, and of the particular qualities of waves. In other words, lost is all the detail that makes surfing exciting. A corollary is hula, especially as depicted in English-language hapa haole songs. Hula is reduced to an attractive display of the exotic female body—a "naughty little wiggle," to quote one of Sonny Cunha's 1909 compositions.

There is much that we can learn about surfing across time and space through the musical practices of surfing communities. Surviving mele from eighteenth- and nineteenth-century Hawai'i show us that surfing was thoroughly integrated into Hawaiian society and the Hawaiian worldview, and that the skillful riding of long *papa olo* surfboards by Hawaiian kings and queens was the ultimate symbol of establishment power. New, reinvented surfing originally found musical inspiration from the mimesis of popular Hawaiian music, especially hapa haole songs, but these already suggested a renegotiation of Hawaiian society where women are objectified, as is surfing. Both are attractions to the islands, even while surfing becomes a major export.

CHAPTER 2

"Surf Music" and the California Surfing Boom

New Surfing Gets a New Sound

Surfin' is the only life
The only way for me.
Now surf, surf with me.

Bom bom dit di dit dip
Bom bom dit di dit dip

—"Surfin'," Brian Wilson and Mike Love, 1961

Mention the phrase *surf music*, and one of two iconic sounds usually comes to mind: the vocal harmonies of the Beach Boys and Jan and Dean, or the instrumental, guitar-driven rock championed by Dick Dale, the Bel-Airs, and a long list of other bands. These two subgenres of what was dubbed "surf music" in 1961 emerged in the Los Angeles area, and each illustrates a different myth about New Surfing. Though the named popular genre Surf Music is not the first, most important, or necessarily best music associated with surfing, it did mark a key moment in the history of surfing as a global cultural practice: the shift of the cultural center of surfing from Hawai'i to California. Thus Surf Music stands as an icon of a watershed moment in the reinvention of surfing.

While Surf Music can be considered to mark a triumphant moment for Californian surfers at the expense of Hawaiians, I will show that the genre garnered mixed responses among surfers then and subsequently. For some surfers the music became and remained an anthem of their youth, but for others then and since it created a problematic popular image of surfing frozen in time while their surfing community moved on and changed. Naming something "Surf Music" may have even limited musicality among some surfers. After the initial popularity of Surf Music, many surfing musicians felt the need to separate, at least publicly, their musicking from their surfing. Eventually Surf Music took on a life of its own and lost any tenuous links it may have had with surfing other than remaining an iconic symbol of early-1960s surfing culture in California. Surfing itself moved in other directions, and surfers sought different musical practices to represent their changing priorities.

If this book is about anything, it is about the intersections of music and surfing before and since Surf Music. Though I find that the genre name Surf Music inadvertently limited musicking directly associated with surfing by subsequent generations, I recognize that the genre marks a significant moment in the history of surfing worldwide. This chapter is about that particular moment when certain musical practices were given the name Surf Music, and about what that act of naming tells us about surfing and surfers then and since.

LET'S GO TO THE BEACH! THE MIDCENTURY RISE OF SOUTHERN CALIFORNIA

The Second World War interrupted surfing to a great extent in California and Hawai'i, but it also introduced new technologies that affected surfing practices in many ways—from the construction of surfboards to the dissemination of ideas about surfing through popular media. As a result, surfing experienced rapid growth, notably in the postwar United States, Australia, and South Africa, but also in Mexico, Peru, Puerto Rico, and other points south. New Surfing soon spread to England, France, and Portugal, and eventually to Japan, Vietnam, Indonesia, China, and other coastal regions of South and East Asia. Surfing was now establishing a global community, and California was well positioned to exploit this emerging market.

The United States emerged from the Second World War as a leading world power, and California played a big role in that transformation. While California's population had been growing steadily since the Gold Rush, the Unites States' entry into the Second World War led to the significant expansion of military bases and government factories in the state. As people moved west to staff these factories and bases, the population of California rose from below 7 million in 1940 to 10.6 million in 1950. After the war, California continued to receive the lion's share of defense funding during the emerging Cold War era. The rate of population growth in the state increased, with more than 15.8 million people in the state by 1960, and two years later California was the most populous state in the Union, with more than 17 million people. More than half of the residents lived in the southernmost ten counties of the state, informally known as Southern California—a region that makes up about one-third of the state's landmass.[1] This includes the coastal counties of San Luis Obispo, Santa Barbara, Ventura, Los Angeles, Orange, and San Diego. These were heady times for Southern California; the United States' film industry was firmly settled in Hollywood, and there was plenty of sun, agriculture, and now plenty of new employment opportunities, many of them providing affluent white-collar work. Life was good. Why not go to the beach?

More people did go to Southern California's beaches, where they encountered repurposed wartime technologies to ease the willing into surfing. Light and easily shaped polyurethane foam (developed during World War II) encased with rigid and waterproof fiberglass (from World War I) began to replace wood as the standard materials for making surfboards by the end of the 1950s. The resulting lighter and more maneuverable surfboards facilitated a boom in surfing popularity. Wetsuits, another wartime technology, made surfing all the more attractive, since even in sunny Southern California, the water is chilly year-round. Whereas the fabrication of objects necessary for surfing had been a DIY (do it yourself) and custom affair, with only a few early commercial attempts, in the 1950s manufacturing these items was suddenly becoming a commercially viable enterprise, and California was at the center of this new industry.

The allure of surfing and the success of the new industry that supplied the emerging surfing community were bolstered by new dryland lifestyle technologies as well. Battery-operated transistor radios brought new musical sounds directly to the beach as DJs began to exploit (and create) a new music-fueled youth-culture concept.[2] The established technology of film was used for the first time to create surfing movies in the 1950s, and those films were always accompanied by recordings of popular music, usually mixed together by the filmmaker using the first commercially available tape recorders. Particularly in Southern California, a seemingly sudden critical mass of surfers collided with postwar optimism, new ideas about music and youth culture, and technologies that brought it all to the beach, setting the stage for the creation of new cultural practices that would define New Surfing.

CALIFORNIA AND THE NEW FACE OF NEW SURFING

In this context of great optimism, increasing wealth, and easy access to beaches, New Surfing began to reach the popular imagination and became linked with California in specific ways that were distinct from the images of surfing in Hawai'i of yesteryear. Most notably, instead of the "black Mercury" described by Jack London half a century earlier (quoted in the previous chapter),[3] the California surfer was white (though tanned), ideally sporting blond hair, male, young, and slightly edgy. Whereas historically in Hawai'i surfing was integral to mainstream society and was celebrated as the ultimate symbol of establishment (royal) power, in California it became associated with antiestablishment play by young men. During the first half of the twentieth century in Hawai'i, when Alexander Hume Ford was promoting surfing among Hawaii's white elite, the face of surfing began to change, yet it still remained a symbol of Hawaiian establishment power. In California, it remained exotic, esoteric, and came to symbolize a stand against midcentury conformism. Though today surfing has become mainstream in many ways, it still retains some of the rebel spirit that it gained in the mid–twentieth century.

In colonial Hawai'i (the late nineteenth century and first half of the twentieth), the typical protagonist of the emerging New Surfing beach-tourist narrative was a relatively well-heeled white man, as seen in English-language popular Hawaiian songs from the first half of the twentieth century. Though some early images promoting California beach tourism were similar to those from Hawai'i, important differences began to appear. In Hawai'i, the centuries of indigenous beachside civilization remained part of the allure, even if only in the form of the female Hawaiian hula dancer and the Waikīkī Beachboy. By contrast, in coastal California indigenous peoples and sacred sites were less visible, sometimes literally paved over.[4] California's beaches were treated as blank slates on which developers could exercise their imaginations. The Los Angeles County attractions of Venice Beach and the Pike amusement area of Long Beach exemplified manmade urban pleasures, middle-class affairs that forever teetered on the edge of respectability.[5]

While city planners worked to clean up the reputations of their cities' beaches, they were swimming against the tide. Southern California's intersection with the Pacific remained in popular conception the domain of outlaws, sailors, beatniks, and increasingly a handful of esoteric surfers—a liminal zone that offered relief from the summer heat but also from the

strictures of Eisenhower-era establishment expectations. The whiff of edginess, captured well by Tom Wolfe's short story "The Pump House Gang,"
about surfers at Windansea Beach, in San Diego, California,[6] mingled with
the sea air as children, young men, and women stripped to their swimsuits
and dipped in the chilly California waters.

Not all strictures of establishment were left inland, however, and in
many ways mainland social norms, good and bad, were pushed to the
edges of the continent with the growing popularity of beach life. For
example, California's beaches remained racially segregated by custom
and sometimes law. Excluded from other local beaches in the area,
African-American beachgoers appropriated a small stretch of polluted
and otherwise abandoned beach in Santa Monica.[7] The spot became
known as Inkwell Beach and fostered a surfer thought to be the United
States' first African-American surfer, Nick Gabaldon, in the late 1940s.
Even today, when no single racial or ethnic group constitutes a majority
in the state of California, coastal areas of the state remain highly segregated and predominantly white. For example, Newport Beach—an
important center of global surfing culture and industry—is one of the
most segregated towns in the state.[8] While white men worked to appropriate surfing in Hawai'i, there it nonetheless remained firmly associated with Hawaiianness in popular conceptions. On the mainland,
however, surfing was becoming increasingly white and male.

My intention here is not to paint midcentury California surfers as
racist misogynists, but to show that even while they were pioneering
New Surfing, which would in time take on a bit of a rebel image, they
nonetheless reflected many of the norms of their times and society. This
unfortunately includes patterns of racial appropriation that are marbled
through popular culture of the mainstream United States. Just as half a
century earlier Alexander Hume Ford went to some pains to show the
world that white men could surf, in the midcentury mainland United
States the history of popular music can be seen as a repeating [stet]
a[stet] pattern of white musicians demonstrating that they could perform genres pioneered by African Americans—jazz, blues, rhythm and
blues, rock 'n' roll, and so forth. My point here is to shine a light on the
racial erasure that too often is part of cultural appropriation. I suspect
that in 1961, as now, every surfer in California respected and paid homage to Hawaiians for the gift of surfing, even while he (maybe even she)
anticipated without reflection that most if not all of the surfers at their
local beach would be white. Similarly, no rock guitarist from the late
1950s on can expect credibility without paying homage to African-

American blues and R & B musicians, even while contemplating a predominantly white audience.

It's hot and the surfs up. I'm just a surfer. Can we leave the politics out of it and just crank up the car radio on the way to the beach? Indeed, can we?

Surf Music can be heard as an anthem of New Surfing that sings of the shift from Hawai'i to California and from Hawaiians to the then–predominantly white surfers of California. Paul Johnson, founding member of the Bel-Airs, a seminal Southern California surf band, today talks about instrumental rock Surf Music as an original regional American folk music expressing the experiences of affluent white kids in Los Angeles suburbs.[9] Though this history challenges (I think fruitfully) scholarly and popular conceptions that link folk music to underprivileged segments of society, and though the musical structures prevalent in Surf Music tell a much more complicated story, Johnson's comments capture something significant about what surfing represented in the postwar American imagination. Johnson and others also speak of 1960s instrumental surf bands as being "garage bands," an early DIY movement, and a precursor to 1970s punk.[10] I expand on this thread in chapter 4.

The year 1961 was a watershed moment for what came to be called Surf Music. Dick Dale was playing his own show at the Rendezvous Ballroom on Balboa Peninsula, Newport Beach, and in September 1961 Dick Dale and the Del-Tones released arguably the first recording self-consciously addressing their surfer audience: "Let's Go Trippin'."[11] A few months earlier a band of junior high and high school boys from the Redondo Beach area, the Bel-Airs, had already recorded "Mr. Moto," a tune that would also become firmly associated with Surf Music though it was not written with surfing in mind. Also in 1961, another Los Angeles–area band of high school students, the Beach Boys, released their first recording, "Surfin'"—the first example of the vocal subgenre of Surf Music. Not only was surfing becoming the "in" thing to do in Southern California; now it also had its own music in both instrumental and song forms. The instrumental-rock and vocal subgenres of Surf Music each have a different yet complementary story to tell about surfing in the mid–twentieth century.[12]

INSTRUMENTAL ROCK BECOMES SURF MUSIC

In the late 1950s and early 1960s, Friday-night dances near urban Southern California beaches supported a number of local bands, such as the Bel-Airs in Redondo Beach, Los Angeles County; and Dick Dale in Newport Beach, Orange County, just south of Los Angeles. These beachside dances tapped into a growing national youth movement and simultaneously attracted at least some of the growing number of Californian surfers. Paul Johnson of the Bel-Airs believes that putting on dances at popular surfing beaches was a chance co-occurrence that led to surfers appropriating already extant instrumental rock as their own. As Johnson explains, at one of the Bel-Airs' dances at Los Angeles's South Bay beaches, a prominent surfer exclaimed, "Wow, man—your music sounds just like it feels out on a wave! It's like . . . 'surf' music, man!"[13] Dick Dale tells a very similar origin story about when instrumental rock was first called "Surf Music," except that he internalizes the story as his own visceral reaction to wave riding: "The style of music I developed, to me at the time, was the feeling I got when I was out there eating it on the waves. It was that good rambling feeling I got when I was locked in a tube with whitewater caving in over my head. I was trying to project the power of the ocean to the people."[14] He claims that the title "King of the Surf Guitar" was given to him by his surfing buddies, who also named many of his tunes.[15]

There are two parts to the origin myths of Surf Music as told by Dale and Johnson. First is the claim by both men that surfers adopted or appropriated their instrumental rock as Surf Music. I find this significant in that it suggests that electric-guitar-led rock resonated with Southern California surfers of the time. At least Dick Dale did surf, and he has asserted that he was trying to capture the feeling of surfing with his guitar playing. Paul Johnson was not a surfer, and he never attached surfing titles to his songs, even when others were calling his music Surf Music. As he remembers it, surfers themselves made the connection with the music the Bel-Airs were playing.[16] In both cases, a link is made between the feeling of surfing and the sound of the music; surfing and instrumental Surf Music were, on some experiential and symbolic level, related.[17]

The second part of this story is that not all the people who wrote and performed so-called Surf Music were surfers or were even thinking about surfing when they composed what came to be called Surf Music. The Bel-Airs' "Mr. Moto" was named after a 1930s film detective played by Peter Lorre, and none of the band members were surfers. They just happened to be playing their music at or near the beach to audiences that included surfers. But what about that perennial surf hit "Walk Don't Run"? It was first recorded by Johnny Smith in 1954, and then in a more familiar style by the Ventures in 1960—both recordings made before anything was called Surf Music and by musicians who, at least at the time, were unassociated with surfing in any way. There are numerous other examples of instrumental-rock pieces recorded before 1961 that later came to be considered Surf Music, even though they were not written with surfing in mind. The Ventures exemplify this. Formed in 1958 in Tacoma, Washington, the band would become the most successful instrumental-rock, guitar-led band of all time. They later were called a surf band only by oblique association, since Surf Music became the default genre name for instrumental-rock bands. Thus while the genre Surf Music has real connections to Southern California surfing in that some surfers in 1961 claimed the music as their own, the genre of instrumental rock was already in place, and many subsequent bands took on the label Surf Music for their music even though they did not surf.

The association of guitar-led instrumental rock with surfing was a trend that remained relatively local through 1962, but in 1963 the Astronauts, from high-mountain Boulder, Colorado, a thousand miles from the closest ocean, released "Baja" in the Surf Music style. That marked a watershed moment for Surf Music as a named genre; suddenly it was a sound with only symbolic (linguistic) links to the practice of surfing, a disconnect that remains today. While there are more surf bands today than there were in 1963, they are just as likely to be in Alabama (Man or AstroMan), Finland (Laika and the Cosmonauts), or Slovenia (the Bitch Boys) as they are to be from a surfing beach town like Newport Beach, California.

Since a number of pieces now considered Surf Music were not created with surfing in mind, what makes any music Surf Music? First, there seems to be an affective feel. A surfer at one of the Bel-Airs' dances proclaims: "Your music sounds just like it feels out on a wave!" Surfer and guitarist Dick Dale explains: "I was trying to project the power of the ocean to the people." Whether the connection is made in the head of a surfer-listener dancing to instrumental rock after a good surfing day, or by a surfer-musician trying to share through music some of the excitement he or she experiences riding ocean waves, the affective connection benefits from the lack of referential specificity in musical sounds. While Dale's loud, fast guitar playing may in fact create in some listeners an affective reaction similar to catching a wave (increased rate of heartbeat, focused attention, sense of elation), any given listener may or may not associate that feeling with surfing. And of course surfing is not all about intense focus and a racing heart. There is a lot of waiting involved, and indeed in large surf, the surfer must endeavor to relax, lower the heart rate, and control breathing.

The second and more enduring link between music and surfing, especially the genre Surf Music, is association: the music is associated with surfing through co-occurrence if not through the original intent of the musicians.[18] The Bel-Airs and Dick Dale were playing on the beaches of Southern California in the summer of 1961, when surfing was becoming the hip thing. Their sound absorbed some of the zeitgeist of the Southern California surfing boom. The music was there, on or near the beaches, at the time, and the sounds were bound up together in the minds of some surfers, who dubbed it "Surf Music." The label stuck.

What are the musical sounds that took on the label Surf Music? Sonically instrumental Surf Music typically includes an electric lead guitar playing the melody, accompanied by an electric bass, a drum kit, and possibly an electric rhythm guitar or piano. Some bands included a saxophone and/or trumpet. Of course such combinations of instruments could perform any number of rock and jazz styles. The distinguishing sound of a surf band is generally described as including guitars played through a reverberation unit, usually called a *reverb*—a device that creates the effect of playing in a large space in which echoes prolong sound. The sonic effect of a guitar played through a reverb unit is often described as "wet"; thus the obvious connection to surfing. Though this timbre or quality is usually mentioned in descriptions of Surf Music, Dick Dale denies its importance, noting that his first surf hits were recorded before guitar reverb units were invented.[19] He emphasizes other features of his guitar setup and the powerful (loud) sound they are capable of producing: heavy-gauge guitar strings and a hundred-watt amplifier driving fifteen-inch JBL speakers—effectively the Fender Showman amp created by Leo Fender to handle Dale's demands. Of course subsequently, loud guitar playing became standard rock 'n' roll aesthetic.

Instrumental-rock Surf Music fetishized power and masculinity. In his often-repeated origin myth of Surf Music, Dick Dale returns to motifs of power. I have seen Dale perform live a few times in recent years, and there, too, I was impressed by the display of power and hypermasculinity.[20] Similar energy can be seen in films of his 1960s performances. Such performances are the stock-in-trade of rock guitar players today, but not yet in Dale's early years. For example, Chuck Berry, arguably rock 'n' roll's first guitar hero, was much more playful onstage. Dale's stage banter and published interviews include an origin myth of the invention of the surf-guitar sound that emphasizes power: he plays his guitar like a drum; he uses very heavy gauge strings on his guitar; he can wear out several guitar picks performing a single song; and of course, he blew out many guitar amplifiers and speakers until Leo Fender created for him the powerful Showman amp.[21] Surf guitar remains a man's genre today, with only a handful of women playing (or being attracted to) the genre.

Both John Blair's and Robert J. Dalley's canonizing discographies of Surf Music[22] describe the sound in terms of style (electric guitar power plus reverb, yet clean, undistorted sounds by later rock standards) and ensemble makeup. However, neither discography talks about the structural form of the music, so I analyzed the musical forms of all the examples on the first CD of the *Cowabunga! The Surf Box* four-CD box set. This box set includes twenty early genre-defining pieces through 1962 either composed as Surf Music or folded into the genre after the fact. Most are instrumental rock, though three are songs, including the Beach Boys' 1961 "Surfin'," the Surfaris' 1962 "Surfer Joe," and Chris Montez and Kathy Young's 1963 single surf hit "Shoot That Curl." When you take these twenty recordings as a definitive example of canonized Surf Music, a very striking pattern emerges: ten of the twenty recordings are in twelve-bar blues form; six of the remaining ten are harmonic-minor mode compositions, emphasizing the major chords built on the fifth and sixth scale degrees, one half step apart.

The two Southern California examples that vie for the privilege of being the first recorded example of the named genre Surf Music exemplify these two musical forms: "Mr. Moto," by the Bel-Airs, and Dick Dale and the Del-Tones' "Let's Go Trippin'," both from 1961. "Mr. Moto" is in D-minor modality. Using timings based on the 1961 recording of "Mr. Moto" as rereleased on the *Cowabunga!* box set, I note that after an introduction that sets the mode, the first melodic theme (which starts at 0:12) is presented accompanied with the chords D minor (the chord on first scale degree), B-flat major (sixth scale degree), and A major (fifth scale degree). The second melodic theme (starting at 0:35) is in what is called the relative major key—F major, in this case. The chords are C major (fifth scale degree) and F major (first scale degree). Then the first melodic theme is repeated (0:48), but in A minor (a modulation to the fifth scale degree), before a return (1:12) of the cool introduction motif followed by repeating the first melodic theme in D minor again, followed by the second theme in the relative major key (1:44), and ending with a return of the introduction motif for the close. This is a nicely shaped, sophisticated composition.

Dick Dale's "Let's Go Trippin'" is an example of twelve-bar blues in E major with the standard progression of major chords: E, A, E, B, A, E (chords built on the first, fourth, and fifth scale degrees). Introduced to the world through African-American blues in the early twentieth century, this basic musical structure is arguably the most enduring North American popular-music form, especially in rock music. Though there is some variation in this formula (the Beach Boys' "Surfin'" breaks the twelve-bar pattern with an eight-plus-one-bar section, for example), ten of the twenty first surf hits employ this basic blues form.

There you have it, guitarists: that's the formula. Come up with a catchy tune in either a twelve-bar blues form or a modal, two-part melody form; add a groovy surf-themed title such as "Surfer's Stomp" (The Mar-Kets, 1961), "Bustin' Surfboards" (The Tornadoes, 1962), or "Surf Beat" (Dick Dale, 1962), and maybe a cool dive-bomber guitar glissando as in "Pipeline" (The Chantays, 1962). Dress your band in matching jackets, go back in time half a century, and you might get some local fame among the surfer crowd. Nothing to it.

Analyzing the forms of these early Surf Music genre hits is not really intended as a guidebook for creating your own pop-music hits, nor is it intended to be critical of the skills of the musicians who created these hits. After all, similar formulas govern most of the classical compositions from Europe that get so much attention and praise. Take the sonata form, for example, which took hold of European composers in the middle of the eighteenth century and remained a popular formula well into the twentieth. Knowing a rhythmic/harmonic formula does not good music make; it is what you do with the formula that makes people want to listen. In the case of Surf Music, these two dominant musical formulas tell us something about the Southern California white middle-class audience that we need to know.

The blues music formula is drawn directly from rhythm and blues of the 1950s, which is drawn directly from African-American blues from earlier decades. The minor modality used in "Mr. Moto" is less common in North American popular music and less specific in pedigree, but minor modality has long been used to suggest the exotic in Western European traditions, and I believe the same is the case with Southern California Surf Music. For Paul Johnson of the Bel-Airs, who created "Mr. Moto," the tune sounded Japanese. Two additional tunes from the twenty analyzed here point to the exotic Other in their titles as well as sound: "Latin'ia," by the Sentinals; and "Miserlou," by Dick Dale. "Latin'ia" is in A minor, but spends most of its time on the E- and F-major cords (fifth and sixth scale degrees, one half step apart). It includes an Afro-Cuban clave rhythm heard in a number of Latin-American popular music genres. "Miserlou" was not composed by Dale but is a well-known Greek folk tune in a mode known as *hijaz* in some Middle Eastern traditions. Thus, a core sonic image in the second-most-common musical form of instrumental Surf Music includes sounds that are suggestive of an exotic Other with their minor modes. It is at least consistent, if not appropriate, that the whitewashed Southern California New Surfing, which took its core activity—surfing—from Hawaiians, gets its first distinct music genre from African Americans and registers a vague sense of the exotic Other in modal tunes.

SONGS ABOUT SURFING

The parallel to instrumental rock Surf Music was songs about surfing, most prominently those by the Beach Boys and their high school friends Jan and Dean. This subgenre of Surf Music shares time and place with instrumental Surf Music, but its origins are distinct. Most surfers did not at first claim the Beach Boys songs as expressive of their sport and lifestyle; it was the other way around. Brian Wilson and his producers noted that surfing was becoming a regional fad, so he wrote songs about surfing, and the band's name was changed from the Pendletones (after the Pendleton shirts favored by many Southern California surfers at the time) to the Beach Boys.[23] While Brian's brother Dennis surfed and probably suggested the surf-themed songs to the band, the other band members did not surf. Sensing the regional popularity of surfing, they tapped into the stoke and wrote songs about the nascent surfing lifestyle and another teen obsession, automobiles. All of their early single releases had a surf-themed song on one side and a hot-rod song on the flip side of a 45 rpm record. Still today an essential accessory for most California surfers is an automobile to carry them and their boards to the beach.

Like their sibling instrumental surf rock, the Beach Boys' songs about surfing contain nothing that alone is entirely new: they were squarely in a late-1950s, early-1960s popular-song-writing vein emphasizing close harmonies with occasional vocables (bom bom dit di dit dip . . .). My ears hear a lineage back to African-American vocal quartets, to early pop bands such as the Ink Spots ("Do I Worry," 1941), then to doo-wop groups such as the Platters in the 1950s ("Only You," 1955; even the guitar intro to this song is strikingly similar to the Beach Boys' later references to surf guitar), and to the production values of early Motown recordings. The tight vocal harmonies that the Beach Boys are rightly praised for can also be seen as tied to African-American music through the medium of barbershop-quartet singing.[24] Like instrumental surf rock with its fondness for the twelve-bar blues form, the vocal version of Surf Music drew many key elements from African-American popular genres. The Beach Boys' first Top 10 hit, "Surfin' U.S.A.," derives its melody and the lyrical hook of naming towns from Chuck Berry's "Sweet Little Sixteen," and Carl Wilson's guitar intro references Berry's playing as well.[25] What made the Beach Boys' music unique was its ability to capture the nation's and indeed the world's imagination about the emerging New Surfing lifestyle now centered in Southern California, as well as the subtle songwriting style and production techniques that identify the Beach Boys' sound.

New genres of music are rarely entirely new in musical form. Surf Music became a recognizable genre when it was attached in the minds of listeners to extramusical phenomena. (Remember that a number of instrumental-rock pieces written and recorded by musicians who did not surf and did not have surfing in mind were later rebranded as Surf Music.) Using musical structures and performance values developed first by African Americans, middle-class white boys and men wrote instrumental pieces and songs about surfing—a cultural practice earlier developed by Hawaiians. Claims that Surf Music was the first music to develop around a sport[26] ignore sports-stadium organs of the early twentieth century, the ancient Persian Zurkhaneh (house of strength) games practiced to the beat of drums, and many other musical practices that are associated with sports—including the most-pertinent example: Hawaiian surfing mele.[27] Neither surfing nor the essence of Surf Music was new, but their intersection in Southern California in the first years of the 1960s marked a new era for both cultural practices.

What do the Beach Boys' and Jan and Dean's songs tell us about New Surfing? First, we are reminded that surfing is now considered Southern Californian and white, even while it gained national and international popularity. Writing about both subgenres, geographer George Carney wrote that surfer rock "established a music identity for Southern California" and that this identity was primarily suburban based, middle-class, and white.[28] Second, we are reminded that surfing is now a man's sport, though the Beach Boys typically took a softer, more romantic, and perhaps more youthful approach to surfing's masculinity than did Dick Dale. The only thing macho about Brian Wilson's surfer in the Beach Boys' 1961 single "Surfin'" is that he is willing to endure the physical hardships of surfer's knots on his knees and getting up at the break of dawn when the surf is good:

Now the dawn is breaking and we really gotta go
But we'll be back here very soon that you better know
Yeah my surfer knots are rising and my board is losing wax
But that won't stop me baby cause you know I'm coming back

New Surfing had defined roles for men and women: men surfed; women were one of the rewards of surfing well. "Surf City," written by the Beach Boys' Brian Wilson but originally recorded by Jan and Dean, promises "two girls for every boy" and reminds us that women don't actually surf, since the singer searches for his surfer girl at parties, not in the surfing lineup. Maybe Wilson's 1963 "Surfer Girl" balances our overly masculine New Surfing culture? Unfortunately not; Wilson may dream of surfing together with his "surfer girl my little surfer girl," but in the song she remains "on the shore, standing by the ocean's roar."

The popular genre Surf Music of the sort described here never really was about surfing per se. Brian Wilson did not surf; Dick Dale did a little bit, but many of the 1960s surf bands were staffed by nonsurfers. This new Surf Music marked surfing as a fad, a trend that said as much about the idea of California as it did about surfing. Just as hapa haole songs were for Waikīkī in the first years of the twentieth century, surfing was now an advertising hook to sell something, be it a song, a T-shirt, or the California Dream. Like the instrumental-rock subgenre, vocal Surf Music soon grew beyond the tenuous links it may have had with actual surfing. It became about an ideal, a lifestyle. This foreshadowed an ongoing trend to use the concept of surfing to brand consumer products. Today one can find so-called surf shops in many American and European cities far from any surfing beach—shops that have all sorts of nice things for sale, but not a single surfboard.

Another thing that Surf Music of the 1960s points out is that the cultural and industrial center of surfing had shifted from Hawai'i to California by the early 1960s. Surf Music was Californian, not Hawaiian. Hawai'i remained and still remains the historical and spiritual center of surfing, but in the 1950s the surfboard-manufacturing industry was centered in California, as were the emerging cultural apparatuses that attached themselves to the practice of wave riding. This included clothing (perhaps surfing's largest consumer product today), magazines, films, and, starting in 1961, music.

The reception of Surf Music was mixed among surfers during its heyday (1961–64), and varied depending on the individual listener's involvement with surfing at the time, and with his or her location. While some, even many, Los Angeles–area surfers latched onto beachside instrumental rock as expressive of their surfing experiences, others thought the Surf Music craze was cheapening their sport and lifestyle. Greg Noll, an established surfboard shaper, surf-film maker, and big-wave-surfing pioneer already in the 1950s, greeted Surf Music with distaste: "The Beach Boys and all the rest of those guys that were jumping on the bandwagon to try and get in on the surf scene, for the most part we hated all that crap. When I had my shop, they'd send music to us and we'd say, 'Thank you very much,' and the minute they'd leave, they go in the trash barrel."[29] Former *Surfer* magazine editor Drew Kampion similarly dismissed the Beach Boys: "As a surfer, we never really considered the Beach Boys to be surfer music frankly. It was overflow from the surf culture, but really it seemed to talk to inland people or something like that."[30] Mike Doyle, an established surfer in the early 1960s, joins the chorus: "I remember the first time I heard the Beach Boys' song 'Surfer Girl' . . . When we heard that whiny, cornball music, we started hissing and hooting because we thought it was so hokey. It was a rip-off. The Beach Boys were stealing our culture. And they didn't even know how to surf!"[31] Doyle goes on, however, to note that he now likes the music of the Beach Boys because he recognizes that they did capture some of the spirit of the era.

Younger nascent surfers, on the other hand, were more likely to embrace the music as evocative of the surfing lifestyle they hoped to achieve. For example, Bill Pitts was born in Oakland, California, in 1949 and moved with his family to Capitola, a beach town just east of Santa Cruz, in 1960. He got his first guitar and surfboard then, and soon was learning to play instrumental Surf Music. For Pitts, who was twelve or thirteen when he first heard instrumental Surf Music, the reverb of the guitar was very evocative of surfing and being underwater, a sensation he enjoyed. He found his passions at that young age. Today he still surfs, and he leads a surf-guitar band, the Concaves.[32] Other surfers I have spoken with in California who were adolescents in the early 1960s similarly like Surf Music, both the instrumental and vocal subgenres, and associate it with their own surfing.

Though in California the ties of Surf Music to surfing itself were tenuous and context specific, they were successfully broadcast nationally and internationally through recordings, radio, TV, and tourist advertising. For example, Surf Music played well in nascent surfing communities overseas; in my imagination, it was heard as reasonably authentic folk music from Southern California, to riff on Paul Johnson's comments. British surfer and surfing historian Roger Mansfield explained to me in a conversation at Newquay, the popular U.K. surfing location that I return to in chapter 4, that in the early 1960s the growing community of surfers was inspired by hearing the Beach Boys singing about surfing and a California lifestyle.[33] Surf Music not only moved eastward, across the United States and to Europe, but also west across the ocean to Hawai'i. In what I read as a reversal of the flow of cultural practices associated with surfing, in 1963 and 1964 the Waikīkī Surf Battle was waged not in the water but at the Waikīkī Shell outdoor auditorium. At the first battle of the bands in 1963, eighteen instrumental surf bands from O'ahu —each representing a high school—played to a screaming audience of teenagers ten thousand strong, breaking the venue's attendance record.[34]

The Waikīkī Surf Battle is significant for many reasons. First is the phenomenon of California-style instrumental Surf Music appearing in Hawai'i, the cultural site from which California received surfing and ideas about surfing music in the first place. This is a clear signal that ideas about surfing now flow in both directions between Hawai'i and California. Second, the ethnicity of the musicians staffing the Hawaiian surf bands throws a little cross-chop into repeated assertions that Surf Music was "white."[35] Photographs on the 1963 *Waikiki Surf Battle* LP suggest that several of the bands consisted of people of color. Most striking is the all-female band Angie and the Originals, which included Angie Pang, C. Pang, Susan Lara, and Janet Lara. It seems that young people in Hawai'i were willing to receive musical inspiration associated with surfing from California while ignoring the racial and gender politics that suggested that New Surfing was somehow white and male. Back on the mainland United States were two surf bands that also add a little color to the whiteness of New Surfing: the Avantis and the Sharks, two early-1960s bands led by brothers Pat and Lolly Vegas (Vasquez).[36] Of Native American and Mexican heritage, the Vegas brothers would later become better known for their 1970s band Redbone, which championed Native American issues.

Are these bands just exceptions that prove the apparent New Surfing rule—set in motion by Alexander Hume Ford back in Waikīkī a century ago with the founding of the Outrigger Canoe Club and reemphasized fifty years later when surfing was suddenly identified with Southern California—that surfers are white? I don't see it that way. These bands are counterhegemonic reminders that, like an ocean of water, ideas about surfing and music cannot be contained, certainly not by racial categories that are ideologically porous. The very idea of whiteness was not the same in 1908 as it was in 1961, and it is different still now. But for all its nonspecificity, absorbing meaning here and dripping with significance there, by the 1960s in popular conceptions a surfer was a white man, darker than his rock-guitar-playing brother only because of his tan.

BAD VIBRATIONS

Almost as quickly as Surf Music emerged in the popular charts, it disappeared; by 1965 the genre—instrumental and vocal—was passé, flat, dead in the water. Songs about fun in the sun no longer resonated with the times by the mid-1960s; President Kennedy's assassination in 1963, the United States' increasing involvement in a war in Vietnam, the growing steam of what came to be called the Civil Rights Movement (including, in the United States, Black Power, the Chicano Movement, the American Indian Movement, and Women's Rights), and the increasing popularity of Motown and the Beatles all marked a different public spirit. The Beach Boys knew this; the bards of Southern California surfing made no mention of surf in their 1966 album *Pet Sounds,* nor did they do so in their number-one hit single "Good Vibrations." Instrumental Surf Music was never that popular in the charts, but it slipped even farther down the lists. Every so often even the most enthusiastic surfers must go to shore and dry off.

But every surfer knows that the waves always come back; the ocean is never still. The genre—especially the instrumental version—returns periodically in what some fans call "waves."[37] Though today there are even more active (and very good) instrumental-rock surf bands than there were in the early 1960s, the excitement does not approach the level reached in that moment when the world looked to California and imagined the boys surfing by day and dancing with their bikini-clad girls by night to the sound of a reverb-dripping guitar.

The fall from the charts of Surf Music, however, was not such a bad thing for surfer-musicians, who often had mixed feelings about the popularization of surfing in the first place. Naming something Surf Music did capture a key moment in the reinvention of surfing, but it also seems to have tied the hands of some surfer-musicians. Half a century later, should you mention music and surfing in the same sentence, many people still think you are talking about the Beach Boys or instrumental rock; this may have encouraged many surfer-musicians to draw a line between their musicking and their surfing, and who can blame them? Not until Jack Johnson's almost accidental popularity as a musician after including a few of his songs on the soundtracks of his surfing movies did surfers begin to once again publicly link their music with their surfing.

In the following chapter, which focuses on surf movies, I show how Surf Music was used in Hollywood films with surfing themes, and also appears in subcultural surf movies made by and for surfers. But even in the early 1960s Surf Music was not fully embraced in the nascent surf-movie industry. When the named genre Surf Music does emerge in surfing communities, it is often used to reference the early 1960s—to serve as a musical cue of an important historical era in New Surfing. Examples include the 2004 surf movie *Riding Giants,* which uses updated versions of classic instrumental-rock Surf Music as the soundtrack for the 1960s historical sections of the film. This and other uses of Surf Music today are decidedly nostalgic. For example, in chapter 4, I show that when Beach Boys songs and instrumental-rock Surf Music are called on to represent surfing in Italy, they are paired with iconography that references 1950s and '60s Southern California. Yet at a U.K. surfing festival linked to a professional surfing contest, 1960s Surf Music has no place. If the surfing community was ever invested in Surf Music in the early 1960s, by 1965 it was moving on and finding new and different ways of musicking about surfing.

CHAPTER 3

Music in Surf Movies

In the beginning, surfing was silent . . . or at least it was on film. Film footage of surfing very rarely has live synchronous sound.[1] The sounds a surfer hears while surfing can be intense, beautiful, and even musical—the hiss of water receding over sand and pebbles at the ocean's edge, the rhythmic dip of your arms in and out of the water while paddling, the roaring crash of waves, the slip of the board down the face of a swell, the whistle of wind, the sudden modulation from loud and high frequencies to muffled and low as you dive underwater. But how do you record these sounds? You don't. Surfing film and video footage is usually shot from shore with a telephoto lens far from the breaking waves, or in the water with a handheld camera encased in a waterproof housing. Both techniques make recording the actual sounds of surfing difficult at best; thus that particular symphony goes unrecorded and remains the private pleasure of surfers.[2]

A surf movie is a silent movie to which the filmmaker adds sound, and that sound always includes music, lots of music, occasionally only music. Without it, even the diehard surfer would find a feature-length compilation of surfing footage tedious. As filmmaker Dana Brown put it to me: "[S]urfing is beautiful, but it is also kind of repetitive, and a lot of times the music can give it a whole different feel."[3] Music can indeed give an otherwise neutral or ambiguous experience a particular feel, an emotional signature. As every filmmaker knows, the combination of moving image and musical sound is powerful. If music and surfing are paired well, musical sounds become an *index*[4] of surfing, creating an emotional experience that neither filmic image nor musical sound would elicit without the other. Writing about the historic conventions of putting music to films, ethnomusicologist Mark Slobin shows how music gives "sonic substance" to filmic images,[5] giving films a cultural context not possible with moving images alone. His ideas apply to surfing films as well. Music adds cultural context to footage of people riding waves; the soundtrack adds meaning. Perhaps for this reason, as I will show in the following chapter, my interviews with surfers from several countries revealed that the pairing of music with films of surfing can define which music is considered surfing music for a generation of surfers. In this chapter I survey and analyze the music used in surf movies that were influential in shaping the musical practices of significant groups of surfers. In particular I draw on interviews with and comments by key surf-movie makers and musicians. I begin in the 1950s with the first surf movies for which we have the original musical soundtracks, and move through the formative boom years of the 1960s, to the VHS era, and on to the present digital formats. These movies provide a clear image of what music was popular among at least some surfers before the named genre Surf Music existed, how some surfing culture brokers responded to that genre, and the musical directions surfers have taken since the 1960s. The music used in surf movies illustrates some of the diversity of musicking among surfers, but it also reveals distinct trends.

WHAT IS A SURF MOVIE?

Surf movies, as I am using the term and as it is generally understood in surfing communities, are films of surfers surfing, made by surfers for surfers. They are a decidedly subcultural phenomenon, and the surf movies that achieve crossover mainstream success are very rare. Up through the 1980s, before videos and then DVDs removed most surf movies from cinemas—or more likely from junior high school auditoriums—and sequestered them in the dens and bedrooms of surfers' homes, a surf-movie screening was a cultural event for the surfing tribe. And this tribe was exclusive; any movie that featured surfing but that targeted a general audience was viewed with great suspicion by surfers.[6]

Surfers need not worry about the overpopularity of their private pleasures with the vast majority of surf movies. Typically they have insubstantial plots and are driven by montages of surfers riding waves. As Dana Brown noted, pretty repetitive stuff. Surfing's most active current historian, Matt Warshaw, summarized fifty years of surf-movie history as a "perpetual groundswell of cinematic mediocrity."[7] Ouch! Yet for many surfers, myself included, watching a skilled surfer on a beautiful wave, or even a wave alone sans surfer, is reasonably compelling, occasionally inspiring, and at the very least, informative about the possibilities of surfing, given a board, a good wave, and enough time and energy to keep trying. To be fair, some surf movies do have themes such as environmentalism (*Pacific Vibrations*), alternative surf-focused lifestyles (*Morning of the Earth*), the discovery of waves in a previously unsurfed location (the list of examples is long), and the antics of young surfers traveling on the cheap in search of waves (as featured in many early surf movies, including all of Bruce Brown's films). There are films that focus on notable surfers (*Searching for Tom Curren*), the introspective musings of surfers (*The Drifter*), and the remarkable accomplishments of a short aloha-filled life (*Heart of the Sea: Kapolioka'ehukai*, about Rell Kapolioka'ehukai Sunn). Some films tackle issues, such as those faced by female surfers (*The Women and the Waves*), or surfing and ageing (*Surfing for Life*). The rare surf movie to achieve crossover success tends toward a documentary format that uses surfing to tap into more universal themes. Bruce Brown's *The Endless Summer* is the standout example with its paired themes of world travel and every student's dream of an endless summer. Even in this movie the simple (and not so simple) pleasure of riding waves remains the focus, and now after nearly half a century *The Endless Summer* still holds the attention of just about any audience of surfers. It is a true surf movie.

Hollywood films containing surfing characters or even a plot about surfing are not surf movies. With rare exception they misrepresent surfers' self-conceptions as a community, and they typically have laughable surfing sequences with close-ups of an ostensibly surfing leading actor interspersed with long shots of his or her actual surfing double. The original Hollywood movie of this sort, *Gidget,* released in 1959, set the standard for lame surfing shots as well as moralistic conclusions that remind us that surfing is not the most important thing in life. Not a few surfers would disagree with that message, and *Gidget* is widely blamed by surfers from that era for overly commercializing and popularizing the sport.[8] Like *Gidget,* the 1964 Hollywood movie *Ride the Wild Surf* is flawed by a moralizing misrepresentation of surfing as cultural practice (a frivolous, risk-taking waste of time, but nothing that a good woman can't cure a man of). At least that movie has some well-filmed big-wave footage of top California surfers Miki Dora and Greg Noll serving—or surfing—as stunt doubles. John Milius's 1978 *Big Wednesday* is the best of the Hollywood surf dramas in its portrayal of the impact of the Vietnam War on surfing communities, as well as hinting at some of the changes in surfing style in the 1970s. The movie with arguably the greatest impact on surfing communities since *Gidget* is the 2002 Hollywood blockbuster *Blue Crush*.[9] The only Hollywood movie since *Gidget* to focus on female surfers, *Blue Crush* is often credited in popular surfing literature with encouraging more women to surf—something most commentators consider a welcome corrective to the heavily male-dominated surfing population. The surfing industry, which is primarily a clothing industry, must have loved the film. But for the purposes of this book, none of the music used in these films became an index of surfing. None is a surf movie.

Music has a more central role in another Hollywood genre known as "beach party" or "beach blanket" movies. This genre of teen-market films was initiated by *Beach Party* (1963), staring Annette Funicello and Frankie Avalon. Both Funicello and Avalon were at least minor TV stars before *Beach Party:* Funicello was previously most famous as an original Mickey Mouse Club Mouseketeer; and Frankie Avalon was a young veteran of Dick Clark's *American Bandstand* and had acted in a few films. After the success of *Beach Party,* the pair went on to make a string of beach-blanket films. All their movies had the same plot; only the scenery changed a bit. Annette and Frankie go with a group of friends to the beach, or skiing, or car racing, or back to the beach; flirtations fly and jealousies are aroused; a nemesis foments a crisis that encourages them to reevaluate and renew their affection for one another; the foe is vanquished and all is well in the world; roll credits . . . These comedies appealed to 1960s teenagers by being slightly edgy (emphasis on *slightly*), and also by featuring popular musicians either loosely written into the plot (Dick Dale stars as himself in both *Beach Party* and *Muscle Beach Party,* infamously playing an electric guitar on the beach without even the pretense of a cable plugged into his instrument) or entirely tangential to the story (James Brown appears out of the snow to sing a song for no apparent reason in *Ski Party;* Stevie Wonder shows up at the white kid's hangout and sings a song with Dale's band in *Muscle Beach Party*). The list of other musicians and bands appearing in beach-party films is long and includes the Pyramids, and Sonny and Cher backed by the Astronauts. Of course another attraction of the genre was mobs of young people frolicking on the beach naked except for surf trunks and bikinis (though Funicello always appears in relatively modest swimming attire).

Even *Ski Party* resolves with a dance on the beach, thus allowing the actors to shed their sweaters and parkas.

Like other Hollywood movies that include surfing, beach-party movies are not surf movies. Actual wave riding is hardly seen in these films, if at all. The surfing footage that did make it into the beach-party films is rarely of any interest to surfers, and sometimes is used for slapstick humor such as when Candy Johnson's dancing causes surfers to wipe out in *Muscle Beach Party*.[10] As a surfer, I find it painful to watch these films. Beach-party movies are yet another manifestation of surfing as an advertising hook to sell something, and many surfers continue to view them as negative exploitations of their affinity group even if they did capture—in an over-the-top manner—a bit of the spirit of the time. In this sense they are viewed with the same contempt that many surfers hold for early 1960s Surf Music.[11] In fact, Brian Wilson of the Beach Boys created some of the music for beach-party films, and, as already mentioned, Dick Dale and the Del-Tones appeared in several beach-party films, as did other surf rock bands of the era. Though beach-party movies certainly projected music-driven fantasies about California beach life and surfing around the world, and therefore affected surfing communities, they were not made by and for surfers. They are commentaries on surfing and surfers made from the outside.

The primary focus of this chapter is on niche-market surf movies made by and for surfers. The core of these movies is footage of surfers riding waves; any plot or narrative story is icing on the cake. Dana Brown was right: music is essential to break the monotony of watching wave after wave. Music is also needed to create an effective emotional connection between the viewer and the filmic image. Especially important for this book, movies offer an insider's view of some of the ways surfing and musicking are brought together; the pairing by a surfer-filmmaker of a surfing sequence with a particular musical sound is in itself a statement about surfing and musicking. These pairings are also influential in establishing certain musics as surfing music.

WHAT WE DON'T KNOW ABOUT SURF-MOVIE MUSIC

Surf movies had their beginning in the 1950s, the first boom period for New Surfing. The early surf-movie makers can be counted on one hand and were all based in Southern California, by then the center of an emerging surfing industry. Bud Browne's *Hawaiian Surfing Movie*, produced in 1953 (he made another film of the same title in 1955), was the first semicommercial surf movie. It was an amateur effort—filmed, edited, advertised (with posters tacked up on light posts near surfing beaches), and then narrated live at screenings by Browne himself— setting a tone for surf-movie making that fit the DIY ethos of surfing at the time perfectly. The premiere of Browne's first film was at John Adams Junior High School in Santa Monica, California, and was successful enough that he quit his job as a teacher to concentrate on making surf movies.[12] With a formula of action-packed surfing sequences interspersed with brief comedy skits, all accompanied by live narration and a mixed tape of music, he went on to make one film a year for the next decade. However, I do not know what music he paired with his films, or even if that music was the same for every screening. Intact versions of his early films do not exist: he made only one print, and would cut some of the footage out for later films.[13] Similar challenges greet anyone curious about early surf movies: some of them are available on VHS and DVD, but many are not. Even when we have available much of the surf-movie footage, as is the case with Browne's films, we rarely have the original soundtracks. Though frustrating for the scholars among us, this situation is also revealing. The surf-movie genre was about the here and now (or the there and then) and not posterity. As Matt Warshaw notes in the introduction to his collection of surf-movie posters, *Surf Movie Tonight,* the point was communal tribal gatherings of surfers indoors, away from the water, for shared moments of surf stoke.[14]

Although many of the details concerning music used in most early surf movies are difficult to confirm, what we do know is compelling. Surf movies during the 1950s and on into the 1970s were, with a few notable exceptions, accompanied by unlicensed soundtracks derived from the filmmakers' personal record collections. As 1960s San Diego surfer Brad Barrett recalls, the practice of deejaying soundtracks to surf footage extended into young surfers' living rooms, where friends would bring 45 rpm records and make their own soundtracks to short 8 mm surf clips sold by *Surfer* magazine. What was considered appropriate music for any given clip varied with the age, experience, and record collection of the individual surfer. Thus the spectrum was wide, extending from the Dave Brubeck Quartet's "Take Five," to Ray Charles's "What'd I Say," to the Fireballs' "Bulldog," to Chet Atkins or Herb Alpert.[15] The creative pairings of music and film made by actual filmmakers also covered a reasonably wide range and is an often-noted characteristic of early and not-so-early surf movies. Former *Surfer* editor Sam George rehearsed this well-worn story to me at a VIP reception before a surf-movie screening in

Santa Barbara, California (at which otherwise unnotable audience members such as me could become a VIP for fifty dollars).[16] The same mixed-tape quality of early films is featured in most mentions of surf movies in the literature on the subject. Though custom-made soundtracks mixed by the filmmaker may have been very effective at largely unregulated live screenings for the surfing faithful, the result now is that the films can't be released on video or DVD since their soundtracks were not licensed, or they are released but with different soundtracks.

Licensing the soundtracks becomes an issue only if you anticipate mainstream theater distribution (as rare then as now for true surf movies) or if you want to openly market the movies on VHS or DVD (modes that became the primary means of distribution beginning in the 1980s for VHS and 1990s for DVD). In other words, any effort to surpass subcultural circulation and to generate commercial success requires a different approach to musicking the film.

What I gather from the firsthand and published accounts of early surf-movie screenings is that well-selected music could make otherwise mundane footage appear great: the unlicensed soundtrack was a big part of the communal surf-movie experience for surfers. The music in these early films linked surfing with popular culture and then, in the 1960s and especially 1970s, with notions of counterculture. Perhaps most important, even during the early 1960s when it was at its peak, the Surf Music genre was used only rarely in surf movies. The relationship between music and surfing never was as simple as a genre called Surf Music.

WHAT WE DO KNOW ABOUT SURF-MOVIE MUSIC

The first surf movie for which we have the original soundtrack is Bruce Brown's 1958 film *Slippery When Wet*. This was also Brown's first film, and it was sponsored by fellow Southern Californian and surfboard maker Dale Velzy, who provided Brown with an all-inclusive five-thousand-dollar budget—the going rate for making a surf movie at the time. Bruce Brown used the format created by Bud Browne: surfing clips interspersed with skits and gags. The first moments of *Slippery When Wet* feature an origin myth for surfing that, while reflecting Brown's signature wry sense of humor, is not dissimilar to other myths that I have heard from other surfers about the human need to engage our oceans (video example 1). This is followed by the most common plot—or what passes for a plot—in surf movies: surfers go in search of waves. Pseudo-travelogues to exotic locations where the waves are ostensibly better, bigger, and more challenging yet less crowded are still the staple of surf movies today. In *Slippery When Wet,* a group of California surfers go to the birthplace of surfing, still-exotic Hawai'i, a scant year before it became the fiftieth U.S. state.

The music for *Slippery When Wet* was created by the Bud Shank Quartet, a West Coast cool jazz ensemble led by Shank on flute and alto saxophone, with Billy Bean on guitar, Gary Peacock on bass, and Chuck Flores on drum set. This is the first soundtrack composed specifically for a surf movie. West Coast jazz was a calmer style than the hard bob jazz from New York City in the 1950s and 1960s, and perfect for Brown's understated narration style. In an introduction he added to the 1990 DVD rerelease of *Slippery When Wet,* Brown relates the story of how the soundtrack was commissioned and created. Employing the same wry sense of humor and penchant for storytelling that make his film narrations so compelling, Brown recalls:

> When the film was sort of edited, I decided it needed some music, so I went up to the Lighthouse in Hermosa Beach, California, where Bud Shank was playing. I asked Bud if he would like to do the music for the film. He said he'd never done music for a film. I said, "That's ok, I've never done a film." He said "Perfect." I gave him the whole music budget; two-hundred and fifty bucks. [Laughs] We couldn't afford a recording studio, so we recorded it in the offices of World-Pacific Records, which was one small room. I sat out in the hall, shined the projector through the mail slot in the door onto the wall; quartet sat inside, played the music.

In a phone interview, I asked Brown if this narrative was how it really happened or just good storytelling. He stuck to his story. When one listens to the soundtrack, it becomes clear that the music was not entirely improvised; there is melodic doubling and other ensemble work that requires premeditation in the form of musical composition and arrangements. In a profile of Shank, Doug Ramsey wrote that Shank composed themes for assigned sequences of the film and then expanded them for the quartet recording.[17] Whatever the details of how the recording was created, Shank and his quartet were responding to filmic images of surfing in some way or another. The result is a feature-length surf movie with a musical soundtrack created by one quartet. The single-source soundtrack was as rare in the surf-movie genre as with other films, but was repeated for several films that I consider here, including Brown's third film, *Barefoot Adventure* (1960), which was also scored by Bud Shank (this time with his quintet). Figure 11 shows a poster for a screening of the film at which Bud Shank performed live.

FIGURE 11. *Barefoot Adventure* film poster featuring Bud Shank, c. 1960. Courtesy of Bruce Brown Films, LLC (www.BruceBrownFilms.com).

Bruce Brown clearly liked Bud Shank's jazz, but as far as I know, Shank was not a surfer, and no one then or now considers him a surf musician. Turino's semiotics model offers a way to understand the link between Shank's flute playing and Brown's vision of surfing. For most viewers of Brown's *Slippery When Wet* and *Barefoot Adventure,* both when the films premiered and today, the relationship between Shank's West Coast jazz (the *sign* in Turino's model) and surfing (the *object*) is indexical—through their co-occurrence in Bruce Brown's films.[18] I doubt that Bud Shank's soundtracks, heard without the films, would conjure images of surfing in the minds of many listeners. Yet the music of the Bud Shank Quartet (and later Quintet) must have been emotionally connected to surfing from Bruce Brown's perspective. From the other direction, Bud Shank and his band did not play music in a vacuum. They performed to the object—the filmic image of surfing projected into a recording studio. On some level, then, Shank's music was presumably influenced by surfing or at least filmic images of surfing. This is what Turino calls a *dicent index sign:* the sign (Shank's jazz, in this case) was affected by the object (surfing) that it stands for. This sort of relationship often becomes the basis for claims of music's authenticity. The ability to play blues authentically, for example, is believed to derive from experiencing hardship. In the previous chapter, I relayed Dick Dale's claims that his guitar playing was a musical representation of the feeling of surfing. Dick Dale did surf at least a little. This makes his playing a dicent index of surfing and lends authenticity to his connection with surfing. How Brown's film footage influenced Shank's musicking would be a very difficult question to answer even if I had managed to interview Shank before he passed away a few years ago. Though I believe analytical studies of how musical sounds change in response to external stimuli are valuable, they are rarely conclusive. The power of music lies not in its ability to mimic other sounds or replicate the exact effect of a different experience, but in suggestion and in the associations we make in our minds and bodies. Pairing visual stimuli with music allows for some wonderful things to blossom in one's mind and body. Perhaps the nonnarrative quality of a film clip of a person dancing across a wave is especially compatible with music—humanity's least referential and therefore most adaptable art form.

In a review published in the *Surfer's Journal* of a recent rerelease of the Bud Shank soundtracks for *Slippery When Wet* and *Barefoot Adventure,* Brad Barrett waxes eloquent about how the music makes the films, keeping the viewer interested even when the filmic image hits a flat spell. He finds that the music for *Slippery When Wet* "really evokes the easygoing life of a surfer" and that the "much more muscular" tone of the *Barefoot Adventure* soundtrack is a perfect match for that film.[19] He goes on to describe particularly effective parings of moving image and music in both films, writing about Shank's tune "Ala Moana"[20] in *Barefoot Adventure* that "[t]his tune epitomizes surfing for me as well as any I've ever heard." He concludes: "You may just find yourself paddling out somewhere and as you drop into that hot little left or right, 'Ala Moana' or 'The Surf And I' will be playing in your head as you come cruising out of the hook."[21] For surfer Barrett, these jazz soundtracks became part of his surfing experience.

Shank's late-1950s and early-1960s California cool jazz resonated with the growing countercultural, counterestablishment, counter-gray-suit trend within Southern California youth communities—a lifestyle that Surf Music historian John Blair describes as "bohemian."[22] Yet I do not want to overplay associations of surfing and counter-anything at this stage. Though surfing has its playful side in that liminal zone offshore from grounded society—something that Brown has great fun with in his films—in the 1950s, rhythm and blues or rock 'n' roll would have been a much more countercultural and edgy choice of music for a soundtrack than West Coast cool jazz.[23] In Bruce Brown's mind at least, Shank's jazz was an appropriate musical pairing with filmic images of surfing. Now, because of Brown's musical choices for his films, the sound of Shank's jazz evokes the possibility of surfing for those of us who view the films.

THE ENDLESS SOUNDTRACK

Bruce Brown's 1964 film *The Endless Summer* is the marquee example of a film made for surfers that went on to have phenomenal crossover success when distributed nationally in 1966 (fig. 12). The premise of the film is simple: two surfers travel around the world, following summer in search of waves (never mind that the best waves are always in the other three seasons). Part documentary travelogue, part quest for the perfect wave, part buddy film, it is peppered with comedic moments and is carried along by Brown's trademark wry narrative and, of course, a fine musical soundtrack.

Brown made his first film in 1958, before surfing had gained mainstream popularity. When he was making *The Endless Summer,* his sixth film, surfing was firmly established in popular culture, including boast-

FIGURE 12. Signed handbill from a South African screening of *The Endless Summer*, c. 1964. Courtesy of Bruce Brown Films, LLC (www.BruceBrownFilms.com).

ing its own popular music—the named genre Surf Music. In the previous chapter, I showed that by 1965 the widespread popularity of Surf Music had passed, but Brown was making *The Endless Summer* from 1962 through 1964, a period when Surf Music was still in its heyday. In an interview, I asked Brown why he had not asked the Beach Boys or Dick Dale to create the soundtrack for his new film. His response was manifold: surfers tended not to like Surf Music at that time (though he likes the Beach Boys now); the Beach Boys sang songs, and he did not use music with lyrics in his films because he thought the text would interfere with his narration; and cost—he could not afford the Beach Boys and probably not Dick Dale.[24] Instead of engaging an established band that would have brought attention to the film, he used for the soundtrack a then-unknown, unrecorded band called the Sandals.

Brown did not seek out the Sandals. The band of young men (most of them still in high school at the time) boldly approached Brown and proposed creating the music for his new film. As Brown recently said when recalling that moment: "I went 'Yeah, fine,' thinking this is going to be a joke. God, they came back a couple weeks later and played the theme, and I went 'Jesus, that's terrific.'"[25] Brown was clearly taken with their whimsical, understated music that combined acoustic and electric guitars with a melodica (a small mouth-blown keyboard reed instrument). He scheduled time for the band in the studios of World-Pacific Records in Hollywood, where they performed and recorded ten of their own compositions for the film, as well as covers of "Jet Black" by Jet Harris and "Driftin'" by Hank Marvin. Both Harris and Marvin were members of the British band the Shadows. The soundtrack includes these recordings made by the Sandals, plus arrangements of their compositions for a small studio ensemble of professional musicians, including brass, woodwinds, and strings.

The Sandals called themselves a surf band. In many ways they fit comfortably within the Surf Music genre—an instrumental guitar-led rock band. Many of the pieces they performed for *The Endless Summer* fall squarely into the instrumental Surf Music style: electric guitar lead and twelve-bar blues. An example is their piece "Out Front," set to the very first footage of actual surfing in the movie. Yet the music most identified with the film is the theme tune, played for the opening sunrise sequence and credits and at various other times throughout the film (sometimes played by the Sandals and at other times arranged for different instruments and performed by the studio ensemble). This composition, awkwardly called "Theme from the Endless Summer," is what originally captured Brown's imagination and got the Sandals their greatest career gig. As played by the Sandals, the theme includes a mix of acoustic guitar (Walter Georis), melodica (Gaston Georis), electric guitar (John Blakeley), bass (John Gibson), and drums (Danny Brawner). This mix of instruments creates an ensemble timbre that is uncharacteristic in the Surf Music genre. In addition, the formal structure of the theme song and of two other compositions used in the film—"Wild as the Sea," heard during the Raglan, New Zealand, scenes; and "Lonely Road," used for several travel sequences—also distinguishes this soundtrack from the Surf Music genre. For example, both "Theme from the Endless Summer" and "Lonely Road" feature harmonically ambiguous guitar ostinatos (repeated patterns) that alternate between two major chords one step removed. Both have slow, sustained-note melodies, repeated without variation—not the virtuosic riffs favored by many Surf Music guitarists—with a bridge beginning on the chord that is the logical resolution of their respective two-chord ostinatos, and both end back in the harmonically ambiguous area of those two-chord ostinatos (video example 2). These slow, introspective compositions, blending acoustic and electric instruments, were not usual fare for the Surf Music genre of the time. And though the other compositions by the Sandals for this movie do fall squarely within the formal standards of Surf Music (primarily twelve-bar blues, though the Sandals tended to favor eight-bar blues), their style never achieves the sonic power of most surf bands of the era.[26] Thus, while Dick Dale had only recently been blowing up prototype Fender amplifiers as he attempted to capture the power of surfing with his guitar, Brown selected a much mellower and subtler version of Surf Music for his greatest film.

To my ear, the original *Endless Summer* recordings by the Sandals reference the Surf Music genre but do not represent it. The choice of the Sandals was shrewd on Bruce Brown's part, and their music contributes to the longevity of the film. Though in 1964 Brown could have emphasized the music that was then as now internationally associated with surfing as an obvious soundtrack for his film, he instead touched the genre lightly. It was a fortuitous decision, since Surf Music was received with some ambivalence, especially, as I showed in chapter 2, among individuals who self-identified as surfers before Surf Music existed as a popular genre. Yet at the same time, for the wider, nonsurfing audience who Brown hoped would also buy tickets for this film, Surf Music was a sonic index for surfing. So Brown chose a surf band to create the soundtrack for his film, but he chose one that played *with* the genre, not *to* it. He seems to have gotten something right. After its initial release in 1964, primarily for his established fan base of surfers, the film was released to critical acclaim a second time in 1966 across the country and abroad, and it remains surfing's movie masterpiece today.

A COUNTERCULTURAL RESPONSE TO SURFING'S SUCCESS

In an article in *Surfer* magazine, Steve Barilotti notes that *The Endless Summer* is the only surf movie that made significant money.[27] Surf movies returned to their subcultural niche after *The Endless Summer,* and though the musical theme of *The Endless Summer* remains a sonic index for surfing, I don't find that surf movies in general established a strong musical identity for the burgeoning New Surfing affinity group. One reason for this, I suggest, was that most of the music used for surf-movie soundtracks was imported—that is, not made by surfers themselves (though several members of the Sandals were surfers).

Music made by surfers themselves and associated directly with surfing, on the other hand, sets up a different paradigm that is significant in the matriculation of the New Surfing community. Epitomizing what Steve Barilotti calls the "surfing-as-art-film"[28] is *The Innermost Limits of Pure Fun.* Filmed and produced in 1969 by George Greenough, a Santa Barbara, California, native then dividing his time between California and Australia, it is a psychedelic pre-MTV music video: no dialogue and no narrative; just music (primarily instrumental), surfing footage, and the occasional groovy handmade graphic by Patty Henoch (Irons) containing key information such as the names of the surfers (fig. 13).

When Greenough needed a soundtrack for his film, he turned to his surfing friend Denny Aaberg, who had an informal band popular at what Aaberg described as "hippy parties" in the Santa Barbara area, near Greenough's California home. The band included Aaberg and Ernie Knapp on guitars and Phil Pritchard on bass. They played primarily in a rhythm-and-blues style. Aaberg wanted to augment the group for the soundtrack and invited Doug (organ and piano) and Dennis (drums) Dragon, siblings in a well-known musical family from the Los Angeles area with whom Aaberg had some connections, to join them. The Dragons brought a jazz, funk, and soul influence to the band, and Dennis was a skilled recording engineer as well as drummer. The group of five musicians took the name "Farm"[29] and set about the challenge of creating the soundtrack for a surf movie that would have no narration.

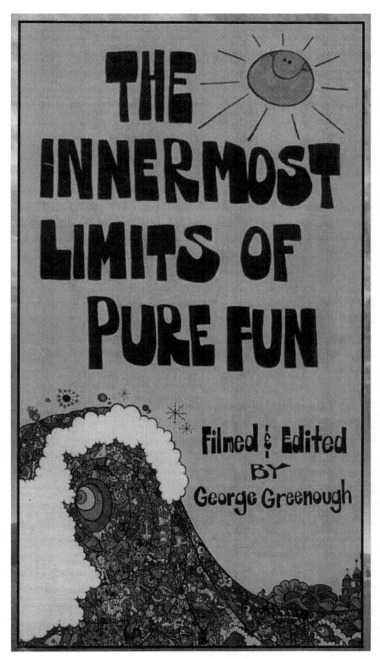

FIGURE 13. Box cover for the 1997 video release of *The Innermost Limits of Pure Fun.* Art created by Patty Irons.

(Unlike the loquacious Bruce Brown, Greenough is a man of few words.) Their method was to meet and jam together, sometimes watching raw cuts of the film for inspiration.

Dennis Dragon, the drummer and recording engineer for Farm, described to me in an interview the context in which one particularly interesting section of the soundtrack was recorded. The film was premiered at the Lobero Theatre in Santa Barbara. Farm had already recorded the soundtrack for the film, but filmmaker Greenough wanted the band to play live for the final "Coming of the Dawn" section of the film during the premiere screening, which is exactly what they did. According to Dragon, playing while watching the film enabled the musicians to "translate directly what their emotions were by viewing [the film] and playing to the footage. . . . [T]he visuals were extremely influential to the music that was being played. I know that seeing the energy 'inside the tube' influenced my drumming tremendously!"[30] Denny Aaberg described this process of playing to the film as direct inspiration for their musicking: "We looked at the movie and tried to kind of mimic what was going on." This process was helped by the fact that, according to Aaberg, individuals in Farm were "deep surfers" and the inspiration for their music "was the sea because of our love for the ocean. Plus we were doing the score for a surfing movie."[31]

Like Bud Shank's at least partially improvised soundtrack for *Slippery When Wet,* some of the music for *The Innermost Limits of Pure Fun* was directly influenced by the filmic image viewed by the musicians while playing.[32] Unlike the Bud Shank Quartet, however, Farm was staffed with surfers responding to surfing images with an insider's perspective—a perspective literally captured by Greenough in the "Coming of the Dawn" sequence, which consists entirely of slow-motion footage taken with a camera strapped to Greenough's back as he surfed waves in a crouched position on a kneeboard or lying on an inflatable mat (fig. 14). As Dragon explained, all the musicians in Farm were surfers, and they knew what being in a tube was like.

The music style and approach used by Farm established a standard that became prominent among some surfing communities and remains so today. This style and approach can be described as a jam band. In the case of Farm, their music is rock-based, sometimes using a blues form (like so many subgenres of primarily U.S. and British popular music that bear the descriptor "rock"), but frequently influenced by jazz-style improvisations (heard most clearly in Doug Dragon's organ solos). The

FIGURE 14. George Greenough riding a kneeboard while filming behind himself into the wave, for *The Innermost Limits of Pure Fun.* Photograph by Howard "Wardie" Ward (www.wardieward.com).

music that Farm created for the "Coming of the Dawn" section of the movie is characteristic (video example 3). It begins with an organ and flute introduction that moves into a section featuring a nylon-string guitar and double bass repeating an eight-beat rhythmic/harmonic ostinato while the organ improvises. This is followed by a more extended five-minute jam built on a four-beat electric bass ostinato under a sixteen-beat harmonic ostinato played primarily on an electric guitar and a drum set. The organ and sometimes a guitar improvise over this foundation. There is also a wordless vocal-ensemble section built around the sixteen-beat harmonic ostinato. The music's interest is not melodic, but rather around what can be called a rhythmic/harmonic groove (the ostinato) over which the organ, electric guitar, and vocalists provide interesting changes in tonal color (timbre). The performance is ostensibly improvised, though the basic structural elements were most certainly worked out in advance. As with similar works by other jam bands (The Grateful Dead, Phish), melodic or harmonic development is not emphasized and is sometimes absent. Interest is created by the pleasure in a repeated pattern or cycle (sometimes described as trancelike or trance inducing) and changing colors (timbres) provided by the improvising instruments.

This type of semi-improvised music is established in the first moments of the film. Just after the opening credits, the tone is set with a five-minute piece built on a four-beat bass ostinato, while other instruments take extended solos in a jazz format. Doug Dragon's organ sets the standard with a jazz-style improvisation that, to my ear, is built around a quote of the African-American spiritual "Wade on the Water," a playful reference to the act of riding a surfboard. Farm also provided two topical songs for the soundtrack, and more conventional twelve- and eight-bar blues improvisations. Note that these blues-form pieces do not sound like instrumental Surf Music that uses the same form. They are distinguished by a generally slower tempo and more varied drum-set patterns, with less reliance on precomposed melodic identities and more emphasis on extended improvisations. All of the music falls squarely into the broad category of rock that was established by the late 1960s. Key for the purposes of this book, however, is the emphasis on extended improvisations within this form.

This style of loosely organized rock-band group-composition/improvisation became a reoccurring theme in surfing communities, and occasionally features in surf movies. For example, *The Innermost Limits* was followed by a few standout surfing-as-art films, including the 1972 Australian production *Morning of the Earth,* another film with no narration but with music made specifically for the film. The film is a statement on self-sufficiency as a surfer: raising one's own food, making one's own boards, and making one's own music. The film featured surfers making their own music, and this is true in that we see surfers play guitars and flutes in the film—but we don't hear them. What we hear is the soundtrack, produced by G. Wayne Thomas, who also wrote and performed some of the songs on the soundtrack, which became very popular in its own right.

Another film remembered for its soundtrack as much as filmic images is *Crystal Voyager* (1973), by David Elfick. The seventy-five-minute movie begins as a documentary about George Greenough and ends with a twenty-three-minute segment that features footage shot by Greenough and a soundtrack consisting solely of the improvisatory group composition "Echoes," from Pink Floyd's 1971 album *Meddle.* Elfick gained permission to use "Echoes" after showing the members of Pink Floyd some of the footage for the film. In return, Pink Floyd was allowed to use Greenough's film footage during their concert performances.[33] *Crystal Voyager* enjoyed long cinematic runs not only in Australian and North American coastal towns, but also in cities such as London, where

London Evening Standard reviewer Alexander Walker famously wrote: "The last 25 minutes is an almost unbroken underwater trip of a thousand translucent tints, accompanied by the electronic music of Pink Floyd pinging out of infinity like an echo sounder. To see it stone cold sober on a wintry morning is exhilarating. To see it 'stoned' as I guess some surf freaks have, must be out of this world."[34] The "Echoes" portion of *Crystal Voyager* is perhaps especially appealing to those who don't surf, since there are actually no surfers seen in the section; in fact, there are no people at all in this twenty-three-minute segment of the film. Like the "Coming of the Dawn" segment—the concluding piece—of Greenough's *Innermost Limits of Pure Fun,* the "Echoes" portion of *Crystal Voyager* consists entirely of shots from a camera strapped to Greenough's back while he surfed, often inside tubular waves, and of footage shot from underwater. While surfers will have experienced similar watery perspectives, such images must be mysterious and even psychedelic to nonsurfers, as suggested by the *London Evening Standard* reviewer. For many viewers, then, surfing—or rather, waves as seen by a surfer—becomes the index sign of Pink Floyd's music. The swirling green waves look like what "Echoes" sounds like.

Of the many other surf movies from the late 1960s and 1970s, I will briefly mention only two: *Pacific Vibrations* (1970, by John Severson) and *Five Summer Stories* (1972, by Jim Freeman and Greg MacGillivray). *Pacific Vibrations* is probably the most famous illustration of my earlier caveat: many surf movies are not available for study because their soundtracks were not licensed. The *Pacific Vibrations* soundtrack featured music by Cream, the Steve Miller Band, Ry Cooder, and many other popular rock bands of the day. In this sense it is representative of surf movies up through the 1980s. The film's poster was created by Rick Griffin, who also designed posters and album covers for rock musicians and bands including Jimi Hendrix and the Grateful Dead. Though most surfers today have never seen the film from start to finish, it survives in the memories of some and the imaginations of many as a film with a great soundtrack.[35] The *Five Summer Stories* soundtrack, on the other hand, was created by Honk, a band from Laguna Beach, California (not far from San Clemente, where the Sandals were from). Like the music for *The Innermost Limits of Pure Fun,* the soundtrack was created specifically for the film, and some of the musicians were surfers. At a roundtable discussion preceding a celebratory screening of *Five Summer Stories* in 2007, Greg MacGillivray explained that music was so important to his vision for the film that they used stereo sound (rare for surf films at the time) and carried their own audio equipment to screenings. He wanted the sound to be better than a live concert.[36] Honk's music is grounded in rhythm and blues but also some sounds associated with country music, including several pieces with banjo (the only use of banjo I have found in a surf movie). The movie also featured some music not played by Honk, such as a solo acoustic-guitar piece played by professional surfer Corky Carol for footage of Carol surfing. This is the first example of a self-accompanied surf-film segment that I have verified, though later a few additional surf movies feature what we might call "auto-soundtracks."

SURFING GETS A JOB (AND GOES DIRECT-TO-VIDEO)

When one is surfing, it is best to catch waves early, before they actually begin to break. There are many advantages to catching a wave as early as possible: once a wave is caught, it is easier to stand and position oneself on the wave for a good, long ride; and in surfing etiquette, the first person to catch the wave has priority; others should yield. Catching a wave early is accomplished only with considerable skill combined with a lot of effort—paddling vigorously on one's surfboard to build up speed matching that of the approaching swell. Catching a wave late, as it is already breaking—called a "late takeoff" or "late drop"—usually requires less physical effort, sometimes just a few strokes or even no paddling, but it carries greater risks. If the surfer does not position himself or herself just right, he or she will wipe out badly and feel the full force of the crashing wave.

This is a metaphor for the 1980s cresting and breaking of the surf movie industry wave. In the 1950s, surf movies were made with little or no sponsorship but with a lot of energy on the part of individual filmmakers, combined with a clear sense of what the surfing community wanted to see and hear. A few individuals managed good careers by making films in this way. They caught the wave early and enjoyed a long ride. By the early 1980s, surf-movie production costs were in the tens of thousands of dollars and would move into the hundreds of thousands by the end of the decade. There was real competition in the lineup now. Much more was at risk financially, but there were also more surfing-related sponsors ready to pay the way. Making a good surf movie was always a lot of work, but now, with major sponsors and product placement, it was a job. But in other ways, the wave of surf movies was "closing out" (breaking all at once—very bad for surfing). Theatrical releases of surf movies dwindled with the mid-1980s direct-to-video releases of films. While filmmakers might get away with bootleg soundtracks to a film they were screening in unregulated school and community halls, they would not get away with openly selling video—and later DVD—copies of their films without first licensing the music on the soundtracks. As a result of the commercial imperative to shift distribution to video sales rather than selling tickets for live screenings, more surf movies began to have licensed soundtracks. An unintended benefit of that trend is that these later films are more readily available for purchase on video or DVD today.

Surfer Jack McCoy began making surf movies in the mid-1970s and is still at it now, thirty-five years later. His films embody, and even led, some of the changes during these three-plus decades. For example, his 1981 film *Storm Riders* (directed by David Lourie and Dick Hoole as well as Jack McCoy, all based in Australia) replaced the fascination with psychedelia and surfing-as-art in 1970s films with a fascination for surfers' fitness and professionalism. The soundtrack for this film is predominantly rock 'n' roll, some of it by well-known groups like the Doors, whose "Riders on the Storm" opens the film, and the Little River Band, whose "Cool Change" plays during the credits. *Storm Riders* was sponsored by Rip Curl Wetsuits and L.K. Communications, and its producers had a large enough budget to license these songs and others for the film. McCoy's films also document the ascendancy of Australian surfers on the international contest circuit, as is seen in video example 4, featuring surfer Mark Richards. This video example illustrates another tendency in McCoy's films: the use of rock music by Australian musicians—in this case, Marc Hunter, who was born in New Zealand but who lived in Australia. An additional musical quality that became a feature of McCoy's later films was the inclusion of music from locations where they filmed some of the surfing: gamelan in Bali, drumming and dance in South Africa, and a hula class in Hawai'i. This use of music from filming locations might be viewed as exoticism today, but McCoy's continued use of diverse musics became much more sophisticated in his later films.

Jack McCoy produced one of the first direct-to-video surf movies, *The Performers* (1984). According to Matt Warshaw, it "signaled the upcoming wholesale change in surf cinema from celluloid to videotape, theater to living room."[37] Warshaw notes that the numbers of VHS and then DVD surf movies rose in the 1990s, but that the quality level plummeted. While seasoned professionals like McCoy, schooled in the era of film, continued to create well-crafted surf movies on tape (though often shot on film and later copied to tape), there was a lot of junk being released. Yet there are some advantages to direct-to-video surf movies that especially younger surfers learned to exploit. With video, a surfer could watch closely the moves of their favorite professional surfers over and over again on their own TV. This experience differed from the tribal gathering at the local junior high school auditorium to view the latest surf movie on the big screen, narrated live by the filmmaker. The differences include how one is likely to experience the music. A VHS or DVD viewer is less likely to hear entire pieces of music that might develop along with a sequence of filmic images, the standout example being the "Echoes" segment of *Crystal Voyagers*. The sonic as well as visual experience is more likely to be fractured, interrupted, paused, rewound, reseen, and reheard as grommet (young, inexperienced but determined) surfers closely study the latest move just before they dash to the beach and try it themselves.

An opinion expressed to me in interviews and casual conversations by surfers in California, Hawai'i, and England is that videographer Taylor Steele set the standard for what music worked best in the new VHS era. These same surfers were also able to name many of the bands whose music was used by Steele for his soundtracks, especially the Southern California punk bands Bad Religion, Pennywise, and Sprung Monkey. These bands were used in Steele's first film, *Momentum,* made in 1992, and they are still considered to be the source of music appropriate for surfing among some surfers today (video example 5). Steele clearly got something right by matching up-and-coming surfers with loud, fast, powerful music. He became the best-selling surf-video maker of the 1990s and 2000s.[38]

Today's most prominent surfer-musician, Jack Johnson, exemplifies how surf videos affected a new generation of surfers. Before becoming a popular music phenomenon, Johnson was a semiprofessional surfer and then surf-film maker, releasing the surf video *Thicker Than Water* in 2000. When I interviewed him in 2010, he directly linked surf movies to the music he personally associated with surfing. He said that surf-film makers such as Jack McCoy and Taylor Steele had a great influence on what music he and other young surfers around him associated with surfing. Though the music selected may have simply reflected the personal taste of the filmmaker, it was a "pretty powerful" connection because they were "all real surfers making these films, and people who really [were] connected with the surf culture."[39] He was very specific in recalling how videos connected music with surfing in his life as he was growing up on the island of Oʻahu, Hawaiʻi, near Pipeline—the most famous wave in the world. He explained how he would watch a video clip of champion surfer Tom Curren over and over again, studying how he surfed, "where his foot was on the board and how far he bent his knee forward, and how he shifted his weight when he did a turn." These clips were accompanied by a musical soundtrack that became part of the surfing experience for Johnson. After studying the clips, he and his friends would run to the beach and try to replicate what they saw in the surfing videos:

> Then we would go out and we would pretend like we were them in the water as kids. And to me I'd have the song that was in the movie in my head the whole time I'd be surfing, and as I was singing a song by the Untouchables— whether it was kind of out loud, actually even humming it almost as I'd surf, or just in my mind—it would make me feel more like I was Tom Curren to hear that song because I had watched the imagery with the music over and over.[40]

Johnson then recalled Taylor Steele's first videos. In Johnson's memory, they initiated a clear shift in surf movies by connecting a type of music that young surfers were listening to with a new generation of surfers. At least in Johnson's case, surf-movie soundtracks also shaped his own music-making in high school, where he formed a punk cover band. Without a doubt, surf videos directly influenced Jack Johnson's surfing and musicking.

WHERE ARE THE WOMEN SURFERS?

In the surf movies and videos mentioned thus far, we could count the number of featured female surfers (and female musicians) on one hand. When we include Hollywood films with surfing themes, the gender balance improves only slightly. Where are the female surfers?

As noted in chapter 1, pre-contact Hawaiian surfing included female surfers, from commoners to princesses and queens. However, New Surfing, reinvented in the twentieth century, is decidedly male dominated. The most prominent role given to women in surf movies, surf magazines, and, as we saw in the previous chapter, Surf Music is as a bikini-clad object of the hypermasculine, heteronormative gaze. Surf movies tend to reinforce this aspect of New Surfing, though every so often a surf movie focused on female surfers takes a step to redress this imbalance. One notable example is *Blue Crush,* a film by Bill Ballard released in 1998 (fig. 15). This film should not be confused with the 2002 Hollywood drama bearing the same title, though that film was reportedly inspired by the original surf movie, and featured many of the same surfers—a few as surfing doubles for the actresses, with others playing themselves.[41] Ballard's *Blue Crush* is a true surf movie: a film of surfers made by surfers for surfers, with no plot. It is distinguished from the surf movies thus far considered in that all the featured surfers in the film are women—women who surf extremely well by any standard. Though surf movies focused on women have been rare (in this chapter they are proportionally overrepresented), the number of women surfing appears to have reached the critical mass that will support more media recognition. For example, *Leave a Message,* a surf movie that claims to be the successor to *Blue Crush,* was produced by the company Nike and released in 2012. The film is a surf movie featuring excellent surfing footage of the best female surfers.

Taken as a whole, the soundtrack for Ballard's *Blue Crush* is different from the soundtracks of male-centered surf movies, though the penchant for punk (Dance Hall Crashers, Ruth Ruth) and reggae (Inner Circle) can be heard as a similarity to other late-1990s and 2000s surf movies. *Blue Crush* distinguishes itself with the inclusion of electronic dance (Crystal Method, Towa Tei), ambient rock and trip-hop (Tranquility Bass, Morcheeba), and, perhaps predictably, music featuring female lead singers (Chaka Khan with Rufus, Skye Edwards with Morcheeba, Amel Larrieux with Towa Tei; video example 6). It is a soundtrack that captures one slice of what young cosmopolitan women in certain places in the late 1990s might have been listening to—surfers or not—with one important caveat: it is music that one would have to look for. It was not U.S. Top 40 fare of the time.

Of course the filmmakers do not source Top 40 hits. As even our most famous surf moviemaker, Bruce Brown, made clear, surf movies couldn't afford to license the most popular music of the day. Yes, at least for the first twenty years of the genre, surf-film makers typically did use the most popular music of the day, but their soundtracks were bootlegs, and for that reason we do not have those movies available today with original soundtracks. But now, in the era of direct-to-video or DVD, filmmakers are compelled to dip slightly below the surface, slightly underground, slightly subcultural (an image surfers are wont to cultivate anyway). In doing so, they are able to come up with excellent soundtracks, sometimes doing the bands they select a great service by promoting their music. For example, Ballard's *Blue Crush* was my

FIGURE 15. Cover for *Blue Crush* DVD, 1998. Bill Ballard, Billygoat Productions.

introduction to all the bands featured on that soundtrack (save one track by Ladysmith Black Mambazo). I have since purchased a few albums by these new-to-me bands.

Of course women themselves have been a subcultural category in the New Surfing paradigm. However, the string of films focused on female surfers in the past decade suggests that this is changing. In addition to *Blue Crush* and *Leave a Message,* there are several standout films: *Heart of the Sea* (2002), about Hawaiian champion surfer and community activist Rell Kapolioka'ehukai Sunn, by Charlotte LaGarde and Lisa Denker; *First Love* (2010), a documentary about three young female surfers from Australia, by Clare Gorman, Clare Pleuckhahn, and Fran Derham; and *Soul Surfer* (2011), a Hollywood production by Sean McNamara about Bethany Hamilton, who lost her arm to a shark while surfing but who continues to surf with one arm. While vastly outnumbered by films that uncritically focus exclusively on male surfers, films focused on female surfers show, at least for those who seek them out, that women can and do surf at the highest levels.

THE RETURN OF SOUL SURFING AND HOMEMADE MUSIC

Not only did Taylor Steele's videos set the standard for direct-to-video surf movies; they also signaled the return of the DIY ethos of surf movies. His paradigm-shifting first film, *Momentum,* was made in 1992 for about five thousand dollars, the same figure Bruce Brown needed for his first film back in 1958—not adjusted for inflation. Anyone with a cheap video camera could make a surf movie, and hundreds of surfers did. In the two decades since Steele's first video, the technology has gotten even less expensive, less cumbersome, and more easily clad in inexpensive waterproofing. Surfing lineups today are dotted with board-mounted and hand-held digital devices shooting everything from experts to rank beginners. Videos of the same range of surfing ability are set to music and uploaded for us all to see on YouTube later that same day. Warshaw's quip about surf movies' legacy of mediocrity applies today more than ever. But within the sea of films, one broad current is especially notable for the music it inspires and carries along—the restoration of the soul surfer.

If in the 1980s the surfing community had to metaphorically get a job to keep up with the multi-million-dollar industry that surfing had become, as it approached and moved into the twenty-first century, it began to return nostalgically to some of the pleasures of its youth, when surfing was for fun—surfing for surfing's sake, the essence of soul surfing. Soul surfing, as defined by Warshaw, is the opposite of competitive and commercialized surfing, and the concept has its roots in the alignment of surfing with the counterculture of the 1960s.[42] The myth of soul surfing is captured best in the 1972 Australian surf movie *Morning of the Earth,* discussed earlier in this chapter, featuring former world champion surfer Nat Young, who lived a nearly subsistence lifestyle for a few years in rural New South Wales, making his own boards, growing his own food, and surfing uncrowded waves. In reality, however, most of us make compromises that prevent us from living to surf. Soul surfing is an aesthetic ideal that, if we are fortunate, we achieve occasionally when we manage to catch a decent wave, arch our back gracefully into a bottom turn, and forget for a moment why it is we ever leave the water.

Then we do leave the water. We run to class, to our jobs, to get the groceries, to mow the lawn, to make our appointments with friends and family. What we crave the rest of the time we are not in the water are books, magazines, and movies that remind us of our own surfing, not just the champion surfers who, by definition, are soulless (though I challenge this idea when I return to soul surfing in chapter 6). This is the niche filled by the return to the soul-surfing-movie subgenre (though it never really went away). The soul-surfing movie inspires and challenges, but with a model that is accessible. With footage of excellent surfing, but not the acrobatics of professional contest surfing, the soul-surfing movie reminds us that we, too, can surf. The music on the soundtracks is also good, sometimes excellent, but equally accessible. If we just get our priorities straight, surf more, and practice guitar more, we, too, could star in such a film. We, too, are surfers; we, too, are musical beings.

I mark the return of soul-surfing films with the 1996 Australian film *Litmus: A Surfing Odyssey,* by Andrew Kidman, Jon Fran, and Mark Sutherland. While clearly inspired by *Morning of the Earth, Litmus* takes the message of surfing self-sufficiency a step further by using a soundtrack made by the filmmakers themselves; most of the music was written by Kidman himself, the soundtrack was recorded by the Val Dusty Experiment in one day, and all of the other filmmakers were also in the band (video example 7).[43] Also of note in the movie is an extended segment featuring film footage of a freely improvised jam on electric guitar by three-time world surfing champion Tom Curren interspersed with footage of Curren surfing. *Litmus* is an introspective movie, its mood complemented by long instrumental improvisations reminiscent of the music that Farm created for *The Innermost Limits of Pure Fun*—except Kidman told me in an interview that they went about the process in a way opposite to what Greenough did: they actually completed the music first and then edited the film to the music.[44] Andrew Kidman also wrote and performed a majority of the music for his 2005 film *Glass Love* and for his 2010 film *Lost in the Ether*. The sense I have in watching these films is that if I dedicated myself to the pursuit, I, too, could surf many of the waves shown in the film. This sense, I feel, is aided by the surfer-filmmaker-musicians who performed the soundtrack, playing music that I might also be able to replicate. This, of course, is part of the affective challenge of DIY projects. It is a subcultural draw; you, too, can contribute.

All of these surf movies are rich with artistic images, shot on film instead of video. While both *Litmus* and *Glass Love* feature top competitive surfers, they are often riding twin-fin surfboards or longboards—types of surfboards that hark back to earlier decades and that generally are not ridden for competitions today. They are nostalgic retro surfboards. Soul surfers make a virtue out of nostalgia. These films may feature the best surfers in the world today, but here they exude soulfulness, emphasizing surfing as a lifestyle instead of a sport. I hear and experience the music as retro, too, emphasizing group effort, musical companionship rather than competition—a jam among competent musicians and songwriters. It is music for sharing, for participation, for singing along with—not for the display of virtuosity. It is homemade music. This was emphasized at a screening of *Glass Love* that I attended in Santa Barbara in May 2005. Andrew Kidman was touring with the film, and he played guitar and sang onstage before the screening. Tom Curren joined him on electric keyboard for a few songs as well—excellent surfers making their own music and their own films: soul surfers.

Jack Johnson may have come of age watching Taylor Steele's high-energy films with intense hardcore punk-rock soundtracks, but when he made his two notable surf films, *Thicker Than Water* (2000, directed with Chris Malloy and Emmett Malloy, fig. 16) and *September Sessions* (2000), he no longer aspired to be a professional surfer. He had earned a degree in film studies, and was well on his way to becoming one of the most successful and most mellow popular music stars of the first decade of the twenty-first century. Johnson's films, too, fall within what I am calling soul-surfing films. Like Kidman's films, Johnson's feature some of the most competitive surfers in the world at the time, and they are similarly introspective and even moody films that stress the pleasures of

FIGURE 16. Cover (back and front) for *Thicker Than Water* soundtrack CD (2000), including an interior photograph of Jack Johnson with camera.

wave riding rather than the thrill of competition. Instead of high-energy punk music, the soundtracks emphasize slower-tempo, mellower music, often with acoustic instruments. The genres include Johnson's own folk rock (video example 8), as well as reggae (Finley Quaye), acoustic blues, and so-called alternative hip-hop (G. Love) and trip-hop (Dan the Automator). Note the similarities with Ballard's *Blue Crush* in terms of popular music genres that appear on the soundtrack. What distinguishes Johnson's surf movies is the inclusion of his own music on their soundtracks. Here he connects with Kidman in being involved in every aspect of creating a surf movie: filming, editing, and performing some of the music for the soundtrack. This points up a core quality of the return or the resurgence of the soul-surfer concept in surfing communities: a broad view of human expressive behaviors associated with surfing beyond wave riding itself. In chapter 6, I return to Kidman and other surfer-musicians who are at the forefront of the return of the soul surfer.

SURF MOVIES, MUSIC, AND THE SURFING COMMUNITY

For surfers, watching surf movies is a corporeal experience. For example, when watching a surf movie, I catch myself leaning from one side to another, sometimes literally catching myself before I fall over on the couch. In a sense I am joining with the surfer in the film and moving with him or her across the face of a wave. This kinetic response is not unlike bodily movement in response to hearing music; it is often involuntary or unconscious. Watching a surf movie, like listening to some music, is literally physically moving. Watching surf movies in a theater with a crowd of other surfers can lead to powerful experiences of what Edward Hall calls *social synchrony* as individuals move with the filmic waves and surfers, and to the musical soundtrack.[45] On the other hand, social synchrony is not often achieved by surfers in the water—not today, with the reigning rule of one person per wave. Part of New Surfing at least is the ideal of being alone, on a wave, miles from anyone except for one or two of your best surfing buddies. (A good ride is always much better if it is witnessed by your buddy.) A surf movie with good music offers a rare opportunity to redress this social isolation. The circle is complete when the soundtrack for a film is also made by a surfer—maybe one who plays guitar pretty well but on a level that you can aspire to on your better days. This reminds us viewers that we are in the loop, that we are part of the tribe of surfers. The subtle message seems to be that we, too, given a little time, could become a film-worthy surfer, and maybe a surf-movie maker and even a musician. Bruce Brown, George Greenough, Jack McCoy, Taylor Steele, Andrew Kidman, and Jack Johnson are just the guys we sit next to in the lineup waiting for waves. Even if they catch more waves than we do, maybe we can jam with them around the fire later on with our guitars and ukuleles . . .

Of course, catching the wave of surf movies, whether early or late, gives the filmmaker considerable influence. In the over half a century of surf-movie history, the music chosen by filmmakers has been very significant for musically socializing surfing communities. The outside world may think of the Beach Boys when the words *music* and *surf* are heard in the same sentence, but surfers are more likely to hear strains of music from their favorite surf movies in their minds' ears.

There is not now and there never was a single genre or style of music that captures the essence of surfing, but the music featured in surf movies does provide a sort of overview of music that surfers connect with. Generally the music of surf movies is at least marginally popular music of the day, sometimes linked to the home region of the filmmaker, as with Bruce Brown's use of Bud Shank's West Coast jazz and the Sandals' subtle take on Surf Music, both local bands with whom Brown had personal connections. Other influential films, such as Greenough's *Innermost Limits of Pure Fun,* followed by Kidman's more recent films, build soundtracks up from the beaches with bands composed in part or entirely of surfers who create music specifically for a surf movie. At least since the 1990s, several trends emerge in surf-movie soundtracks (and at surfing festivals, as we will see in the following chapter): high-energy punk rock (or other music sometimes described as "heavy") and down-tempo music including folk rock, singer-songwriter, acoustic hip-hop, and reggae, much of it performed by surfers themselves. This is a shift from some of the early surf movies, such as Brown's *Endless Summer,* that included popular genres of the day played by one band (in Brown's case, the Sandals), paired with more typical Hollywood soundtrack fare of musical arrangements played by an unnamed group of studio musicians. With rare exceptions, anything that smacks of classic Surf Music is gone from surf movies. Since the 1970s, the trend has been to draw the soundtrack from existing recordings of music popular at the time, or for the filmmaker to gather his musically inclined friends in a studio and ask them to create a soundtrack.

What is unchanged, however, is the realization since the earliest surf movies in the 1950s that pairing music with surf movies is an aesthetic necessity. I am ready to take it a step further and propose that, as with any significant human social grouping, surfers need musical practices to imagine themselves in a community. The surfing affinity group requires music.

CHAPTER 4

Two Festivals and Three Genres of Music

Every year dozens of surf-related festivals are held where we might expect: Hawai'i; the West, East, and Gulf Coasts of the United States; Australia; and South Africa. There are too many festivals to list here, and almost all of them feature live music. While it might have made sense to focus on festivals close to my home in California (there are plenty), I have instead decided to present two case studies from Europe: the first in Italy, near Livorno, on the Mediterranean, where surfing waves only occasionally grace the otherwise pleasant beaches; and the second in the surf-crazed town of Newquay, Cornwall, United Kingdom, which is attached to an international surfing contest. By moving beyond the obvious centers of the global surfing community, we gain new perspectives on that community. These two very different festivals in Europe, which I attended during the summer of 2009, point out some of the range of musics associated with surfing internationally. They also bring into relief many of the interpretive issues and questions at the heart of this book.

SURFER JOE SUMMER FESTIVAL, ITALY

On 24 July 2009, my wife, Ruth, and I flew to Pisa, Italy, rented a car, and headed a few miles down the Mediterranean coast on the S1 to Calafuria, the site of the 2009 Surfer Joe Summer Festival. The festival was held on the patio of a restaurant and nightclub that sits alone on a cliff over the sea, just south of the industrial port city Livorno. Because the festival was hosted at the same location in 2008, we had some idea of what the site would be like from photographs and videos posted on the Surfer Joe Web site. But by the time we found the festival, the sun had set, and we would not see until the following day the full beauty of the location with its stone tower and rock cliffs overlooking the Mediterranean. Still, the effect of the warm patio cooled by the sea lapping against the rocks in the dim light some meters below was intoxicating.

Crammed onto the patio between the restaurant and the sea were two stages: the larger, primary stage on the edge of the patio with its back to the sea (seen in figs. 17 and 21 below), and a smaller, secondary stage on a narrow porch attached to the lower level of the building (partially seen in fig. 19 below). Also on the patio were two bars serving drinks, and stalls selling CDs, vintage vinyl, T-shirts, bathing suits, and other music- and beach-related items. Corporate sponsors such as Shark Energy Drink, Vodaphone, and a few others had their logos on display. From the patio one could also enter the downstairs of the building, which housed the restaurant. In this basementlike room, cut into the stone cliff and open only toward the patio looking over the sea, were additional vendors displaying and selling merchandise, including an array of new and vintage guitars. In one corner of this room a local surfboard shaper, Marco Rizzo, creator of Dr.ank Surfboards, displayed several of his handmade and tastefully colorful boards. Though we heard a few people speaking English with British accents, most of those present were conversing in Italian. The age range was perhaps typical for a nightclub in Europe: most individuals appeared to be in their late teens to midthirties, with fewer individuals in each subsequent decade of age acquisition. I felt older than most on the patio, but vainly noted that I was not the oldest fellow there. The festival had the feel of a summer beach party, with a distinctive retro vibe provided by the Surfer Joe logo, the costumes of several bands and a few audience members, and much of the music heard. This was not a large festival setting, but a relatively compact and enclosed space. Nonetheless, the atmosphere was festive, and attention was focused on the spirit of the Surfer Joe Summer Festival.

The music, however, distinguished this particular beach party from what one might expect in 2009. Sometimes aurally clashing with a techno disco in the club above the patio, the music at the Surfer Joe Summer Festival, with a few exceptions, referenced the circumscribed genre of Surf Music.

The Surfer Joe Summer Festival is a music festival, not a surf festival. Surfing is present at the festival as an idea and as a symbol of the genre Surf Music. The inclusion of Dr.ank's surfboards and other icons of wave riding offers a tenuous symbolic link to the cultural practice of surfing itself. Yet, as I hope to show, symbolic associations are meaningful and important. And, as I point out in other parts of this book, Turino and Peirce's system of semiotic interpretation shows us that associative meanings continue to change—a chaining effect of meanings.[1] For our purposes here, the Surfer Joe Summer Festival shows how symbolic associations can generate meaning and become part of the story of music and surfing today.

History of the Festival

The Surfer Joe Summer Festival is the creation of Lorenzo Valdambrini, an Italian musician with two Surf Music bands, Wadadli Riders (specializing in instrumental rock) and the Pipelines (a Beach Boys–style band emphasizing vocal harmonies; fig. 17). In spring 2002, Valdambrini created the Web site surferjoemusic.com to promote the Italian Surf Music scene. Then in the winter of 2003 he began producing shows featuring bands playing Surf Music at several venues in Italy, followed by a series of "Surfin' Sundays" events that paired Italian and international bands. The summer was rounded out with the first Summer Festival of Surf Music, held on the beach at Marina di Massa, a small town north of Pisa. The second Summer Festival, in 2004, was in Calcinaia, Pisa. Then Valdambrini moved to Antigua and did not host another Surfer Joe Summer Festival until 2008, this time in Calafuria, at the same location where the festival was again held in 2009. Valdambrini has since opened Surfer Joe's Diner, situated on the beach in Livorno, and he now hosts the festival there. The Surfer Joe festivals have all been held on or near the coast of Tuscany, where there is a modest surfing community hungry for the rare surfable waves that occasionally grace their beaches.

Lorenzo Valdambrini's motivations for creating the festival seem clear: as a fan of both the instrumental-rock and vocal-harmony genres of early-1960s Surf Music, he has created a platform for bringing together and promoting Italian and international Surf Music bands. He has succeeded in establishing a virtual community of fans of this music, and he has brought them together for numerous concerts and a handful of festivals. Valdambrini is also able to promote his own two bands, the

FIGURE 17. The Pipelines on the main stage at the Surfer Joe Summer Festival. with Lorenzo Valdambrini, arm raised, leading the singing, 25 July 2009. Photograph by the author.

Pipelines and the Wadadli Riders, and place them with other Surf Music bands. He shares with many of the musicians I have met who play classic genre Surf Music an intense passion for the music. With his professional skills as a Web designer, his knack for organizing events, and his inexhaustible enthusiasm, Valdambrini has created a music scene focused on Surf Music in Italy.

Valdambrini is not a surfer himself, and his festival is first and foremost about music, but he actively tries to bring surfing and Surf Music together when possible by seeking the sponsorship of surfing brands and by having surfing products such as surfboards at the festival. Yet he told me that he believes the sport of surfing and Surf Music have little connection now and that although it was a cool alternative music that surfers listened to in the 1960s, Surf Music seems to have lost that immediate connection.[2] Thus Surfer Joe is also deliberately nostalgic, a nostalgia that is reinforced by the design graphics of the Web site and printed literature about the festival. Take, for example, the Surfer Joe mascot (fig. 18a) compared to the cartoon character Murphy, created by Rick Griffin and featured semiregularly in *Surfer* magazine from 1961 to 1987 (fig. 18b). Some of the bands and audience also sported clothing and haircuts referencing certain youth styles of the mid-twentieth-century United States. However, unlike many Southern California Surf Music events that fea-

FIGURE 18b. Untitled (Murphy Surfin' around the World), by Rick Griffin, 1964. From Gordon T. McClelland's collection. Reproduced Courtesy of Ida Griffin and the Rick Griffin Estate.

FIGURE 18a. Surfer Joe trademark created by Fred Lammers (www.surferjoemusic.com).

ture original bands and musicians who had hits in the 1960s, all the musicians at the Italian festival were relatively young. Their references to midcentury style were nostalgic, not a reenactment of their youth.

This deliberate nostalgia was balanced by updated versions of 1960s-style instrumental rock, usually in the form of aggressive renditions punked up sonically as well as performatively. For example, the band I Fantomatici, with their matching boardshorts, flip-flops, white shirts, and leis, looked like a throwback to 1961 in their uniformity, and they played instrumental rock from that era. Looking at the band before they played, one might mistake them for the young Beach Boys or Jan and Dean, and on their CDs they sound like a band that could have been playing the Redondo Beach area of Southern California in 1963. However, in live performances their act is more aggressive, with a hard edge that counterpoints their retro nice-boy costumes. Similarly, Ex Presidenti from Italy, a band I will discuss in more detail later, usually performs in midcentury-style suits or dinner jackets. However, as their lead guitarist and singer, Gian Maria Vaglietti, explained to me, at the 2009 Surfer Joe Summer Festival they had been asked to mount the stage before they had time to change into their costumes. They made the best of it; bassist Francesco Peloso stripped to the waist and presented himself in a manner consistent with their aggressive punk vocal style

FIGURE 19. Ex Presidenti at the Surfer Joe Summer Festival: Gian Maria Vaglietti (left) and Francesco Peloso, 24 July 2009 (www.expresidenti.com). Photograph by the author.

(fig. 19). Indeed, Vaglietti considers his band's music to be what he called "surf punk."[3] A band from Sardinia, Hangee 5 (a reference to a surfing stance in which the surfer rides with one foot on the nose of the board, "hanging five" toes over the front edge), performed punk versions of standard surf rock from the 1960s as well as some of their own songs. Note that, as the festival poster reveals, all the bands that stray too far from 1960s-style Surf Music were presented on the smaller, second stage (fig. 20a–b). All the bands on the main stage performed instrumental rock or vocal-style Surf Music—their own compositions and covers of classic Surf Music from the 1960s.

FIGURE 20a–b. Surfer Joe Summer Festival 2009 poster, front and back.

SUMMER FESTIVAL

24→26 JULY ▸ CALAFURIA LIVORNO ▸ ITALY

A great event completely dedicated to surf music with live bands from everywhere, dj sets, exhibitions & more for 3 days of absolute fun !!

FREE ADMISSION

Music and concerts from 3 pm
Local bars & restaurant

DJ SETS

Iaso ' Snoopy ' Captainzerbo
SPAF Combo - Lucabeat - Stivaletto DJ's

HOST FOR THE SHOW

Unsteady Freddie (N.Y.C.)

Info line:
+39 347-5143166 / +39 347-1490186
www.surferjoemusic.com/festival

THANKS TO...

M. CASALE BAUER   TECNOCASA   mosrite of California

FRIDAY JULY 24
HOT ROD SURFERS (Italy)
THE BRADIPOS IV (Italy)
THE PIPELINES (Italy)
Surf/Punk on Second Stage
EX PRESIDENT I (Italy)
Jack Johnson's Tribute
RODEO CLOWNS (Italy)

SATURDAY JULY 25
PSYCHO SURFERS (Italy)
I FANTOMATICI (Italy)
WADADLI RIDERS (Antigua)
also feat. REV HANK of
URBAN SURF KINGS (Canada)
LOS TWANG MARVELS (Germany)
THE KILAUEAS (Germany)
POLLO DEL MAR (USA)
Garage Day on Second Stage
JUMPIN' QUAILS (Italy)
THE HANGEE V (Italy)

SUNDAY JULY 26
COWABUNGA GO-GO (Hungary)
LES ARONDES (France)
LOS CORONAS (Spain)
THE MADEIRA (USA)
Beatles' Music on Second Stage
THE SHUFFLES (Italy)
Special Performance of
DOCTEUR LEGUME et Les Surfwerks

Three Bands, Three Approaches

Three different bands that performed at the Surfer Joe Summer Festival in 2009 illustrate different ways that musicking can be connected to surfing—or not.

Pollo Del Mar was the headline band Saturday night. They are from San Francisco, California, where they formed in 1994. The band consists of two guitarists (Jono Jones and Ferenc Dobronyi), bass (Jeff Turner), and drums (Jeremy Rexford)—a classic surf-band lineup. Pollo Del Mar is an instrumental rock band, a self-proclaimed Surf Music band "of surf music's 'Third Wave.'"[4] As their position as the headline band for the festival on Saturday would suggest, they are a critically acclaimed band in this genre, with an active international touring schedule. They were emblematic of the sort of music the Summer Joe Summer Festival was all about (fig. 21).

Before Pollo Del Mar went onstage Saturday night, I met guitarist Ferenc Dobronyi, who happened to be sitting near me and my wife while other bands played. Hearing us speaking English, he struck up a conversation that we maintained on and off for several hours. We had plenty of time, since Pollo Del Mar did not go onstage until about 3:15 A.M. Sunday. Dobronyi was curious about what brought Ruth and me to the festival. I explained my research interest in music associated with surfing, and he quickly picked up on the general thrust of my research (and the place of his band in it). He had his laptop open and running during most of our conversation, and he mentioned our meeting in a blog he was writing then and there. Picking up on the words I carefully chose to represent my interests, in the blog he wrote that my research was on "music associated with surfing," and then he went on: "Not surf music, but music associated with surfing, so his story begins in the 1800s with Hawaiian chants and gets up to date with Jack Johnson. Somewhere in there will be a chapter about my beloved reverb instrumentals, but only a small one."[5]

Dobronyi also touched on a theme I encounter frequently with musicians specializing in instrumental Surf Music. They don't believe that their music has strong connections with the act of wave riding. Though he surfed some when he was young, he makes no direct connections between his own surfing and his music. In fact, he seemed a little frustrated with some surfers who get attention playing so called "surf music" when he believes what they are playing is not Surf Music. According to Dobronyi, the genre Surf Music is divorced from surfing

FIGURE 21. Pollo Del Mar onstage at the Surfer Joe Summer Festival, 26 July 2009 (www.pollodelmar.com). Photograph by the author.

itself and is now music that should be appreciated on its own terms. In Dobronyi's conception, the sport of surfing may have some historical significance for inspiring some of the early musicians who pioneered the genre, and the connection to surfing certainly helped popularize the genre, but surfing is not directly associated with the music today.

The second band I consider is Ex Presidenti, which performed at the Surfer Joe Summer Festival Friday night, the first day of the festival (fig. 19 above). This band is from Maranello, near Modena, in the north central part of Italy. As guitarist and singer Gian Maria Vaglietti explained to me, Maranello is better known for its fast cars than for surfing. (The Ferrari car factory is there.) Nevertheless, in his own words, Gian is "obsessed" with surfing, and he travels to go surfing whenever he can.[6] All the original members of his band when it formed in 1997 were also surfers, and most of their songs are about surfing and an imagined surfing lifestyle, including references to California.

Ex Presidenti calls itself a "surf punk" band, and the guitar (Vaglietti), bass (Francesco Peloso), drum set (Alex Oltramari), and vocal (all) styles they use do sound like punk rock. They occasionally reference the patently un-punk Beach Boys—one of Vaglietti's inspirations—along with other California bands such as the punk band NOFX.[7] Ex Presidenti derives its name from the feature film *Point Break,* in which four California surfers rob banks while wearing masks of three ex-presidents of the United States. Vaglietti writes the music and song texts, and did the graphics for their first CD, *Pirati.* The art on the CD is a mix of pirate themes (skull and crossbones, frigates, treasure chests) and surfing themes (idyllic beaches, tubing waves, surfboards). The songs, too, reference pirates and surfing, but the emphasis is on surfing. Even the title song, "Pirati," is about surfing (audio example 4).

This band, therefore, stood out at the Surfer Joe Festival as a band that was deeply interested in the sport of surfing and making music about surfing. However, their music did not fall in the Surf Music genre. I speculate that the band's base so far from the Mediterranean Sea, and even farther from an ocean where more reliable surf can be expected, may intensify their obsession with surfing. Gian Vaglietti said as much to me, stating that he thought I might find it strange that he is so interested in surfing when he lives inland and can surf only a few times a year. But this does not stop him from actively imagining California and a surfing lifestyle. Such acts of imagination are consistent with perceptions of surfing as a subculture and what geographer Nick Ford and sociologist David Brown call "the consensus narratives of surfing culture" that enable individuals to identify with surfing in a number of ways, both in and out of the water.[8] Musicking about surfing is clearly a way that Gian Vaglietti engages with the surfing lifestyle even when miles from any sea.

The third band that I will consider here is Rodeo Clowns, a Jack Johnson tribute band headed by Andrea Lo Coco on acoustic guitar and vocals, supported by Federico Bellini on bass (substituting for Fabrizio Balesi) and Francesco Zerbino on drums. The name of Lo Coco's band is taken from Jack Johnson's song "Rodeo Clowns," first released on G.

Love & Special Sauce's 1999 album *Philadelphonic*. Rodeo Clowns was performing when we first arrived at the festival site, and it was simultaneously an odd and confirming sensation to hear Jack Johnson songs performed in English by a fellow wearing shorts, a T-shirt, and flip-flops who looked like a surfer and a bit like Johnson himself, and who played an acoustic guitar similar in appearance to Johnson's. This opening act at the Surfer Joe Summer Festival was an Italian trio that covered today's most popular Hawaiian surfer-musician.

Speaking with Lo Coco after his performance, I discovered that he is a surfer who talks about the sport with some authority. He told me that he started performing covers of songs by Donovan Frankenreiter, who, like Jack Johnson, is an accomplished surfer turned professional musician.[9] Thus his musical inspirations center on two surfing musicians, both of whom are held in high esteem in the global surfing community, and both of whom are currently popular as musicians well beyond that surfing community. Johnson and Frankenreiter share some recognizable stylistic traits: an emphasis on acoustic instruments, small ensembles, and understated vocals. Rhythmically, many of their songs reference reggae (a sharp, timbrally high-register mark of the offbeat), but the emphasis on acoustic instruments creates the impression of music one might hear around a fire on the beach rather than in a dance hall or from a mobile block-party sound system in Jamaica.

Surfer Joe: Some Conclusions

The Surfer Joe Summer Festival tells the story of music associated with surfing over the last fifty years in a striking way. Lorenzo Valdambrini's vision for Surfer Joe is squarely on instrumental rock à la Dick Dale and the Surfaries from the early 1960s, as well as songs about surfing à la the Beach Boys from the same era. However, the link to surfing among the headlining bands was symbolic, not through active surfing. Yet Valdambrini's vision for the festival is wide enough to include Lo Coco's Rodeo Clowns Jack Johnson cover band as well as Ex Presidenti's surf punk, with both bands staffed by passionate surfers. Also included were what Valdambrini called "garage" bands on the second stage, including a group called Jumpin' Quails, described to me by drummer Diego Bolognese as "garage-surf." There was a clear division of priority between the bands that played classic genre Surf Music—all presented on the main stage—and groups offering surf punk, garage, and Jack Johnson tributes, who were generally presented on the second, smaller stage. This prioritization of the festival is clearly represented by the lists of bands on the back of the festival poster (fig. 20b above). But the deeper connections with surfing tended to surface there on the second stage. The same could be said for Marco Rizzo of Dr.ank Surfboards: he was not on the main stage, but his presence at the festival site was a tangible link to surfing.

For a festival that focuses on classic Surf Music in a beach area with marginal surf at best, the Surfer Joe Summer Festival has surprising relevance for my interest in music and the sport of surfing. This is a result of Lorenzo Valdambrini's deliberate attempts to engage the surfing community, even though he is not himself a surfer. The festival also, I believe, results in some Italian surfers making identity connections to classic Surf Music and more recently created surf punk. This in part may result from their critical distance from California—a distance that requires one to imagine a California-style surfing life, including some of the music that first popularized that image.

RELENTLESS BOARDMASTERS, UNITED KINGDOM

Less than two weeks after the Surfer Joe Summer Festival in Italy, I attended the Relentless Boardmasters Surf, Skate, and Music Festival in the town of Newquay, on the coast of the peninsula that is Cornwall, in the southwest of the United Kingdom, with the Celtic Sea to the north and west, and the English Channel to the south (fig. 22a–b). This was a very different event from the Surfer Joe Summer Festival. The Relentless Boardmasters Festival had two main sites—one at Fistral Beach in Newquay proper, and a second a few miles north at Watergate Bay. Newquay is the center of surfing in the United Kingdom. It is a British-style surf town with a fine surfing beach between two headlands that define the town. The Watergate Bay site is just outside Newquay in a pasture overlooking a beautiful and much less crowded beach (fig. 23). With four stages, several bars, and many other amusements, the Watergate Bay site is the primary music venue. It ran for two days: Friday and Saturday, 7 and 8 August. The Fistral Beach portion of the festival began on Wednesday, 5 August, and ran through to Sunday, 9 August. It centered on a professional surfing contest. Wednesday and Thursday evenings, and again on Sunday evening, at the Newquay Fistral Beach venue, were the "Beach Sessions"—a single-stage music event in an eight-hundred-person-capacity tent set up for the occasion. I decided to focus on these

FIGURE 22a–b. Relentless Boardmasters 2009 poster, front *(above)* and back *(next page)*.

Relentless BOARDMASTERS
IN ASSOCIATION WITH **VANS**

★★★★★ SURF ★★★★★
★ MEN'S 5 STAR WQS EVENT
★ $120,000 PRIZE PURSE
  (HIGHEST EVER IN ENGLAND)
★ 100+ OF THE WORLDS BEST SURFERS

MUSIC FESTIVAL AT WATERGATE BAY
★ 7th-8th AUGUST ★

★★★★★★★★★ MAIN STAGE ★★★★★★★★★

THE STREETS   *Cypress Hill*

CALVIN HARRIS   **SUPER FURRY ANIMALS**   *Roots Manuva*   **Isaac yr pip**

THE KING BLUES ★ DREADZONE ★ ASH GRUNWALD ★ WILL & THE PEOPLE
MASTER SHORTIE ★ BEN HOWARD ★ MAX TUOHY ★ BACK BEAT SOUNDSYSTEM

★★★★★★★★ *Relentless* STAGE ★★★★★★★★

NOISETTES *Keisha SellOut*

PETE & THE PIRATES ★ FILTHY DUKES ★ TOMMY SPARKS ★ FIONN REGAN
THE DYKEENIES ★ SKY LARKIN ★ FANFARLO ★ WALLIS BIRD ★ HAUNTS ★ THE SEA
CHEW LIPS ★ RUTH KEALY ★ ROSIE & THE GOLDBUG ★ AUCTION FOR THE PROMISE CLUB

★★★★★★★★★ VANS MUSIC STAGE ★★★★★★★★★
OFF THE WALL

BRAKES   **THE GHOST OF A THOUSAND**

THE EXCERTS ★ PULLED APART BY HORSES ★ DINOSAUR PILE UP ★ THE PLIGHT
FAILSAFE ★ OUTCRY COLLECTIVE ★ THIS CITY ★ HEXES ★ JETTBLACK
THE COMPUTERS ★ TELEGRAPH ★ SHARKS ★ ULTERIOR ★ TURBOWOLF
GENTLEMANS PISTOLS ★ SSS ★ SURTENOIR ★ DON BROCO ★ SAN PABLO ★ EVERYTHING BURNS

★ PLUS ALL NEW JAGERMEISTER LOCAL STAGE ★

★★★★★★★★ *Relentless* BEACH SESSIONS ★★★★★★★★

★★★★★ VANS ★★★★★
SUMMER SESSIONS
★ VERT SKATE COMP
★ BMX MINI RAMP COMP
★ WOODEN WAVES PRO STREET
  SKATE COMP
★ $25,000 PRIZE PURSE

WED 5th	THUR 6th	SUN 9th
THE BLACKOUT	*Pete Murray*	**SNEAKY SOUND SYSTEM**
WE ARE THE OCEAN	**BEN HOWARD**	
EVERYTHING BURNS	**ROB SAWYER**	
DOWNTOWN RIOTS	MAX TUOHY	
	BOY WHO TRAPPED THE SUN	JELLY JAZZ

★ TICKET PRICES ★

THE CHARGER
(all inclusive 5 day ticket)....SOLD OUT
WATERGATE W/E.....................$54.99*
WATERGATE DAY.....................$29.99*
BEACH SESSIONS....................$14.50*

*Tickets purchased on the door are
more expensive. See website

Tickets also available from
Ticketmaster on 0844 847 2517

TICKETS & INFO AVAILABLE AT
WWW.RELENTLESSBOARDMASTERS.COM

FIGURE 23. Watergate Bay seen from the Relentless Boardmasters festival site, 7 August 2009. Photograph by the author.

performances—the Beach Sessions—because they seemed to hold more promise for my particular interests and because they corresponded with the surf contest: as the surfing contest wrapped up late each afternoon, the Beach Sessions concerts commenced just a few steps away.

The festival was an unmistakable presence on Fistral Beach. In addition to the large tent, complete with a patio and a bar serving food and drinks, there was a towering arch at the entrance to the festival, a festival village where vendors were showing and selling their surf- and skateboard-related wares, and several mountainous skateboarding and BMX bike ramps. Additional structures on the beach served the surfing contest: a shelter for contest judges, a separate shelter for contestants, loudspeakers, official time clocks, and so forth. Banners bearing the brand names of the festival sponsors—Relentless (an energy drink) and Vans (shoes favored by skateboarders and other sportswear)—flew in the wind in any direction one looked (fig. 24).

Upon arrival, I found my way to the pressroom to pick up my media pass and packet of press materials. The festival was a major event. Millions of British pounds were being spent. The media was out in full force.

FIGURE 24. Fistral Beach during the Relentless Boardmasters surfing contest and festival, 5 August 2009. Photograph by the author.

History of the Contest and Festival

The Boardmasters event is the descendant of the first professional surfing contest in the United Kingdom. That contest was in 1981, was also held at Newquay, and was sponsored by the British wetsuit company Gul and the Newquay Surfing Centre.[10] The contest has been held every year since except for one, making the 2009 contest the twenty-eighth. From 2001 to 2008 the primary sponsor was Rip Curl, a wetsuit and surfwear company. At the core of Relentless Boardmasters is the surfing contest, a World Qualifying Series event in which surfers compete for a spot on the World Championship Tour of the Association of Surfing Professionals (ASP). In some past and subsequent years the contest included women's qualifying events, but not in 2009. Female surfers were not completely absent from the 2009 event, however; the festival did include Animal Surf Academy Girls Only Days with professional women surfers, sponsored by Animal (a surfing apparel company). Also at the festival were competitions in vertical-ramp skateboarding and BMX cycling. Skateboarding has been part of the festival since at least the late 1990s.

Since 1999 the contest has been managed by Sports Vision, an events and marketing company based in London. When Sports Vision started managing the contest it was primarily a surfing event with secondary skateboarding events. According to James Rodd, Event Marketing Manager for Sports Vision, the festival used to run for two weeks and only later was pared down to the five-day event that it is now[11]. Boardmasters was also originally about sports; music became an official and major component of the festival only later.

Music at the Festival

I have not been able to determine exactly when music first became an official part of the Boardmasters festivals. Based on news releases and archived Web guides for summertime events in the United Kingdom, including the official Boardmasters Web pages, one can see that music events in the town of Newquay were generally mentioned alongside information about the surfing contest since at least 2002. Yet music events were likely to have been at least loosely associated with the contest from the earliest years. Young surfers and fans like to party just like everyone else, and Newquay was a summer vacation spot for beach lovers of all ages long before the surfing contests started. I suspect that informal links with music in local clubs began immediately with the original 1981 professional surfing contest in Newquay.

The official music festival component of the Boardmasters event was added in 2005 as a way to boost sponsorship revenue. New sources of money were needed when the city of Newquay sold the parking area at Fistral Beach where they hold the surfing and skating events and the new owners started to charge Sports Vision for the use of the space. The festival organizers decided to pair the contest with a music festival at nearby Watergate Bay. The event was called the Nokia Unleashed Music Festival and was conceived of as a tie-in with the surfing contest, but Rodd notes that a lot of the attendees did not necessarily make that connection.[12] Whereas the surfing contest events were free to the public, a fee was charged for the music festival: in 2005 the cost was £19.50 (about thirty-five dollars) for Friday, £25 (forty-four dollars) for Saturday, or £39.50 (seventy dollars) for the weekend. In 2009, the tickets cost £29.99 (fifty dollars) for either Friday or Saturday or £54.99 (ninety dollars) for the weekend—more at the door. The Beach Sessions were £14.50 (twenty-five dollars) each evening and £17.50 (thirty dollars) at the door.[13] These were premium prices for events that anticipated large audiences.

Central Questions

My interpretive process at the Boardmasters festival moved in the opposite direction from what it took at the Surfer Joe Summer Festival. At the Italian festival there was a genre of music labeled "surf," but I had to ask what that music and the festival had to do with surfing and the surfing community. At the Boardmasters event, I started with surfing and a healthy contingent of a British and international surfing community, and then asked how the music featured at the festival connected with that community. The music components of the Newquay festival were far from the Surf Music genre celebrated at the festival in Italy. In fact, I find no references to Surf Music in any of the information available about Boardmasters historically, or at the festival I attended. Instead, I experienced examples of what former *Surfer* editor Sam George calls "surfing music," and by this he means music that surfers like.[14] But for this to be a meaningful ethnographic question, it must extend beyond personal preferences of individual surfers. Instead, there needs to be some consensus that contributes to social grouping: what social psychologists call *social identity,* as distinct from, though linked with, the concept of *self.*[15] This, of course, is the challenge of this book, but I think also an important challenge for music studies in general. Links between a music and a place (Irish fiddling and Ireland, for example) remain meaningful, but they can be limiting (Irish fiddling can be heard outside Ireland; and within Ireland one can hear many different musics). Facile links between music and the identity of musicians are also dangerous. The best Irish fiddler in the pub may not have heritage ties to Ireland, just as the best Surf Music guitarist may never have ridden a wave. Is there any meaningful connection between place, music, surfing, and surfers? Can we talk about surfers as *a* community with *a* music?

I approached this question at the Boardmasters Festival by asking different individuals with particular roles at the festival—organizers, musicians, and surfers—about how they do or do not associate music and surfing. Then I conclude with summary observations about the different types of music heard and not heard there.

Organizers. James Rodd, the Sports Vision manager introduced above, agreed to sit with me in the pressroom for a recorded interview. I asked him directly about the connections between music and surfing: "What does music have to do with surfing?" He explained that not everyone in Newquay was there for the surfing and that the festival organizers have to provide what he called "commercial" music for the general audience, but that the festival organizers also make an effort to "get the vibe right" and include what he termed "surfy" music as well.[16] Rodd mentioned Pete Murray, an Australian acoustic songwriter, who was playing the Beach Sessions later that evening, as having a surfy sound. When I asked Rodd to explain what he meant by a "surfy" sound, he laughed, saying music was not his strong point, but then he went on to describe two contrasting styles that I find informative: laid-back and punk rock. Rodd made a connection between laid-back, acoustic, singer-songwriter music and surfing, while what he called a "punky attitude" is more closely associated with skateboarding. Yet skateboarding, as Rodd noted, owes its early popularity to surfers riding skateboards when there were no waves. Skateboarding is a bit more gritty, he said, and this lends itself to punk and rock music. In Rodd's conception, surfing music was more mellow, in line with his perceived roots of surfing. Thus, what may seem like contrasting aesthetics are linked through the entangled histories of surfing and skateboarding.

Rodd also pointed out that the music festival at Watergate Bay has four stages, each with a different emphasis, as can be seen on the back side of the festival's poster (fig. 22b above). While two of the big stages were devoted to contemporary music, in Rodd's terms, the main stage did include sets by surfers Ben Howard from Devon, United Kingdom, and Tristan Prettyman from San Diego (the latter scheduled after the posters were printed). In addition, one of the stages held a lot of punk rock, which Rodd associates with surfing and skateboarding, and the smallest stage, the Jägermeister Stage, was billed as "local," featuring bands from Cornwall, the county where the festival is held and a place that is known for its surfing beaches. Rodd believed that the Cornish (that is, from Cornwall) bands would appeal to local surfers. He volunteered that the festival has received some criticism for taking the focus off surfing, but he believes that this is a misconception. He stressed that the music was for the competing surfers as well as the general public. In my conversations with some of the competitive surfers, several were indeed excited about the music parts of the festival.

Musicians. The main focus of my fieldwork was the Beach Sessions on Wednesday and Thursday nights, the days when the surfing contest was held. The lineups for these two nights were very different. On Wednesday all the bands could be described as punk or derived from punk;[17] the headline band was the Blackout, from Wales, and they were preceded by We Are the Ocean, from the town of Loughton, northeast of London, and the local Cornish bands Everything Burns and Downtown Riots. I was able to talk to members of all of these bands, and none of them had strong surfing connections; none identified as a surfer. Dan Brown, the so-called screaming vocals singer for We Are the Ocean, told me he has done some surfing, but he downplayed any connection, noting that even the name of the band is derived from bassist Jack Spence's old e-mail address, not from any affinity with the ocean. When I mentioned my interest in connections between surfing and music, Spence and Tom Whittaker (drums) said they thought there really was no connection with surfing, but that their music did connect with skateboarding. Spence commented that it really depended on what individual surfers liked, and that he has noticed some surfers wearing "heavy T-shirts" (shirts bearing the brand of heavy-metal and punk bands).

The differing appeal of the lineups Wednesday evening versus Thursday evening could be seen in the people in attendance. The audience for Wednesday evening skewed toward early teens to young twenties (fig. 25). Thursday night all the bands featured acoustic guitars, a symbolic and sonic step away from the "heavy" electric bands of the previous evening. The audience was a bit older than the night before—late teens to late twenties (fig. 26). There was no mosh pit as there was the previous evening.

Thursday I was able to talk with Rob Sawyer, also from Australia; Max Tuohy, from London; and Ben Howard, a surfer from Devon—all performers that evening. I will focus on Ben Howard, not because the answers to all my questions lie with surfing musicians, but because he challenges the very issues at the core of this book.

Devon is the county east of Cornwall and has coasts to both the south and north. Howard grew up in rural southern Devon, and has been both surfing and writing songs since he was a boy. These are his two passions, but when I asked him if he wrote songs about surfing, he replied: "I tend not to . . . I think it's easy to drop into the sort of surfing-music clichés if you start writing about surfing, the ocean, and things like that. I mean, I do reference it a fair amount, for sure. But that's because it has been a

FIGURE 25. Frontline audience at the Relentless Boardmasters "Beach Sessions" concert, 5 August 2009. Photograph by the author.

FIGURE 26. Frontline audience at the Relentless Boardmasters "Beach Sessions" concert, 6 August 2009. Photograph by the author.

FIGURE 27. Ben Howard performing at the Relentless Boardmasters "Beach Sessions," 6 August 2009. Photograph by the author.

part of growing up really. I have always surfed. I've always played music" (fig. 27).[18] That he is not trying to write specifically for a surfer audience came up repeatedly in our interview. Howard said he liked happy upbeat music when he is getting ready to surf, but that this is not the sort of music he writes: "No one's going to get amped before a surf listening to this [his songs]" he said. His music may be more appropriate after surfing, what he called "postsurf music" (audio example 5). As a surfer and as an individual, he likes to listen to different sorts of music for different purposes at different times. The clear message I got from Howard is that being a surfer does not make him appreciate, listen to, or write any particular music. The same could be said for surfers as a whole. They are not a unified audience.

Yet there does seem to be some sense that there is such a thing as a surfing lifestyle, and that this may call for music. Howard described his own surfing lifestyle as "hedonistic. . . . At the end of the day we live . . . like, surfers. We sort of live quite hedonistic lifestyles as such, and you always need a soundtrack to do that, don't you? You always need a few tunes to amp you up [before surfing] or pull you down afterwards." Owain Davies, a friend of Howard's who helps him manage his affairs and who helped me organize this interview, spoke up in agreement, adding that "music is just such a big part of the surf lifestyle." Then Howard quipped, laughing: "Surfing without music would be *nothing.*"

Howard and Davies had realistic views of the commercial appeal of music associated with surfing as well. At the time Howard was sponsored by Quiksilver, a large international surfing brand based in Australia. Quiksilver helped promote Howard's music and his performances, and he would wear one of the company's T-shirts. Before his performance at the Beach Sessions bar, I asked him and Davies to estimate how many of the hundreds of people present were into surfing. Howard replied that they were probably all into surfing, but then he looked around and added that only about twenty actually surfed. He went on to say that surfing was "quite cool at the moment" but that there would be a backlash. "I think everyone will start listening to slit punk soon, and Jack Johnson will be a thing of the past, and surfing will be for all those weirdos who don't work a proper job," he added, reasserting the countercultural roots of surfing's popular image created in California in the 1950s and '60s.

But for now, surfing or at least the idea of surfing is popular and sells things. A surfing festival attracts a lot of people, and if there is music on the beach after the contest heats, all the better. Quiksilver sees the commercial value in this and, like the festival organizers, sees music as a way of extending brand appeal. Nonetheless, Howard still seems surprised that his music is being attached to surfing: "We've kind of never pushed the whole surfing scene. I've never thought of my music as being something that surfers would particularly like. But it's worked quite well. I surf and play music, and people seem to really enjoy the tunes. Quiksilver has really helped push us in the surfing scene, and people really like it though. I mean, I've been really quite surprised." Davies added, "At the end of the day, it's more about the music than the surfing, isn't it?" Howard agreed, but noted that the Quiksilver gigs were usually on the coast, and that this had the added bonus of allowing them to surf on the same day that he performed his music.

Surfers. Friday, as the surfing contest moved toward its conclusion, I made my way to the competitors' staging area to talk to surfers about connections between surfing and music. Tucked high on the cliffs, with clear views of the waves where the competition was taking place, this area included a massage tent and a bar serving fresh fruit, energy drinks, and other snacks. A few tables and deck chairs bearing the Relentless logo provided nice perches for watching the surfing. There I found surfers who were preparing to compete, others who had already been eliminated, and a few of their surfing friends. Explaining my research interests, I asked four surfers if and how they associated music and surfing.

David Young, a friend of one of the competitors, replied that one band he associated with surfing is Blink-182, a Southern California punk-rock band more commonly, in my experience, associated with skateboarding. Young then moved directly to music that is featured on surfing films, mentioning specifically Taylor Steele's films and the bands Bad Religion and Pennywise, both punk bands (also described as melodic hardcore, hardcore punk, and skate punk [Pennywise] on Wikipedia) from Southern California.

Then I put the same questions to Jarrad Sullivan, an Australian surfer who had been in the contest, and his friend Reubin Pearce. Their responses took the form of a conversation between them. Pearce said that music is a personal choice of the surfer, though films help to associate music with surfing. "Surf-rocking-punk" and hip-hop were among the styles he mentioned. He noted that a lot of underground U.S. bands are promoted in surf films, as are a few U.K. bands such as Block Party. Once again Taylor Steele's films in particular were mentioned. Sullivan and Pearce also mentioned that the metal band Metallica is led by surfers.

I then talked with Ryan Arthur from Laguna Beach, California. He said that before a contest heat, he listens to different types of music, from hard rock to gospel. Ryan has been playing drums since he was eight, and he used to be in a rock and reggae band, but he got cut from the band because he was surfing too much. In his opinion the relationships between surfing and music are very important. Following up on my interview with Ben Howard and his comments about music before and after surfing, I asked Arthur if he listened to different music after a surfing session. He replied that if it was a good session, he might be still amped and want rock music. His key phrase was: "It depends."

Relentless Music: Some Conclusions

On the Celtic Sea in the capital of British surfing at a professional surfing competition, the branded genre Surf Music found no home on any of the many stages, contrasting markedly with the Surfer Joe Summer Festival in Calafuria, Italy. Still, music is associated with surfing in a number of sometimes contrasting and possibly conflicting ways. At the Boardmasters festival, the individuals I interviewed—festival organizers, musicians, and surfers—stressed that there is no single type of music most associated with surfing, and that first and foremost it depends on the individual surfer. The musicians and the festival organizer also noted that not everyone at the festival was a surfer and that the music could not address surfers alone. However, two perhaps contrasting themes kept returning concerning music appropriate for surfing or a perceived surfing lifestyle: "laid-back" (read acoustic) music versus punk rock. For example, James Rodd with Sports Vision used the term "surfy" to describe acoustic songwriter Pete Murray, as well as acoustic music in general, as somehow appropriate for surfers (an interesting step away from the 1960s surf guitar, which is by definition electric). Rodd also spoke of punk music as being appealing to surfers, though probably more so to skateboarders, while noting the links between the two board-sports.

This acoustic, mellow aesthetic contrasted with punk rock was also manifest in the lineups at the Beach Sessions: punk-oriented bands Wednesday night, and acoustic bands Thursday. Here, too, connections were made between punk and skateboarding, though also with surfing. Dan Brown of the punk (post-hardcore) band We Are the Ocean drew a line from punk through surfing to skateboarding. Ben Howard, the Devonshire surfing songwriter sponsored by Quiksilver, spoke of music to amp up surfers for a surfing session, but that this was not his music. His was more introspective (again suggesting acoustic guitars) and probably more appropriate for a postsurf listening session. Also prominent in my interviews was the specter of Jack Johnson (who most typically performs on acoustic guitar), and an association of relatively mellow, acoustic music with the equally vague concept of a surfing lifestyle.

The professional surfers, however, were more consistent in connecting punk-rock music to their own surfing.

Much can be made of the polemic between mellow surfing music and punk skateboarding music. Any practitioner will quickly note the back-and-forth of influence between surfing and skateboarding, and now snowboarding. There are visceral similarities and contrasts between the sports: the shared feeling of flow and glide versus "gritty" skateboarding, and the different implications of falling—wiping out—on pavement, in the water, or on snow. Surfing requires waiting, floating, fluid motion, wipeouts cushioned by water. The edgy, dangerous surfing we see in films, in commercials, and in countless magazines is a small fraction of what most surfers ever do. Yet even small-wave surfing is today much influenced by skateboarding: surfers "getting air" is derived from the skateboarding "Ollie," for example. A "floater" on a surfboard is similar to a "rail grind" on a skateboard or snowboard. That board riders of all sorts might share some musical interests should not be too surprising.

Garage and punk music also have deep links with both Surf Music and the lifestyle of surfing. In at least the U.S. origin myths of punk music, garage bands play an important role, and those who write about Surf Music like to equate early 1960s surf bands with early punk and the DIY movement. For example, Phil Dirt, a radio DJ in the San Francisco area who was influential in reviving interest in Surf Music, talks about surf bands as "the first generation of punk bands."[19] Surf Music discographer John Blair calls early Southern California surf rock bands "garage bands" and links them to later punk bands.[20] Punk music scholar Bill Osgerby also makes connections between early punk and Southern California surf bands.[21] Though we can quibble about the history of punk rock and its relationship to 1960s Surf Music, there are two ways in which punk seems to be an important genre or style for surfers and surfing today. First, the idea that early Surf Music bands were proto-punk is important to some musicians. For example, Paul Johnson, a guitarist who cowrote and recorded "Mr. Moto," arguably the first instrumental rock piece that later took the genre label Surf Music, also thinks Surf Music was the original punk music, or was at least the seed of punk. He recalls that in the early 1980s punks started coming to Surf Music shows, and that in turn the 1980s revival of Surf Music is indebted to punk. In his mind, surf, garage, and punk are genres all related in their directness and simplicity.[22] Connections are made from the punk side as well.

Sam Bolle, the former bass player for Agent Orange, a Southern California band that bills itself as a punk/surf grind band, told me that he considered Surf Music to be the first punk.[23] I met Bolle at a festival in Los Angeles billed as a beach party. I noted then that Bolle not only played with Agent Orange but later that same day played bass for Dick Dale. Surfers, especially younger surfers (in their twenties), also link punk to surfing, not through classic Surf Music but through surf films, most particularly Taylor Steele's films.

TWO FESTIVALS, THREE GENRES OF MUSIC

The Surfer Joe Summer Festival and the Relentless Boardmasters Festival come to the question of music and surfing from very different directions. The Surfer Joe Summer Festival starts with a music genre that includes the word *surf* in its title, while Boardmasters begins as a surfing contest. In Italy, where surfing requires considerable patience, the surfers I met were quite passionate about the sport, and about making music around the idea of surfing. In Newquay, Ben Howard (the Devonshire surfer who was sponsored by Quiksilver not as surfer but as a musician) says emphatically that he does not write songs about surfing. He felt his music might be more appropriate for postsurf calming-down sessions, what he jokingly called "postsurf music."

Playing with his "postsurf music" comment a bit, I find it descriptive of the musical practices I have documented among surfers in the twenty-first century. The named genre Surf Music from the early 1960s helped popularize the sport of surfing and the idea of a surfing lifestyle, but it seems to have had a chilling effect on making music about surfing. Once that genre became passé, it was difficult to make music about surfing without being considered passé yourself, being accused of cheapening surfing, or falling prey to any number of other criticisms from surfers who held the act of riding waves dear. Today, then, in this postsurf-music era, those musicians who are identified with the sport (Donavon Frankenreiter, Jack Johnson, Ben Howard, Tristan Prettyman, and so forth) make only subtle references to surfing if at all.

Taking a step or two away from these festivals for perspective, however, one can see that music associated with surfing since the 1960s at least does fall within a fairly narrow spectrum. All the music at both festivals could be considered *popular*—a problematic category, but no less problematic than *folk* and *classical,* categories of music featured at neither festival. Guitars were prominent in all the bands at both festivals. Most of the bands were staffed exclusively by men. From the vast array of genres and subgenres of popular music, three rise to the surface at these two festivals: Surf Music (Italy only), punk rock, and acoustic rock. In the next two chapters, I show that my interviews with professional surfer-musicians and what I call soul surfer-musicians tend to support this finding.

CHAPTER 5

The Pro Surfer Sings

Any member of the Hawaiian *ali'i* (royalty) with real stature would have been accompanied by a chanter who sang his or her praises. One such chanter was an old woman who accompanied Naihe, the chief from the turn of the eighteenth to nineteenth century introduced in chapter 1. We know of this chanter from a historical legend in which Naihe was challenged to a surfing match in Hilo, some distance from his Ka'u home on the island of Hawai'i.[1] After the long journey, Naihe let his chanter go off and rest while he paddled out for the contest, only to learn once he was in the water that the contest rules did not allow a competitor to return to shore until he heard his personal surf chant. The jealous chiefs had withheld this rule from Naihe, knowing that his chanter was elderly and would be excused from the event after their journey, and that Naihe's honor would not allow him to break contest rules no matter how capricious they might be. The intention was to strand Naihe in the water, probably during a rising swell that would make getting to shore increasingly difficult and possibly lethal for even an accomplished surfer. But a local chief had pity on Naihe and sent for his chanter, who hurried back to the contest site and chanted Naihe's surf mele over the rising swell, thus allowing him to once again return to shore triumphant.

This legend not only reminds us that the first professional musicians linked to surfing were in Hawai'i, but also illustrates consistent themes that come up in my interviews and historical research: both surfing and musicking can be life giving, and the two seem to go together. All human societies create music, and there are very few if any human activities that aren't enhanced with a bit of music. It is striking how some of the most influential and competitive surfers in history have also been active and accomplished musicians. Indeed, Hawaiian King Kalākaua was not only an accomplished surfer who adopted the surfing chant for chief Naihe as his own, but also an accomplished musician. The surfing musician is not a New Surfing invention. Might it be that the subjective nature of beautiful surfing—as opposed to objective measures of accomplishment in many other sports—attracts people who have particular interests in that most subjective of arts, music? Is there really something musical about surfing, as so many have suggested?

While definitive answers to these questions may not be possible, in this chapter I address them by looking at the life stories of surfing musicians. Included are a surprising number of professional and semiprofessional surfers who have second or parallel careers as musicians, as well as scenes where lifelong surfers actively integrate musicking with their surfing lifestyle.

THE ORIGINAL BEACHBOYS

Hawaiian surfers kept pace in the transformative twentieth century, adapting new musical practices to their surfing-based lifestyle. The prototypes of surfer-musicians for New Surfing were the Waikīkī Beachboys. Affable fonts of local knowledge as well as complicated representations of Hawaiian masculinity during an era when the Hawaiian female was promoted as the embodiment of Hawai'i,[2] the Beachboys provided a wide range of services to affluent Waikīkī hotel guests, including surfing lessons, canoe rides, lifeguarding, and entertainment on land, strumming their ukuleles and guitars while singing. In the nineteen-teens a small group of the more musically inclined Beachboys began performing evenings on the Moana Hotel's pier for tips. During the golden era of elite tourism to Hawai'i up to the start of the Second World War, the Beachboys attended to—and made music with—the likes of Bing Crosby and other mainland stars (fig. 28).[3] A few Hawaiian Beachboys went on to have careers as musicians, including Squeeze Kamana, Chick Daniels, and Pua Kealoha.

Worldwide the best-known Waikīkī surfer-musician is Olympic gold medalist swimmer and surfing ambassador Duke Kahanamoku. He was loosely affiliated with the Beachboys during the golden era and joined

FIGURE 28. From left: Pua Kealoha, Chick Daniels, Bing Crosby, and Joe Minor at Waikīkī Beach, 1936. Note that Kealoha and Daniels are sitting on a wooden surfboard. Photograph by N. R. Farbman. Image courtesy of the Bishop Museum, Honolulu, Oʻahu, Hawaiʻi (www.bishopmuseum.org).

them in oceanside musicking. He strummed his ukulele poolside to calm his nerves at the 1912 Stockholm Olympics,[4] and is seen in figure 29 sitting at the edge of a pool with a guitar in Chicago in 1918. After World War II, he and some of his then-senior Beachboys colleagues parlayed their fame into music-performance opportunities as mass tourism to Hawaiʻi increased.

Just as Kahanamoku was never a professional surfer in the modern sense, he was never a professional musician—nor a professional swimmer, for that matter. (He carefully guarded his amateur status so that he could compete in the Olympics.) However, he used his considerable skills as a waterman to eke out a modest living as a minor celebrity that included a bit of musicking, as well as acting for Hollywood films and television programs. The mechanisms for capitalizing on lifestyle-sport celebrity were not in place for most of Kahanamoku's lifetime, but in 1961 disc jockey Kimo Wilder McVay became the aging surfer's manager and provided him with some late-in-life financial success.

FIGURE 29. Duke Kahanamoku playing a guitar at a swimming pool, Chicago, Illinois, 1918. Image courtesy of Chicago History Museum (glass negative; SDN-061582) (www.chicagohs.org).

McVay licensed the Duke Kahanamoku name, branded his Waikīkī showroom, where Don Ho performed with the surfer's name, and established a line of merchandise.[5] The Duke Kahanamoku Invitational Surfing Championships event was founded in 1965. Kahanamoku became the modern era's first branded surfing icon, if only for a few years. Duke Kahanamoku died in 1968, but the value of his licensed name continued to grow and is worth more now than it ever was during his lifetime, with restaurants bearing his name on three Hawaiian islands and in two California cities. In addition, he is honored with memorial statues in Waikīkī; at Freshwater Beach in Sydney, Australia; and at Huntington Beach, California. And the U.S. Postal Service issued a stamp in his honor in 2002. Though a traditional Hawaiian-style surfer in many ways, Kahanamoku became the prototype for later New Surfing musicians who would combine surfing with music—and, in some cases, acting and modeling—to make ends meet or even amass considerable wealth.

NEW SURFING AND THE PROFESSIONAL SURFER MUSICIAN

On the surface, it seems uncanny how many current or former professional and semiprofessional surfers have extended their public image through music or even have had second careers as musicians. Not too deep below the surface, however, we see that the entertainment industry and other commercial enterprises have long been hungry for young, fit bodies to sing, dance, act, and otherwise display themselves for mainstream consumption. Figure 29, for example, is in many ways a typical representation of Duke Kahanamoku, revealing his naked torso and powerful shoulders. Toby Miller in his book *Sportsex* shows the many ways that multinational capitalism capitalizes on the athlete's body, ultimately benefiting first-world industries and reaffirming heteronormative, masculinist, and white power.[6] While some of the stories I tell here include resistance to the commodification of the surfer's body for capitalists needs, New Surfing nonetheless is centered in the industrial first world, where everything is for sale. And I don't pretend to write from a position of charitable purity; indeed I hope that you, dear reader, paid money for this book. While we surfers like to think that surfing is somehow musical—and it may be—we also need to remember that there is a well-established trend of commercial interest in the athlete (wet or dry) by entertainment industries, including the music industry.

Here I focus on musicians who perform some form of popular music, since this is the music featured in most surfing films and at surfing festivals, and is most exploited by commercial interests, including the surfing industry. Currently the most obvious examples are free surfer Donavon Frankenreiter from California, and former semipro surfer, then filmmaker, Jack Johnson from Hawai'i. Frankenreiter was one of the first free surfers in the industry[7] (a *free surfer* is sponsored by a surfing brand to travel, surf, and be photographed for surfing magazines and publicity), and it was on this foundation as a media personality that he built his career as a songwriter and performer. Jack Johnson gave Frankenreiter a big boost as a professional musician in 2003 by offering to produce his first album (*Donavon Frankenreiter,* released in 2004).[8] Today both Johnson and Frankenreiter are international music stars, touring with their bands and releasing albums. Though few achieve their level of popular success, there are many other examples of leading surfers who develop second careers as musicians. This includes three-time world surfing champion and one of the most influential surfers of the late twentieth century, Tom Curren from California; two-time world longboard champion Beau Young from Australia; Timmy Curran, a former professional surfer who is now a musician, having released three albums to date; and José Romero, who represented Chile at the Huntington Beach (California) championships before turning his focus to music and becoming a top Chilean mix master performing under the pseudonym DJ Bitman or Latin Bitman.

We can compile an even longer list of professional surfers who tap into musicking as a way of boosting their public image. After all, being a professional surfer is not ultimately about winning contests, but about media image.[9] For example, among the first generation of California New Surfers to have careers in the sport was Charles "Corky" Carroll. Arguably the first professional surfer and a frequent contest champion of the 1960s and early 1970s, he was a master of getting media attention with his antics. Carroll recorded several albums singing and playing guitar, including *Laid Back* in 1971 and *A Surfer for President* in 1979, and he still performs live regularly in Mexico and Southern California. The list of professional surfers who also make music as part of their public image includes ten-time world champion Kelly Slater, who in 1998 together with fellow pro surfers Rob Machado and Peter King recorded an album, *Songs from the Pipe*. Slater has performed onstage with the rock band Pearl Jam and popular singer-songwriter Ben Harper. Veteran big-wave surfer Titus Kinimaka from Kaua'i, Hawai'i, has released several recordings of Hawaiian music. Free surfer Rob Machado recently formed a band that created the soundtrack for a surf film that he also starred in, *Melali: The Drifter Sessions*.

Just as professional female surfers are fewer in number than their male counterparts, it is more difficult to identify women who move between the worlds of professional surfing and musicking, but there are some outstanding examples. Two-time world longboard champion Daize Shayne (Sarah Rose) is also a Roxy model, and rock singer and songwriter. (Roxy is a women's clothing line by surfwear company Quiksilver). British singer and guitarist October Hamlyn-Wright gains valuable publicity with her surfing prowess. For example, she was profiled in the August 2010 *Surfgirl Magazine,* published in the United Kingdom. Australian Stephanie Gilmore, the 2007 women's world champion, is sponsored by Cole Clark guitars. Former semipro Hawaiian surfer and now semipro musician Kelli Heath was part of the Hawaiian female group the Girlas and has performed with Jack Johnson and Paula Fuga. Tristan Prettyman from San Diego was a competitive surfer in her teens and a Roxy model, and is now a songwriter and performer with three albums released and an active touring schedule.

No list of notable surfer-musicians proves the often-repeated claim that surfing and music go hand in hand. That is not the point. Any significant grouping of people will find musical expression. That is part of being human. Surfing being reinvented in the twentieth century as a lifestyle sport makes it all the more likely that participants in the lifestyle—in the affinity group—will seek out musical expression. The question then becomes, What sort of meanings and connections do individuals within this group give to musicking in relation to their surfing? How does one enhance the other?

The ways that surfing musicians talk about the two practices do suggest a few possible explanations. To that end, here I offer case studies of three individual surfing musicians so that we might learn about surfing and music through their voices.

Kelli Heath

Kelli Heath is a guitarist, singer, and songwriter who was part of the Hawaiian band the Girlas, which released an album in 2006 and was featured at the 2007 Kokua Festival, in Waikīkī. Now she is working as a solo musician. Born in 1983 on the island of Oʻahu, Hawaiʻi, where she still lives today, her surfing and music-making are tied to the islands, where her family has deep roots in surfing culture. Her grandfather, Fran Heath, was a noted surfer from Hawaiʻi in the 1930s and ʻ40s and an early adapter of the "hot curl" board—a solid wooden, finless board with a V-shaped tail section that allowed for riding a tighter angle on a larger wave. Figure 30 shows Kelli riding a modern reproduction of a board much like one her grandfather would have ridden. Growing up by and often in the water, she was stand-up surfing by the age of thirteen and became a competitive longboarder a few years after that. In her high school years she was a sponsored surfer and was winning contests, but she realized that surfing was not going to be how she made her living. There was not that much money to be had for a female longboarder, even one who was a very good surfer. As she told me in an interview, she or her sponsors would pay upward of five hundred

FIGURE 30. Kelli Heath surfing a 1930s–'40s-style solid wood "hot curl" surfboard at Waikīkī, 2004. Photograph by Paul Teruya.

dollars to get her to a contest, which she would win, only to walk away with a T-shirt and a check for a mere one hundred dollars. The economics was not working.[10] But the real reason she stopped surfing competitively was that it was taking too much fun out of surfing itself. While she liked the complex mix of competition and camaraderie at a surfing contest, and she enjoyed winning the occasional trophy and having her abilities appreciated, it was beginning to alter her reasons for surfing. She wanted to return to surfing for fun—for herself.

At the same time, at about age eighteen she was also beginning to focus her energy on music, especially playing guitar. She credits a family friend and fellow surfer, Chuck Brown, with teaching her to play the guitar informally at the family home. He tuned the guitar Hawaiian slack-key (open tuning) style, and showed her bits of a song by playing it, then handing her the guitar so that she could try. She learned her first songs this way, handing a single guitar back and forth with her teacher. She says that her interest in competitive surfing began to wane just as she started getting serious about the guitar, facilitating a smooth transition of her energies from one expressive medium to the other:

> There was kind of an overlap of a couple of years. I was about eighteen when I really got into learning guitar. . . . At the same time, I was still surfing con-

tests but it was phasing out a little. And then I started getting into the guitar more, and it was like a big cross-fade, a very nice smooth transition between surfing all the time, and then wanting to play music all the time. And they're two extremely different—they can be two extremely different lifestyles. Surfing is more of a daytime, early morning, get up with the sun and go jump in the water [activity]. And for a musician . . . it all goes down at night. Once the sun rises, I just want to check out and go to sleep.[11]

When I asked Kelli if she connected her surfing with her music-making, she replied, "Not consciously," but then in the next breath she started to elaborate on ways that surfing and musicking were related in her experience:

They are both very solitary activities for me, especially when I'm creating music. And surfing is a very, was a very solitary sport for me. It's just you and your instrument and whatever you want to do with it, or you and your surfboard and whatever, however you want to play with it. So in that sense, it [surfing and musicking] is very much the same activity.

Kelli then reflected on how both creating music and surfing brought her to a similar mental state of heightened awareness or intensified sensitivity that was also paradoxically a feeling of nothingness. She described both as a "switch," an instant turning from one way of being in the world to another where her experiences were focused.

They were both activities that just kind of . . . they pulled me out of whatever world I was in, situation I was in, or state of mind I was in. And either intensified whatever you're going through, or took you away from it. And those are the only two things that have ever done that for me . . . Kind of like a switch . . . It's like leaving. When you jump in the water, you're leaving shore and going out into the ocean. It's the same feeling when I pick up the guitar. I'm kind of leaving something behind and going to explore something else.

She further elaborated that with surfing, there are layers of "leaving." Paddling out and then paddling for a wave are one form of departure, but then riding a wave is something altogether different: "From the moment I'm standing and riding to the moment I kick out [exit the wave], I'm in one place. When I kick out, I'm in an entirely different place. . . . The way my mind focuses on being on the wave versus trying to catch the wave, or paddling back out for the lineup . . . it's like you're flipping that switch again."

The state achieved when riding a wave is described by Kelli as "nothingness":

My mind races when I'm paddling. But riding the wave, there's nothing. I can't think of anything that I've thought, or anything. No song in my head or anything . . . It's just nothingness. I guess it's the closest I've ever come to just being in a moment and not having any other thought running through my head and just doing exactly what I'm doing. Just putting the pressure on the board and cross-stepping or adjusting and having nothing in your head and not thinking about what you're doing. It's the, the . . . that classic metaphor of riding the wave except you actually are riding a wave. You kind of let the water push you around and you respond. And if you don't think about it, you achieve this state—this state of harmony with nature or with yourself, or with whatever [*laughs*] and you just let it take you. You let it, you let it affect you, and you respond, and then it affects you again, and you respond. And I guess that in itself is the building block of creativity. It's just being affected and responding. And that's a big part of songwriting for me . . . just being able to be affected by something.

This is as good a statement about the mental state of what Mihaly Csikszentmihalyi calls "flow" as I have encountered—an optimal experience where intense concentration on an activity causes distractions to disappear, and one experiences harmony within and with one's environment.[12] Though Kelli says that she does not enter the water consciously to achieve this state, it clearly calls her back to the water. She also recognizes this state of flow as creatively potent: "And I guess when I'm singing, that's the place I want to be . . . not thinking. . . . When I'm singing, and start thinking about things, then you're not in the moment. So I guess riding a wave just throws you into a moment and there's nothing else to think about. That's what I've got to do when I sing."

Focusing her attention on music later in life, she finds that she needs to work harder to achieve this state of nothingness or creative flow with musicking than she does with surfing. Aware of this, she feels that her surfing informs her music in specific ways. She left competitive surfing because it pushed her toward more aggressive riding styles that she did not enjoy as much as what she describes as a more organic response to the wave. Similarly with her songwriting: Kelli believes that she is more successful if she sticks with simpler words and melodies—with what she calls an "organic" and "simpler" sound. She summarizes: "My whole . . . musical journey is just trying to get back . . . get back to nearing what I did with surfing. And it felt better to not struggle . . . when I was in the water."

Surfing and musicking are related for Kelli Heath through the profound mental states they both offer her—both an intensification and focus of feeling, and also a profound feeling of nothingness brought on by clearing the mind of distractions and focusing on and responding to the moment. Yet she, like other contemporary surfing musicians I have interviewed, is reluctant to write songs specifically about surfing: "It's probably because surfing is a sacred thing that I don't want to destroy with words." But she does use water as a metaphor in songs, illustrated most obviously by the song "H2O," released by the Girlas on their album *Now or Never* (audio example 6). Therefore, while surfing and music-making are paired experiences in Kelli Heath's life, sometimes competing for her energy and time, and while there are some qualities of being in the moment that she has learned from surfing and that she strives for with her music, it would, nonetheless, be very difficult to say exactly how her musical sounds are directly affected by surfing.

Tom Curren

With the era-defining style combination of speed, power, and grace, Tom Curren was a three-time surfing world champion (1985, 1986, and 1990). He is still regularly encountered in surfing magazines and is often described as one of the most influential surfers of the late twentieth century. Tom was born in Newport Beach, California, in 1964, and was raised in Santa Barbara, California, where he lives today. His father, Pat Curren, was a pioneering big-wave surfer and is still an influential surfboard shaper. Tom started stand-up surfing at age six when on vacation with his parents. By the time he was eighteen years old he was sponsored by Rip Curl wetsuits and Ocean Pacific beachwear for forty thousand dollars a year. Ten years later (early 1990s) he signed a two-million-dollar, five-year contract with Rip Curl. He is still sponsored by Rip Curl not only to surf, but also just to be Tom Curren.[13] In this way he is following in Duke Kahanamoku's path by realizing his valuable personal branding potential, but Curren was able to capitalize on this from a young age.

In an interview, he explained to me that his first musical instrument was the drum kit, which he began playing at age eight or nine, and that he focused on the guitar at age fourteen.[14] In addition to the music in his parents' limited record collection (he mentioned specifically Simon and Garfunkel, Bob Dylan, and a recording of Hawaiian music, probably *James Michener's Favorite Music of the South Sea Islands* from 1965), he considers two youthful influences to have been the greatest shaping forces on his desire to play music. One was the record collections and listening preferences of some university students who rented accommodations from his parents. The second was the musical soundtracks of surfing movies: "That was a really big part of surfing for us, because we didn't have so many videos coming out all the time. So whatever came out tended to have really good music." The films that he mentioned, however, were not necessarily surf movies: Chuck Wein's *Rainbow Bridge* (1972), featuring Jimi Hendrix (and incidentally a few shots of surfing); and the 1970 concert film *Woodstock*. Two surf movies that he singled out were Jack McCoy's *The Performers* (1984) and George Greenough's *Crystal Voyager* (1973), especially the latter's concluding twenty-three-minute segment with Pink Floyd's "Echoes" as the soundtrack (see chapter 3). He recalls *Crystal Voyager* as providing the first mental connection that he made between surfing and music, with the possible exception of the Beach Boys.

When I asked him how I might better understand the connections between surfing and artistic behavior, Tom tended to engage ideas about rhythm, and also the concept of being "in the pocket"—a term used in both music and surfing. In surfing parlance, being "in the pocket" means riding on the steepest section of a wave, where the greatest power is found—the ideal spot. Tom described being in the pocket as "tapping into the power of the wave in a way that results in really fantastic fun." He compared this to drumming and, for example, playing a fast drum fill. If you land on the beat, he explained, it is like doing a good surfing maneuver and landing in the pocket, where the power is. On the other hand, if while drumming you do not land on the beat, you mess up the other musicians—a musical wipeout.[15] I hear this as a surfing analogy for staying with the flow of rhythm—staying with the movement and power of musical sounds. For Curren, this means staying in time with other musicians; it is a collaborative effort. The corollary in surfing would seem to be collaboration with the wave itself—staying in time with the rhythm of the ocean.

Curren's musicking reveals a progression over the past twenty years that parallels stages in his surfing career: he established himself early with that combination of speed, power, and grace but then mellowed a bit, focusing on grace and becoming increasingly introspective. His semithrash band, Skipping Urchins (with Tom playing drums), did a whirlwind tour of East and West Coast U.S. surfing spots in 1993. His first album, *Ocean Surf Aces* (sometimes also written as *Ocean Surfaces*) was recorded at about the same time but is much jazzier. It is an instrumental album, with Curren playing guitar and drums. A decade later, when he released his eponymous album, his sound had mellowed considerably and features a blend of electric and acoustic guitars. All of the nine tracks are songs sung by Curren, and some of them would not be out of place on a country-and-western radio station's playlist. I have seen Curren perform live a number of times. He can play a full solo set—occasionally using an almost comically small acoustic guitar— but at most of the shows I have seen he has fronted a band playing electric guitar or electric piano. He is able to gather around him good musicians—some of them fellow surfers, but not all. Many of the songs contain Christian messages, though one usually has to listen carefully for them. None is overtly about surfing.

As we saw in chapter 4, surfing brands do sponsor musicians, but Curren made it clear to me that he is not sponsored by Rip Curl to play music; in his self-conception, surfing and music are separate businesses. He believes that for younger professional surfers today there may be more opportunities to blend sponsorship from surfing companies for different activities (surfing, musicking, painting). Curren notes that many surfers do have some creative outlet in addition to surfing, such as painting, photography, or music. Like so many of Tom's explanations, his thoughts tend toward the practical. As he explained, the waves are not always consistent; one cannot surf all the time, so even someone who surfs a lot will still have time to develop other interests. Why not music, or painting, or photography? Today articles in surfing magazines frequently feature surfers' artistic talents, but this was not the case in the 1980s, during Curren's most competitive surfing years.

The times I have seen Tom Curren perform in the Santa Barbara area, the events have always been linked to the surfing community in some way: twice before the screening of surfing movies, at the local maritime museum for the opening of a surfing-themed exhibit, at a Concert for the Coast environmental festival (fig. 31), and at a restau-rant/bar for a Surfrider Foundation fund-raiser. All of these events were closely linked to the local surfing community. Though he does not write songs about surfing, fellow surfers make up a significant proportion of his audience. Is it because he is such an influential and artistic surfer that at least some of us also want to hear what he has to say while mak-ing music? I think yes, and believe that his music and surfing careers are deeply symbiotic.

I noted in chapter 3 that Curren was featured in Andrew Kidman's movie *Litmus,* playing an extended electric-guitar solo. The filmic image of Curren playing guitar was interspersed with footage of him surfing; he was therefore providing an auto-soundtrack for his own surfing.

FIGURE 31. Tom Curren (foreground) performing at the Concert for the Coast environmental festival, 30 May 2009, Isla Vista, California. Isla Vista is the unincorporated coastal neighborhood adjoining the campus of the University of California, Santa Barbara. Photograph by the author.

Previously, in 1997, Sonny Miller's film *Searching for Tom Curren* also included music performed by Curren on the soundtrack. Writer and surfer Jay DiMartino claims that the combination of Curren's era-defining surfing accompanied in this movie by his own guitar playing "single-handedly put a guitar in the hand of every pro surfer for the next decade," and he listed the likes of Jack Johnson and Donavon Frankenreiter as those who were influenced by Curren to take up guitar.[16] Kidman and surfer-artist Joe Curren (Tom's younger brother) made very similar comments to me several years earlier in an interview. Drawing such clear lines of influence is not my objective here, though I do think it is true that when the surfer heralded as the best in the world at the time decided to go public as a guitar player, the surfing community took notice.

Jack Johnson

Jack Johnson is a busy man, a true superstar popular musician who fills the premier auditoriums in North America, Europe, New Zealand, Australia, and Japan. Yet he is also famously chilled out and takes time for himself, his family, and surfing. Born in 1975 on Oʻahu, Hawaiʻi, Johnson also has family ties to California. I was able to interview Johnson at his home in Hawaiʻi. When I arrived he was walking up the beach, board under arm, from his morning surf, and after the interview he loaned me one of his surfboards and recommended where I should paddle out (valuable local knowledge). Completely comfortable in his own skin and gracious during our interview, he also had his demands: no photos, no details about the location of his house, and no names of his children in print. Johnson is media savvy.

Johnson started by agreeing with my comments about the named genre Surf Music being problematic for the surfing musician, or at least presenting some challenges. He explained that when being interviewed in a place that does not have a prominent surfing culture—Germany was the example he used—he may have to spend half the interview explaining why he does not sound like Dick Dale or the Beach Boys. He hastens to add that Dick Dale and the Beach Boys probably did represent musically an early moment when surfing was a new subculture, but that the next generation wanted different music that better represented their time. He recommended looking to surf films for music that resonates with surfers: "I think films are always a pretty good representation of what surfers were listening to during that time, mostly because it was surfers making the films."[17] At some point—probably in the 1980s, according to Johnson—surfing grew beyond a relatively unified subculture and into what he calls pop culture and even the mainstream: "It's such a mainstream deal now that you get people surfing for so many different reasons. So you are going to get people listening to so many different types of music . . . You've got people who listen to stuff like what I might make, and you've got people who don't want any of that mellow stuff . . . There's hardcore stuff, there's everything in between. There's hip-hop. There are surf movies that have all hip-hop music. So it all depends."

Even though Johnson came of age musically over thirty years after the Surf Music genre had its heyday, he did not want his music to be classified as Surf Music "because," he said, "it seemed kind of limiting and wasn't really what I felt like I was going for. I was trying to make something that wasn't going to be classified just as Surf Music. I don't really mind the label now, being known, kind of, as the surf guy." By that time (2010) he already had four platinum-selling albums behind him, and he was finally comfortable addressing surfing more or less directly in the songs that he was working on for his fifth album, *To the Sea*. Of course everyone already knew he was a surfer; Mikael Wood of *Entertainment Weekly* called him "the most successful surf bum in history,"[18] and several years earlier comedian Andy Samberg had parodied his laid-back surfer lifestyle in several skits for *Saturday Night Live*. Still, his role as a surfer plays differently in different contexts. Here in coastal California, many fans seem to understand Johnson as a surfer. Fair enough: surfing is pretty inescapable here. Yet Johnson literally has hundreds of thousands of fans who live far from the sea and have never even tried surfing. While some fans may hear a surfer singing when they listen to Johnson, for others that part of his identity is not salient. Had he presented himself to the world as a surf musician from the get-go, I suspect he might not have been quite so successful.

Johnson talks about surfing and musicking being the yin and yang in his life—his two passions (somewhere behind his wife and family). When the pressure to perform in one venue—surfing or music—begins to threaten his enjoyment, he finds balance with the other. Though he has been making music and surfing since he was a boy, it was surfing that first presented itself as a career possibility. This generated pressure that eventually was balanced with musicking. Now it goes the other way. Rather than trying to bring attention to himself as a surfer (job number one for a professional surfer), he uses surfing as a means to get away from attention, to escape the pressure of performing music onstage before thousands of people. But of course each feeds the other: "I get a lot of my lyrics while I'm out surfing. You know, it's a time to reflect on everything I've been seeing in life. It's not like I'm actually singing about seeing a fish swim underneath me and things like that so much as it is time to actually think about the process, everything that has been going on in the rest of my life. So, they do balance each other in a way."

Johnson grew up on the North Shore of Oʻahu, the epicenter of competitive surfing in Hawaiʻi. He was sponsored by Quiksilver from about the age of thirteen and recalls the excitement of seeing photographs of himself in some surfing magazines, and hanging out with the best young surfers such as Rob Machado and Kelly Slater, but he could also see a downside to it all: "Once I was about sixteen or seventeen, I had a few pictures [in surfing magazines] and it was all pretty intriguing, and then I started noticing that a lot of our friends that were five years ahead of us were already on the downhill. By the age of twenty you were either going to be happening, or you weren't going to have sponsors anymore. And I saw that people who loved surfing a few years before were bitter about it."

His response was to pull back from competitive surfing, if for no other reason than to ensure that it did not ruin the pleasure he takes in surfing. He decided to attend college and was accepted at the University of California, Santa Barbara—not a bad choice for a surfer since the campus is on the coast, though the consistency and quality of waves is several steps down from the North Shore of Oʻahu. He majored in film studies while all the time developing his songwriting and performing skills.

Fans will note that Jack Johnson's music is famously mellow. He mentioned it himself several times in our interview, joking that he has received the Hawaiian version of the Grammy Award for the best rock album, when off the islands his music might not even be called rock. Yet his music-making was not always so mellow. The first band he was in when in high school was a punk rock cover band, playing the music of Minor Threat, Descendents, Fugazi, and Bad Religion. As already noted, his taste for punk rock was fueled by the surfing movies he was watching at the time—a time when he aspired to be a professional surfer. His musical style seems to have changed when Johnson decided to leave Hawaiʻi and seek a college degree.

Johnson lived in a neighborhood called Isla Vista when he was in college. Nestled between the campus, the Pacific Ocean, and a wetland nature reserve, Isla Vista is well known regionally and even nationally for its sometimes-raucous student parties. It is also an incubator for popular music bands. While some of the bands demand attention by being loud, Johnson's Isla Vista songwriting took a turn toward the mellow with an emphasis on acoustic guitar and subtle lyrics. Some of the songs he wrote there are featured on his debut album, *Brushfire Fairytales* (2000), and helped solidify his signature sound.

It seems that while in college and living in Isla Vista, he was nostalgic for the Hawaiian Islands and the backyard and beachside barbecues with acoustic guitars and ukuleles that he recalled from his youth. In our interview, he reminisced about those barbecues and told me about the influence of the sound of waves and birds on his music. For him, mellow music is normal. It works in Hawai'i, where he grew up and still lives. It worked in Isla Vista, too.

I experience some cognitive dissonance when I think about Hawaiian surfing—especially surfing on the North Shore of O'ahu, where the waves can be deadly—and the characteristically mellow music associated with Hawai'i. Why don't Hawaiian surfers create heavy, loud, powerful music that reflects the power and danger of Hawaii's most sought-after waves? Jack Johnson grew up surfing Pipeline, one of the most powerful and dangerous waves in the world; it even has a classic early-1960s instrumental surf-rock tune named after it.[19] Dick Dale speaks of his efforts to express the power of surfing with his aggressive guitar playing, but Dale never surfed anything as violent as the waves Johnson has surfed in Hawai'i and around the world. I asked Johnson why his music was so much mellower than Dick Dale's, for instance. He responded that energy can be expressed in different ways, but that when surfing big waves, the surfer must respond with calm: "I think one of the things you learn in big surf is that the one thing you have to do is stay calm. If you let the energy of the waves get you that intense, then you probably won't be able to do it. . . . If you feed off the energy too much you're going to panic." Thus his mellow music can be heard as the measured response of an accomplished surfer who knows how to ride waves that would leave most of us clinging to dry land.

MUSIC AND PROFESSIONAL SURFING

These case studies—though spanning nearly a century of musicking by surfers who in one way or another made a profession out of surfing and music—are only a thin slice of the pie. There are important musical scenes in Australia, South Africa, France, Bali, the Republic of Ireland, the United Kingdom, Brazil, Mexico, the East Coast of the United States, and so many other places where the surfing affinity group has outposts and beachheads. I am also focused here on musicians who play in broadly conceived popular genres, and each musician featured in this chapter happens to play guitar. I have not included case studies of Richard Tognetti, violinist and artistic director of the Australian Chamber Orchestra, or David Weiss, the recently retired principle oboist of the Los Angeles Philharmonic and Professor of Oboe at the University of Southern California Thornton School of Music, who also teaches surfing. There are many more stories to be told.

One finding in case studies here corresponds nicely with the studies of festivals presented in chapter 4: individuals involved in competitive surfing tend toward faster, louder music, often punk rock. This was Jack Johnson's preferred music when he was a sponsored competitive surfer; Tom Curren seems to have moved into more mellow music as he reduced his competitive surfing (though he still rocks when he wants to). Kelli Heath did not like what competitive surfing scene was doing to her surfing and balanced her energies with music-making. Maybe aggressiveness is necessary for competitive surfing and certain musics are better for getting one in that mood, as suggested by competition surfers at the Boardmasters festival and surfing contest in Newquay, United Kingdom. But mellower, often acoustic music also has a key place among surfers, not just to cool down with after an intense surfing session, but also to promote calm when facing waves of size and consequence.

From my interviews and conversations with competitive surfers summarized in this chapter and in chapter 4, some trends linking certain musical tendencies with surfing do emerge. Yet all is held in balance. The "heavy" music preferred by competitive surfers for preparing mentally for a contest may be balanced by more mellow music postsurf, but this does not mean that all good surfing requires or even benefits from raising one's heart rate in preparation. As Jack Johnson pointed out, getting amped up may not be the wisest approach to surfing large, dangerous waves. Instead, a different, more reflective approach that promotes calm and focus can be sought. Music seems to have a role in a variety of surfing conditions, if only just to allow the surfer to return to shore, as was the case with Chief Naihe in the Hawai'i of yesteryear.

The tension between getting amped up for competitive surfing and seeking a state of calm before paddling out in large waves can be illuminated by a key quality of surfing itself that vexes the media-driven contest industry. Neptune is fickle, and waves of size and quality are fleeting. Even at the best surfing spots on the globe, good waves are the exception rather than the norm. Surfing itself relies on exceptional weather events sending ocean swells often thousands of miles to arrive at the right angle over an ever-changing near-shore sea-floor contour in such a way that the swells rise and break as rideable waves at exactly the spot where surfers are waiting in anticipation. Most surfers, like most surfing-contest organizers, take what they can get rather than holding out for perfect conditions. Only a handful of contests are centered on big waves: the Eddie Aikeau at Waimea Bay, Oʻahu, held only when waves are a minimum of twenty feet high; and the Mavericks Invitational held at Half Moon Bay, California, scheduled only when waves are predicted to be around forty feet. As a consequence, neither of these contests is held every year for lack of adequate waves. The surfing competitions that drive the industry, on the other hand, must go on and therefore are often held in less than favorable conditions—conditions where contestants seem to benefit from "amping up" for big performances in small, often choppy, marginal waves.

It is all about riding the wave that comes your way, but also knowing when to let a set pass beneath your board while keeping your eyes on the horizon. All the surfers featured in this chapter knew when to paddle away from the contest zone and take up the guitar. Yes, Tom Curren still surfs the occasional contest, vexing surfers in their youthful prime, but he also knows how to get in the pocket with a rock band. Both Jack Johnson and Kelli Heath surf better than the vast majority of surfers in the water today, but many more individuals tap their feet to their tunes than have ever watched with awe their grace on a wave. All three surfing musicians talk about personal expression, balance, and timing. For all three, musicking today offers a way of extending creative performativity first expressed through surfing. However, while Jack Johnson and Kelli Heath use music as an antidote to competitive surfing, for Tom Curren and other especially successful contest surfers, from Corky Carroll to Beau Young and Daize Shayne, musicking can be a way to promote their personal brand image—a technique pioneered by Duke Kahanamoku and a few of his fellow Waikīkī Beachboys before professional surfing was redefined by the New Surfing contest industry.

CHAPTER 6

The Soul Surfer Sings

There is something about the pro surfer who becomes a pro musician, or at least extends his or her brand through music, that grabs one's attention. Multinational capitalism, especially entertainment industries, know this and have long exploited the singing, dancing, acting, modeling athletic body.[1] But what about the rest of the surfers? Does their strumming a ukulele on the beach count for much in this story about music and surfing? I certainly hope so. While professional surfers and musicians capture something of the ideals of the communities they represent, they also tend to be exaggerations (and this, of course, excites the entertainment industry that in turn drives professional surfing and popular music). Surf magazines, movies, and popular music all feed on exaggerations. Then there is the rest of the surfing/musicking community. If I may speak for the fragment of this global affinity group that I am familiar with, I will note that most of us get in the water when we can, before or after our paying jobs. Most of our surfing is on two- to four-foot waves. A six-foot day is a real treat; eight-foot waves start to separate the wheat from the chaff; anything over ten feet makes us think twice about paddling out. And that is just fine—great, in fact. We form the backbone of the surfing community; we hold this tribe together. We'll enjoy the punishing waves of Pipeline, Mavericks, and Teahupo'o in the magazines and films, thank you very much. We may be soul surfers, but we have not given up on our bodies quite yet.

We are similarly comfortable singing and playing an instrument among our circle of friends and family, occasionally at an open-mike night at the local bar, but not before hundreds, thousands, or tens of thousands. We prefer to engage in what Thomas Turino calls *participatory performance* rather than *presentational performance.*[2] We are happy singing along with our friends rather than performing for a distinctly defined audience (though as I show below, a few of us can take the heat of the stage lights). In popular music this performer/audience divide was largely manufactured at about the same time surfing was reinvented. In the nineteenth and early twentieth centuries, for example, popular music products were sheet music and instruments—items that enabled active participation in musicking. This began to change with the introduction of recordings and radios, and eventually for some the very conception of music shifted from something one did to something one bought and listened to.[3] Or this is what the music industry wants, but people resist. Turn the radio off and hand me my guitar . . .

Though the surfing industry is doing its best to make surfing a spectator sport, every surfer I know would rather be out there surfing an average three-foot day than watching pro surfers riding twenty-foot giants on TV or even live from the beach. That's because we are soul surfers: we surf for the pleasure of the ride; we surf because our soul cries out for it. Does the surfer have the same impulse to make music rather than consume it?

There is little agreement about what *soul surfing* means, as Matt Warshaw explains in his *Encyclopedia of Surfing* entry on the term. I introduced the concept of the soul surfer in chapter 3, on surf movies, where I tied it to a return to a DIY spirit in filmmaking. I use the concept of soul surfing to emphasize approaches to surfing as a cultural, aesthetic, meaningful practice rather than as a competitive sport. As I suggested in chapter 3, soul surfing seeks to be inclusive rather exclusionary. I suspect most surfers think of themselves as soul surfers at least some of the time. Here I use the term *soul surfer* to refer to people who surf because it has become somehow deeply meaningful to them. Soul surfers often take a decidedly aesthetic and even philosophical approach to surfing that enables them to connect surfing to other aspects of their lives. Surfing is not exceptional in this tendency; there are many books about other sports that employ a philosophical approach and that attach great meaning to the pleasures and struggles of play.

This chapter tells something of the stories of several individuals and groups of soul surfers for whom surfing pervades their musicking on some significant level. A few make their living playing music, a few have brushes with the surfing industry, but most are just engaged surfers and musicians who bring the two cultural practices together to feed their souls. Most of the examples I use here are from California and Hawai'i, though as with every idea presented in this book, they flow around the world, where they are reinterpreted by local surfing communities.

TRANSPORTING ICONIC MODELS: BEACH BOYS AND GIRLS ON THE MAINLAND

Those original twentieth-century professional surfers—the Waikīkī Beachboys—were also prototypical soul surfers of the emerging New Surfing era. While setting up successful and sometimes lucrative businesses teaching surfing, offering canoe rides, entertaining with ukulele and song, and serving as all-around guides for wealthy early-twentieth-century tourists to Hawai'i, they were, as Isaiah Helekunihi Walker's research shows us, also defending their rights to the surf zone, where they could "forge their own identities in contrast to colonial categories."[4] In other words, they were using surfing to feed their souls as Hawaiians on their own land and in their own waters as the islands were colonized by primarily mainland-U.S. business interests. They were soul surfers even while engaging the new colonial economy to sustain their material needs. In my estimation, then, the Waikīkī Beachboys serve as the models for both professional surfers and soul surfers. I write more about musicking and surfing in Hawai'i below, but first I return to a particular beach in Southern California where some of the spirit of the Waikīkī Beachboys is evoked through mimesis, if not in context, meaning, and function.

On any summertime Wednesday afternoon starting at four o'clock, in the southern reaches of San Onofre State Beach, just south of San Clemente, California, one can find a group of men and women sitting on chairs in the sand playing guitars, ukuleles, and other assorted instruments. They call themselves the Bamboo Room Philharmonic. Though there are hundreds of ukulele clubs around the world preserving at least some of the mix of Hawaiian traditional and hapa haole repertoire together with 1930s and 1940s jazz standards, the Bamboo Room Philharmonic boasts the greatest continuity and connection to the roots of New Surfing. I introduced the musical scene at San Onofre in chapter 1 and described how the originators of the surfing and musical style there drew directly from imagined and actual experiences in Hawai'i since the 1930s (see figs. 7 and 8 in chapter 1). At the time, Hawaiian music, especially hapa haole, was popular on the radio on the mainland United States. Southern California surfers sought out Hawaiian musical acts, and they were plentiful in the region, especially in the Los Angeles area.[5] According to early California surfer and musician E. J. Oshier, "Hawai'i to us was like what heaven is for religious people."[6] Notable Hawaiian musicians even graced the Bamboo Room Philharmonic, including Waikīkī Beachboy and professional musician Pua Kealoha (see fig. 28 in the previous chapter). He was just one of a number of professional musicians—such as Los Angeles session musician Ron Cook and uku- lele player and teacher Pat Enos from Hawai'i—who have found their way to the Bamboo Room Philharmonic over the years.

The informal gathering of musicians at San Onofre has been going continuously since the 1930s, pausing only for a few years during the Second World War. Though the repertoire has changed over those nearly eighty years, and is no longer the 98 to 99 percent Hawaiian content that Oshier claimed made up the prewar repertoire, the group as a whole still prizes everything Hawaiian. Figure 32 shows a September 2007 gather- ing of the Bamboo Room Philharmonic, including Bill Tapia, an accom- plished ukulele performer from Hawai'i living in Southern California, age ninety-nine when I took this photograph. That afternoon I noted the group playing "Hanohano Hawai'i" (traditional), "Beautiful Kaua'i" (by Rudolph Farden, 1965), and several other Hawaiian-language pieces mixed in with jazz standards, such as "Sweet Sue" and "Baby Be Blue." I have sat with the Bamboo Room Philharmonic on several occasions over the years, and this mix is representative.

But there is more going on with the Bamboo Room Philharmonic than a group of mostly-senior men on the beach, playing mostly music of their youth. The San Onofre scene was highly instrumental in the early adoption of surfing in California, the reinvention of surfing, and even the subsequent globalization of a surfing lifestyle. Many of California's pioneering surfers in the early century frequented San Onofre. It was the site of the Pacific Coast Surf Riding Championships from 1938 to 1941. (As a favored contest site, the relatively gentle Waikīkī-like breaks of San Onofre were surpassed in the 1980s by the more consistent and shapely breaks called Trestles just a mile up the beach.) Still today, icons of California surfing culture are regulars at San Onofre's music sessions.

The prewar weekend camping excursions to San Onofre by young surfers—warmed by burning piles of old tires and lubricated by gallon jugs of cheap wine[7]—have been supplanted by more family-oriented

FIGURE 32. Bamboo Room Philharmonic, San Onofre, 5 September 2007. Moving from left to right across the photo, a vertical line reaches the heads of individuals in this order: Fred Thomas, Sandy, Gigi Thomas, Bill Tapia (back to camera with dark hat and shirt), Hal Landis (on gut-bucket bass), Donna Ostercamp, Ron Cook, Joe Ostercamp, Roxanne Moores, Jack George, David Weisenthal, Bill Breau, Mike McCaffrey (behind Breau), Bob "Jake" Jacobs, unidentified, Wally Tucker, Pat Enos, Kay Cook, Nancy Enos, and Anne Breau. Photograph by the author.

gatherings. Today second- and third-generation members of the San Onofre Surfing Club (established in 1952) speak of being raised on the beach, getting their first jobs through beach contacts, and celebrating their retirements on the beach. Passing members are memorialized on the beach. The San Onofre Surfing Club offers a utopian corner for the lives of its members, complete with a music soundtrack.

Just a few steps up the beach from the habitual gathering spot of the Bamboo Room Philharmonic can be found, every weekend, the

Hawaiian Surf Club of San Onofre. Founded in 1990, this relatively recent group was started by Hawaiian surfers living in Southern California. While prizing Hawaiian connections, the club is open to all who share a respect for Hawaiian hospitality and 'ohana (family, kin). The San Onofre Surfing Club and the newer Hawaiian Surf Club of San Onofre are not directly competitive, and there is some crossover among the personnel. Yet the creation of the Hawaiian Surf Club of San Onofre does suggest something about the assumption of whiteness in New Surfing, even among groups that actively pay homage to Hawaiian cultural practices.

Glenn Alapag is a musician who has earned a leadership role in the Hawaiian Surf Club. He moved from Hawai'i to California to go to college in 1969, when he as nineteen. He had no intention of staying in California, but he ended up making his life here. His musical interest in high school in Hawai'i was the popular music of the day, especially rock 'n' roll, but somewhat ironically he ended up playing much more Hawaiian music when he moved to California. He explained that once away from Hawai'i, he and his friends "were drawn to our roots. . . . The crew that we hung out with on weekends were people that had the same roots—the same Hawaiian culture and background that we did. So we started playing a lot of music."[8]

Alapag's description of surfing combined with cooking food and making music on the beach sounds a lot like what Ka'au Crater Boys— a band from Hawai'i whose music Alapag recommend to me—celebrate in song (see below). In Alapag's words: "Music doesn't dictate the surfing. Surfing is just another art form. But when you can tie the two together and have good music, and when you come in after surfing, you come in and just pick up the ukulele and start jamming with the guys on the beach making music, hey, you know, it just makes the day a little more well-rounded . . . I mean, when you're not surfing, you're on the land; [when] you're not eating, you're playing music."[9] In this way, the Hawaiian Surf Club of San Onofre seeks to replicate some of the feel of a weekend afternoon on the beach in rural Hawai'i.

Here at San Onofre, with both the San Onofre Surfing Club and the Hawaiian Surf Club, surfing and Hawaiian songs accompanied by guitars and ukuleles, with the occasional hula, were and are icons of an imagined Hawaiian surfing lifestyle. While we might imagine similarities with a lost era of simpler times in Waikīkī, where some of the music and even the waves are strikingly similar, the context is very different. The Waikīkī Beachboys' musicking and surfing were servicing wealthy tourists on the one hand, and preserving core essences of Hawaiian masculinity on the other. In most cases, however, the surfing musicians of San Onofre are not servicing tourists, offering surfing lessons, or songs for tips. Thus while the performative content both in the water and on the sand with ukuleles may be similar to pre-1950s Waikīkī, the social context is of a different order. On the one hand it decommercializes surfing by insulating it from the tourist industry (though I should note that San Onofre is a California state beach, is featured in tourism guides, and is one of the most visited state parks in California). In this sense it may tap into some shred of pre-reinvention Hawaiian surfing. On the other hand, the San Onofre scene represents New Surfing: it is the site of early California surfing contests, and participation is based on individual choice—an affinity group—not the ubiquitous social lifeways that gave meaning to pre-contact Hawaiian surfing. Select cultural practices from or associated with Hawai'i are reimagined by surfers in California and become icons of a romanticized distant paradise where all is well.

The various musical scenes among surfers at San Onofre are not the heirs of some sort of pre-contact Hawaiian essences, while both organized clubs there do pay homage to Hawai'i in their own ways. The laid-back San Onofre scene that pairs surfing with ukuleles and guitars became a model for a surfing lifestyle in the first half of the twentieth century decades before Dick Dale plugged in his Fender guitar and rebranded surf music in the early 1960s. If I have learned anything from my interviews with present-day surfing musicians, it is that today's surfing music owes as much to the Waikīkī Beachboys, and the "boys and girls" of the Bamboo Room Philharmonic, as it does to Dick Dale and the Beach Boys of Hawthorn, California.

URBAN 'OHANA

Traveling seventy miles up the coast, past storied California surfing spots—including Redondo Beach, where George Freeth arguably launched Californian surfing—we find ourselves in Manhattan Beach, one of the several small beach cities that make up the greater Los Angeles metropolitan area. Just three miles south of L.A. Airport, every inch of Manhattan Beach is valuable real estate, and public beach access is a common good that the Los Angeles elite would buy up if it weren't for the efforts of the California Coastal Commission, established in 1972 to, among other things, ensure public access to the state's shoreline.

With a just few modest clapboard cottages still holding out against newly built multistory structures displaying pretensions of grandeur, this is a dense, urban beach town that feels like it is worlds away from San Onofre. Yet even here the spirit of Hawaiian aloha and the Waikīkī Beachboys is evoked if one knows where to look.

It is Saturday, the second day of December 2006, and I am up at 6:30 A.M., treated to a breakfast of eggs and avocado on an English muffin by my host Nancy Cook, long-time surfer and Hawaiian-music enthusiast. She drives with me to a municipal parking lot that spans the distance between 26th and 27th Streets, just a block from the beach, and introduces me to some of the Manhattan Beach Crew, including Al Lee and Laurie Armer, who are suiting up and heading out with their boards. Once in the water, I manage to find Mike Goodin and Gene Lyon, whom I had met the evening before at a Hawaiian restaurant—Bob's, in Gardena, another nearby suburb of sprawling Los Angeles. We surf nice three-foot glassy sets until about 9:30. Back in the parking lot, we peel off our wetsuits before Al, Gene, and Mike set out a few chairs, tune up their ukuleles, and begin playing and singing a mix of hapa haole and popular standards interspersed with a few of their own compositions while our wetsuits hang in the sun to dry (fig. 33 and audio example 7). It's a warm, sunny Southern California morning in the dead of winter, and there is music in the parking lot. And you wonder why there are so many people in L.A. . . .

Maybe it is exactly this density of population that encourages these surfers to be so polite, so engaging, and so willing to immediately take me into their posse (as a group who surf together is sometimes called). Even at my home breaks in Santa Barbara and Goleta I rarely experience such neighborliness or deliberate cultivation of 'ohana. 'Ohana, sharing, and joy are themes that kept returning in my conversations about both surfing and musicking with the Manhattan Beach Crew. Mike Goodin's take on it was both practical and poetic: "An important part of being able to surf in a particular area is that you maintain the connection with the people that you surf with. I hate to say 'localism,' but it does help if you are known by the local crew. So, yes, talking with people before and after surfing is almost de rigueur. And I think the same could be said of music jam sessions."[10] The "localism" that he referred to is the dark underside of New Surfing, the aggressive and even violent behavior toward surfers who are deemed to be outsiders at some surfing breaks. Mike's observations are common sense, but he and

FIGURE 33. Manhattan Beach surfing musicians, 2 December 2006. Left to right: Laurie Armer, Mike Goodin, Alan Lee, and Gene Lyon. Photograph by the author.

the other Manhattan Beach Crew surfers cultivate the positive when it comes to sharing the water and surfing:

> You do get to know a person's personality out in the water; whether they are aggressive or willing to share. You also have lots of time to talk (depending on the conditions). But you get to know people. They are open. Maybe we think that what is "said on the water, stays on the water." The one thing I believe is that we were all trying to improve our skills . . . both surfing and ukulele . . . and we would show off in the water, and then show off in the parking lot. All in good fun.

Mike describes the relationship between surfers as "familial" and then goes on to compare the intricate negotiations between surfers in the lineup to that of players in an orchestra.

> We are a relatively small minority of the overall population, and when you talk with someone else who surfs, you immediately have this connection to them: A shared experience that is not necessarily understood by the public at large. An understanding of the reading of the conditions. An understanding of the effort involved in maintaining your physical ability to enjoy the sport. An understanding of engaging in a sport that is seen by some still

as counterculture and self-centered. While it is true that each surfer is surfing alone, they are really amongst a whole orchestra of other surfers, sharing waves when appropriate, and dominating when necessary, but in the end, hopefully, they are all sharing a session that allows each person to advance their ability while not inhibiting the more advanced or truly gifted from also enjoying and expressing their skills. The same could be said of musicians. When they get together and jam, there is an immediate, shared understanding of an experience and ability to perform. Each person has their own skill level. I have been in many jam sessions where accomplished musicians essentially tutor neophytes, but in the end, everyone has had a good time.

These accounts counter without actually contradicting some comments by other surfers who represent surfing as somehow selfish whereas music-making can be shared. Manhattan Beach Crew surfers Al Lee and Gene Lyon—in an animated conversation in which one would interject agreement and commentary while the other was speaking—compared the spirit of aloha and 'ohana that they find playing Hawaiian traditional and hapa haole music to surfing in a way that counters localism and surfing selfishness. I asked them if this spirit of aloha and sharing had anything to do with surfing:

> Gene: You know, I think surfing probably has something to do with the mode of the heart.
>
> Al: I think . . . I, I do in the sense that if the people understand surfing, then it's kind of the same thing. You know, they're more welcoming instead of being on the other side of that. What we talked about a little earlier—about being territorial. You know [adopting an aggressive voice] "This is my surf spot." [back to his normal voice] Is it? . . . [laughs]
>   If you're in position for a wave . . . if you just gave it up [laughing] to somebody. You just give it up to somebody . . .
>
> Gene: It's a gift . . .
>
> Al: and let them enjoy it
>
> Gene: It's a gift . . .
>
> Al: You know how much you feel better than if you just kind of . . .
>
> Gene: . . . take all the waves.
>
> Al: [sounding aggressive, tense] . . . try to outpaddle the other guy to get in the position to get it.
>
> Gene: It's about sharing.
>
> Al: You're going to just let it go, and hey, man . . .
>
> Gene: It's your time . . .
>
> Al: Yeah . . .

Gene: . . . to shine.

   Al: I'm not going to paddle-battle, you know, battle-paddle you for that wave. Enjoy it.

Gene: Yeah. You're in a better spot.

   Al: And it feels so good to do that, you know. So I think in this whole same conversation—just like the sharing of the music—you play it but you want to share with other people and have them be a part of it.

Gene: Yeah, our venues are definitely interactive, you know.

   Al: So that right there is the joy, I think . . .

Gene: It is the joy.

   Al: . . . to, uh . . .

Gene: share . . .

   Al: . . . yeah, to share. *[laughs]*

This is the wisdom of soul surfers. It is a lot more fun if one keeps the focus on just that: fun. Not that they don't surf hard. In my notes taken after my first surf with the Manhattan Beach Crew in 2006 when the waves were three feet and glassy, I noted that Gene was always on the move and caught many waves—one measure of a good surfer. The second time I surfed with them was in 2007. The waves were in chest- to head-high sets and fast, and the lineup was much more crowded. There was real intensity to the session. I recall Laurie Armer surfing on a shortboard (we were all on longboards the first time we surfed) with such energy that I did not recognize her until we were back at the parking lot. Still, the emphasis—both in the water and in the parking lot with ukuleles in hand—was on sharing, appreciating each other's skills, and having some fun. Soul surfing.

The musical and narrative links to Hawai'i made by individuals active in both the surfing and music scenes at San Onofre, by the Manhattan Beach Crew, and by others, especially from California, with whom I have spoken bears more research. First, any engagement with posited "Hawaiian music" needs to take into consideration that it, like most music, is highly mediated. Even the songbooks published in Hawai'i that I analyzed in chapter 1 are mediated products of the music industry. *Johnny Noble's Book of Famous Hawaiian Melodies* was published in New York, but Noble was from Hawai'i and worked primarily in Hawai'i. All three of the songbooks by Cunha, Noble, and King directly reference tourism to Hawai'i; Noble even reproduces a document created by the Hawaii Tourist Bureau (see fig. 9, chap. 1). Second, concepts of *aloha* and *'ohana* are also highly mediated, often for the benefit of the tourism industry, but the surfing industry also has a stake in representing Hawai'i as welcoming. What *aloha* and *'ohana* might mean to a native Hawaiian speaker may vary significantly from how those terms are used by surfers in California and elsewhere, even those with family and heritage ties to Hawai'i such as Al Lee, Gene Lyon, and Glenn Alapag. While cultivating expressions of love and family by any group of people is a good thing, one must be careful not to essentialize a people's interpretation of even these seemingly most basic of human needs. Love and family may be basic human needs, but the meanings of love and family are culturally constructed and enacted, and differ around the world.[11] Can we fully separate the many Hawaiian-language uses of term *aloha* from the many companies that use the same word in their band name, for example? While I hope surfers in California and around the world can find ways to use surfing and possibly other ideas from Hawai'i, including aloha and 'ohana, to create a better world, we also need to be sure we are not exploiting the very people who gave us these ideas.

MODERN HAWAIIAN BEACHBOYS (AND GIRLS)

In the ocean, things tend to go in circles and cycles: waves, currents, trends. When talking about surfing, things tend to return to Hawai'i, where it all began.

Pua was sixty years old when I met her in the village of Hau'ula, on the northeast side of O'ahu, Hawai'i, in 2010, at the Aloha Ko'olauloa festival celebrating Hawaiian-language instruction at the village elementary school. Pua was playing ukulele and singing with the Nani Haunani Serenaders when I arrived. After their performance, I introduced myself to Pua. Learning that she still surfs, I asked her what I needed to know about music and surfing. She responded by moving her arms and shoulders forward and back and saying that it is all about rhythm, back and forth. She explained that one can't fight the water and waves but must move with them: the tide that takes you out will also bring you back in; even a child growing up in Hawai'i knows this. Then she sang a mele that she said she sings on the beach. In our conversation, she integrated surfing, swimming, dance, song, and traditional Hawaiian land-use practices into a description of her life ambi-

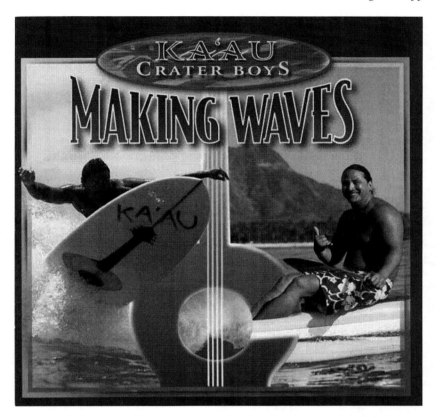

FIGURE 34. Cover of Kaʻau Crater Boys' 1996 CD *Making Waves*. On the left is Troy Fernandez, surfing, and on the right is Ernie Cruz in an outrigger canoe, another traditional Hawaiian wave-riding vessel. Use courtesy of Roy Sakuma Productions, Inc. © 1996.

tions and philosophy. It all flowed together like the fish, sand, and seaweed in a waxing and waning tide.

I was in Hauʻula to meet Ernie Cruz Jr., a surfer and a musician of considerable accomplishment. He is best known for his work with ukulele player Troy Fernandez in their band Kaʻau Crater Boys, one of the most popular Hawaiian contemporary bands in the 1990s (fig. 34). Their recordings won three Nā Hōkū Hanohano awards (informally called the Hawaiian Grammy Awards) and are still heard frequently on Hawaiian popular radio stations. Both Troy and Ernie are avid surfers, and Kaʻau Crater Boys released several songs about surfing, including "Surf" and "Makaha." As the title suggests "Surf" is an anthem to the pleasures of wave riding, but surfing is linked to musicking in several ways:

> Surf is the only way I say to make
> Music with the ocean day by day
> I surf all day play music all night and I
> Just can't wait till the morning light to go
>
> *Chorus:* Surf ooh ooh wa ooh, Surf
> Everybody go surf ooh wa ooh, Surf, Surf
>
> ("Surf," by Troy Fernandez. Use courtesy of Roy Sakuma Productions, Inc. ©
> 1993.)

Just reading the text, one could think this song was by the Beach Boys of California. Ka'au Crater Boys' sound was similar to that of the Beach Boys with their harmony singing and nonsense syllables (ooh wa ooh). However, the lyrics elsewhere in the song place the band in Hawai'i, on the island of O'ahu, where both Cruz and Fernandez were born and raised and still live:

> Waimea, Sunset, Pipeline, Haleiwa, Velzyland
> Bomburas, Rock Piles, Ala Moana and
> Keiser Bowl. Everybody go . . . *[chorus]*

This type of place naming, verbally mapping the island, is reminiscent of mele that contain lists of prominent surfing spots.[12]

Their hit song "Makaha" celebrates a specific well-known surfing spot on the west side of O'ahu, miles away from the tourist hotels, both literally and figuratively (audio example 8). The west side is considered to be a place where traditional Hawaiian ways survive, and where haole surfers are advised to surf with heightened respect, if at all. The song suggests that for some Hawaiians, Makaha is a place where a surfer and musician can feed his or her soul:

> There's a place, on the west side
> Called Makaha, Makaha yeah.
> All the braddahs and sistahs,
> Surfing big waves and hanging around
> Playing music and having some fun
> At Makaha, Makaha yeah
> We're going to Makaha, Makaha yeah.
>
> ("Makaha," by Troy Fernandez. Use courtesy of Roy Sakuma Productions, Inc.
> © 1996.)

The song goes on to name some of the "braddahs and sistahs," all of them west-side surfing legends: Braddah Mel (Mel Pu'u, who inspires younger west-side surfers), Braddah Russ (Rusty Keaulana, world champion longboarder), Sistah Rell (the much-lamented Rell Kapolioka'ehukai Sunn, "Queen of Makaha," who died at age forty-seven of cancer), and Uncle Buff (Buffalo Keaulana, 1950s Waikīkī Beachboy, 1960 Makaha International champion, and now informally known as the "Mayor of Makaha"). Here, too, this song recalls the naming function of mele.

Another difference between the Ka'au Crater Boys and the Beach Boys is that the former use acoustic guitars and ukulele as their primary instruments rather than electric guitars. They also have a mild reggae feel to some of their songs, with a characteristic moderate tempo punctuated on the upbeat by ukulele and guitar, while the bass emphasizes the downbeat. Especially easy to hear in "Makaha," this style is sometimes called "Jawaiian" (Jamaican-Hawaiian), though there is a move among some Hawaiians to change the genre name to "reggae-based Hawaiian music."[13] Finally, the greatest difference for the purposes of this book is that unlike the Beach Boys, the Ka'au Crater Boys are avid surfers, and thus their surfing songs are expressions of their own experiences.

This afternoon in Hau'ula, Ernie Cruz Jr. is performing with guitarist Todd Adamski. Ernie is wearing a Hawaiian Surfers Union T-shirt like the one he is wearing for the photo on the cover of his 2001 solo album *Portraits*. The songs on *Portraits* are markedly different from those Cruz did with Ka'au Crater Boys in a number of ways. Only one makes reference to surfing. After his show at Hau'ula, I asked Cruz what connections he makes between his surfing and his music, and his response was pragmatic: "Once you get a guitar or a surfboard, it cost you . . . (he makes a round zero shape with his hand). Then you can get whatever pleasure you can out if it."[14]

He has a real point. Though Ernie Cruz Jr. was half of one of the most popular groups in Hawaii in the 1990s, music is his avocation; working as a longshoreman assures that he can pay his bills. The songs on *Portraits* take pleasure in things Hawaiian and hark back to the music of the 1970s Hawaiian Renaissance, when there was a concerted effort to restore Hawaiian-language use and other cultural practices. Prominent in the Hawaiian Renaissance was Gabby Pahinui and his band, the Sons of Hawaii. They actively sought out Hawaiian-language songs and popularized them using slack-key guitars, ukuleles, and lap steel guitars—all instruments associated with Hawai'i, and all celebrated on Cruz's *Portraits*. (I return to the Hawaiian Renaissance below.) Cruz's heritage is Hawaiian . . . and German, and Japanese, and. . . . As he told me, the Hawaiian element of his heritage is amplified in his experience because

FIGURE 35. Eddie Kamae (left) accompanied by Mike Kaawa at the Waikīkī Elks Club, 15 January 2008. Photograph by the author.

he was born and raised there on the islands.[15] On his solo album, Cruz sings Hawaiian-language and Hawaiian-/English-language songs in praise of Hawaii's beauty ("Fires of Pele," "Ka Makani," "Hana Calls"), and two songs calling for Hawaiian sovereignty ("Where Are the Brothers" and "Ua Mau"[16]). Could it be that after his popular success in Ka'au Crater Boys, Ernie Cruz Jr. needed to tend to his Hawaiian soul?

Tending to things Hawaiian is at the core of the musicking of Mike Kaawa. An avid bodysurfer, Kaawa makes music grounded in the legacy of the Hawaiian Renaissance. I met him at the Elks Club, in Diamond Head, Waikīkī, where he was performing with Eddie Kamae (fig. 35), one of the founding members of the Sons of Hawaii. Kaawa's songs, often with texts in Hawaiian and/or English by his wife and champion bodysurfer Malissa Kealiihokulani Tongg, celebrate the beauty of the islands and local beaches and the excitement of bodysurfing. Eddie Kamae did me a good turn when, after I told him about my research, he pointed me toward Mike Kaawa.

The musical collaborations of Kaawa and Tongg stick close to what they call their "Hawaiian roots," a theme that was ever present when I interviewed them on the deck at the Elks Club, overlooking some of the world's most famous surfing breaks: Tonggs (named after Malissa's grandfather),[17] Ricebowl, Old Man's, and Castles. Both were born and raised on Oʻahu, and their passion for bodysurfing and the interrelated idea of Hawaiian roots are two things that bring Mike and Malissa together. Mike's first solo album, *Hwn Boy* (1999), includes several cowritten songs about bodysurfing: "Kūlaʻilaʻi" and "Panics," both named after noted bodysurfing breaks. Malissa wrote the lyrics in Hawaiian, and Mike composed the music. A third piece on the album, "Sandys," is a solo-guitar composition by Mike about another body-surfing spot. On Kaawa's next solo album, *Hwn Groove* (2003) is a song cowritten by Mike and Malissa called "Sunrise @ Sandy's" also about bodysurfing. Both Mike and Malissa described the pleasure they received when local bodysurfers at these spots recognized and appreciated these songs.

In our interview I asked them if there was anything especially musical about surfing or being on the beach. Malissa commented on the rhythm in the waves. Mike added that there is a lot of movement of the waves that inspires an intensity of sound. Music inspired by the waves "certainly wouldn't be a ballad," he quipped. Later in our interview, Malissa added: "When you're surfing though, there's a . . . I guess my take on it, I guess it's not everyone's, but there's a smoothness to it, like a flow that you got going on . . . I, I got going on. When I'm swimming, there's a certain kind of nice, even flow . . . I try to carry that through the music."[18]

The intensity, movement, and flow that Mike and Malissa express with their poetry and music are accomplished within a style that Mike describes as Hawaiian. When I asked Mike to explain what he means by Hawaiian music, he said, "Hawaiian lyrics, Hawaiian instruments, stories that talk about Hawaiian issues." This he contextualized within his own family history of playing music, especially slack-key guitar—a style of guitar emphasizing finger picking and open tunings. Mike Kaawa signed the notes to his album *Hwn Groove*: "From my heart and soul Hawaiian music shall always flow—Hwn Boy" (his nickname). It is indicative that from that heart and soul flow songs and instrumentals about that most intimate form of surfing, bodysurfing.

All of these Hawaiian groups and individuals focus on Hawaiʻi in different ways. Pua's primary concern expressed to me was traditional Hawaiian patterns of land use. Her musicking and surfing, too, flowed out of her sense of being Hawaiian. The Kaʻau Crater Boys may borrow a bit of Jamaican reggae style in their music, but when they sing about surfing, it is distinctively Hawaiian, naming Hawaiian breaks and key Hawaiian surfers. On his own, Ernie Cruz Jr. harks back to the Hawaiian Renaissance and forward with new songs about Hawaiian sovereignty. Mike and Malissa continue the tradition of the Sons of Hawaii by singing older Hawaiian songs and writing new songs in Hawaiian, including songs about bodysurfing, and emphasizing a distinctively Hawaiian approach to the guitar.

I hear all of these musicians as an expression of the success of the Hawaiian Renaissance, though its influence on surfing is not yet fully understood. Isaiah Helekunihi Walker's work in *Waves of Resistance* links the Renaissance with the 1960s Save Our Surf environmental group that worked to stop the coastal development and dredging that threatened surfing breaks.[19] The Hawaiian Renaissance encouraged (and accomplished) the revival of Hawaiian cultural practices, such as language, mele, and hula, but as Walker notes, surfing did not need revival since it was still going strong. In fact, the surf zone was the sole remaining uncolonized place where Hawaiians could assert their dominance and express themselves on their own terms.[20]

Hawaiian music did not need revival, either, since Hawaiian-language singing never ceased, even if some singers were not fully conversant in the language. Yet by the mid-1900s, several generations had been raised in an era when use of the Hawaiian language was discouraged. Hawaiian-language songs were old songs, the songs of one's parents and grandparents. With the Hawaiian Renaissance, the arduous task of reversing that trend began. Hawaiian-language instruction resumed in schools, and Hawaiian-language songs were suddenly in the charts and on the radio again. Music became a key tool in the Hawaiian Renaissance, especially in the hands of the popular Sons of Hawaii, who actively researched and recorded old Hawaiian songs and encouraged new ones to be created.[21] Pua, Cruz, Kaawa, and Tongg show the success of the Hawaiian Renaissance with their fluency in Hawaiian cultural practices including language, hula, and even the playing of ukuleles and slack-key guitars. If we accept Walker's thesis, and I do, we know that surfing also played an important role in maintaining some (reimagined) sense of Hawaiian identity.

GLOBAL SOUL SURFING

Here I have focused on Californian and Hawaiian soul surfers, but there are soul surfers around the world at every surfing beach. Given more time and space, I would have profiled Neil Halstead, the principal singer of the British band Mojave 3, who learned to surf when on tour in California, and subsequently moved from London to Newquay to be near the sea. He says surfing changed his life and may have even saved him.[22] I also would have returned to the Ex Presidenti's, Gian Maria Vaglietti (introduced in chapter 4), who lives inland in Italy yet is obsessed with surfing and writes songs about an imagined California surfing lifestyle. And then there is Peggy Oki, surfer and skateboarder for the Zephyr team memorialized in Stacy Peralta's 2001 documentary film *Dogtown and Z-Boys,* who continues to balance skating, surfing, rock climbing, mountain biking, playing her viola, painting, and environmental activism. At some point, in some way, and even if only for fleeting moments, all surfers are soul surfers.

This does not, however, get us very far if our goal is to clarify what *soul surfing* means, but then, I don't want to define the term. It has to mean different things for different surfers. For Ernie Cruz Jr., it could mean finding a nexus between surfing and musicking that helps him keep body and soul together while making a living doing the backbreaking work of a longshoreman on the very docks that have historically exported Hawaii's wealth. His views of Hawai'i, surfing, and music cannot be the same as those of E.J. Oshier, who seventy years earlier preceded Cruz Jr. in playing ukulele and singing Hawaiian-language songs. For Oshier, surfing and playing music on the beaches of California in the 1930s, Hawai'i was an essentialized ideal, the idyllic font of surfing and good music, though Oshier would not visit Hawai'i himself until the 1970s.[23] Soul surfing, like surfing itself, is different things to different souls.

Though the stories I tell here are but a few, several themes emerge. I note that soul surfers in California tend to reference Hawai'i, pay homage to Hawai'i, and attach key aesthetics themes of their surfing lifestyle to Hawaiian terms and concepts. I interpret this as both a recognition of the debt owed to Hawaiians for surfing, and also as a use of Hawai'i as an icon of surfing authenticity. By the acquisition and display of knowledge about and experience with all things Hawaiian, a surfer accrues cultural capital in the surfing community, perhaps especially in California, with its long historical ties to Hawai'i. I suspect that the mainland-U.S, and especially Californian, focus on Hawai'i among surfers is in part a reaction to the colonial history of Hawai'i and its close links to California via the shipping trade and the centuries of exchange of people between the continent and the islands. As far a as surfing is concerned, Californians have benefited from the relationship and have played a leading role in displacing Hawaiians from primacy in the surfing industry if not from surfing lineups. Thus in some cases California soul surfers may be seeking atonement even as they pay homage to Hawaiʻi in their musicking. Hawaiian surfers, on the other hand, do not tend to sing about surfing in California. They, too, sing about Hawaiʻi, and the changing social and political conditions of island surfing.

Even though Hawaiʻi has been marketed worldwide as a sort of paradise or soul-soothing heaven on earth, surfers from Europe are just as likely to imagine surfing paradise in California as in Hawaiʻi. Gian Vaglietti writes surf-punk songs about California; Neil Halstead found his surfing salvation in California. Yet Peggy Oki, who grew up in gritty Venice, California, and now lives two minutes from Rincon, one of the state's best surfing spots, prefers the warmer waters of somewhere else, anywhere else. As if exiled from the surfing Garden of Eden, the global soul surfer is doomed to wander in search of surf—the basic theme of so many surf movies. Or does the true soul surfer find paradise at his or her home beach? In the following chapter, I show that some Australian surfers know that paradise may be on their own coasts, or nearby islands. My admittedly limited experience with surfing musicians from Australia suggests that they are not as prone toward songs about California or Hawaiʻi. Ultimately, whether through lines in a song or lines drawn on the face of a wave, many soul surfers realize that paradise is experienced in fleeting moments on ocean waves or in the sound waves of music.

CHAPTER 7

Playing Together and
Solitary Play

Why Surfers Need Music

Stylish surfing is most important to me. Music also comes
in waves, and surfing with style means timing and rhythm,
I think I surf like Jamiroquai, but I wish I surfed more like
Jimi Hendrix!

—Stephanie Gilmore[1]

In this concluding chapter I draw out key themes from examples of how
surfers talk about musicking in an effort to understand something of
significance about surfers as an affinity group. I offer some of the words
of surfers gleaned from my own interviews as well as from interviews in
surfing magazines, films, newspapers, and books. My focus is on the
New Surfing era, and most of these surfers and some of their words
were introduced in previous chapters. My goal in this final chapter is to
show why some surfers may need to be actively involved in musicking,
and why music may be beneficial or even necessary for realizing a sense
of community among surfers.

TWO THEMES

From the words of the surfers featured in this study, two themes
emerge. The first is a set of what I will call *homologies:* claims that
musicking and surfing are in some fundamental way the same. *Homology* generally means sameness or relation, a correspondence. Sometimes this is expressed as an *analogy*—a comparative figure of speech,
such as the epigraph at the beginning of this chapter—but often surfers

have put it to me as a fact of physics: *sound waves and ocean waves are the same.*

The second theme that emerges from the way surfers talk about musicking and surfing I summarize as *community sharing*. This theme derives from a key distinction that many surfers make between the two cultural practices of musicking and surfing: while the surfing affinity group gathers around the cultural practice of surfing, surfing itself can be difficult to share, whereas musicking is ideally a shared activity.

Taking these two themes together, we begin to see why and how musicking is important, the role it has in creating a sense of self and group identity, and some of the ways it is effective not just in expressing but also in creating an experience similar to that of surfing. Ultimately, I propose, musicking allows surfers to give expression to, and to reexperience in a shared context, the corporal experience that draws them into the ocean.

The interaction of the individual surfer-musician with ocean waves or with other musicians is frequently described as requiring skills of improvisation. Though sometimes surfing musicians talk about musicking as being a performance—sharing their music with a relatively more passive listening audience—more often I find that the ideal is sharing among a group who are all contributing what they can to the musicking. Mike Goodin's description in the previous chapter of a good session at Manhattan Beach exemplifies this perspective. Additionally, making music allows wave riders to bond on dry land when not surfing. The participatory quality of shared musicking, therefore, allows for a collective expression of group identity unachievable in the water.

Homology: Waves Is Waves

As presented by surfers included in this study, homologies take several forms. First is the claim by some that sound waves and water waves are in essence the same; they are both waves and behave like waves behave. Surfers and musicians, therefore, are tapping into the same phenomenon. A second and often related connection made between musicking and surfing concerns conceptions of rhythm. Both playing music and riding waves require timing, getting into the groove. Finally, a more general response is that surfing and musicking generate the same affective feelings or peak experiences. These feelings and experiences are sometimes called *flow,* but they are also described as sensations of timelessness, moments of nonthought or nonthinking—or their seeming opposite, moments of intense focus or presentness.

Here are some of the ways surfers speak about music and surfing being fundamentally similar or even the same. Surfer-musician Samuel Bonanno, proprietor of Kapa Boutique and Music Store on the Hawaiian island of Kaua'i, put it to me in an informal conversation most eloquently. He said: "Music and surfing are the same thing . . . Sound and music are both just waves." He went on to say that the origins of life are where the sea meets the land, and that we all descend from this place. For him, music replaces the feeling of surfing when he can't be there in that meeting zone, actually surfing.[2] For Bonanno, not only are musicking and surfing in essence the same; they are the essence of being. Tim Donnelly, in the beginning of an article of his about music that appeared in the magazine *Surfers Path,* approaches the same idea in a poetic mixing of metaphors: "The waves of sound and the waves of water are the translucent and connective engines that universally flow through our saltwater veins."[3]

Jack Johnson's understanding of the unity of sound and ocean waves is expressed on the level of wave frequencies, important for both surfing and musicking:

> Well, you're dealing with wave frequencies with both [music and surfing]. I have always loved tuning, tuning the guitar, ever since I first learned it. When you get the harmonics, when you go "doo, doo" [singing two different but nearly identical pitches] and you hear it go "woowoowoowoo" [speeding up] you can kind of play with it. . . . I've always tripped out on that a little bit, just the sound waves and the waves in the ocean. Trying to understand them, because you can . . . they can either seem really confusing or you can make some sense of it with the ocean. Being able to predict swells and wind patterns and stuff, on the ocean.[4]

Johnson's "woowoowoowoo" was imitating vocally what musicians call the beating of overtones that are audible when tuning, for example, one guitar string to another. As the pitch of one string comes close to matching that of a second, the beating slows down, and it disappears when the two strings are exactly the same pitch. The same thing happens with ocean waves, but the wavelength (roughly synonymous with "frequency") is much greater, so surfers experience the "beating" (Johnson's "woowoowoowoo") as periodic sets of larger waves.[5] The harmonic beating, created by two slightly different pitch frequencies, is audible as a variation in amplitude (volume or loudness); we hear the rhythmic increases in volume as beating. With ocean waves, this increase in volume corresponds to the sets of larger waves that the surfer waits for with anticipation.

Bobbing in the lineup, surfers use another term also commonly uttered by musicians: *interval*. When we are talking about music, interval is the distance between two pitches; the pitch D is one whole step above the pitch C, for example. When talking about water waves, *interval* refers to the time in seconds between one wave and the next—the longer, the better. Johnson's and so many other surfers' words suggest that they understand something of the universality of waves and that this is one of the ways that they link playing with ocean waves and playing music.

Homologies permeate the discourse in and about the film *Life Like Liquid,* by Australian free surfer Dave Rastovich. For example, Rastovich states: "Through so many ocean experiences and so many days spent listening to music I have come to wonder if sound waves and ocean waves are actually the same thing. The only difference being that they are moving through different mediums."[6]

Of course, all of these surfing musicians are right: waves are a universal phenomenon and are at the core of our sensorial and temporal experiences. In his book *The Wave Watcher's Companion,* Gavin Pretor-Pinney illustrates with his signature combination of wit and scientific inquiry the fact that waves are energy that can be seen (light waves), heard, felt, surfed (ocean waves), and so forth.[7] Christian philosopher and surfer Peter Kreeft agrees with physicists that waves are a "fundamental force of energy throughout this universe" and builds on that to propose that waves are the "fingerprint of God" and surfing is a "foretaste of heaven."[8] Bob L. Sturm turned wave energy literally into sound to create several musical compositions for his album *Music from the Oceans.*[9] He sonified ocean-wave patterns measured by wave buoys, effectively speeding them up so that we can hear the wave patterns. Waves is waves.

The second way I document the homologies between sound waves and water waves, musicking and surfing, is expressed in terms of *rhythm.* For example, surfer and popular Hawaiian musician John Cruz talks about surfing and rhythm poetically, slipping seamlessly between surfing and musicking: "Melodies . . . there's always rhythm. The water . . . always rhythm. When you're swimming . . . bouncing . . . floating on top . . . with little bubbles that form on the board . . . there's always rhythm. When you're working a wave, it's all rhythm— get the groove and figure out what pattern this wave is gonna be. When

I watch surfers that have the spot wired, [I] almost know what song they're going to play."[10]

Australian author, musician, and surfer Andrew Crockett makes strikingly similar comments about surfing and musicking both requiring not just rhythm, but also submission and attentive "feeling":

> I think there is something there as well that attracts people to surfing and music, where you have to fit in to . . . you're submissive to the wave. If you're trying to fit in with a band and they're playing like a blues in a four-four beat, you can't just sit in there and play . . . some kind of different timing. . . . The best bit of surfing is when you're feeling the wave and you're trying to fit in with the wave. It's a good feeling, 'cause you feel . . . I don't know, you just feel . . . You can't describe the feeling, but it's the same with music. Like when you have to fit in with it. And it's a nice feeling to fit in with that rhythm.[11]

Crockett goes on to describe surfers who, though doing technically difficult maneuvers, don't quite feel the rhythm of the wave but instead appear to fight against the wave. In contrast, he continues, "other surfers, they really feel the groove so beautifully that when you watch them, when you watch someone who's like that, it's really nice to watch. And it's the same with music. When you listen to someone that can feel the groove really well, there's no edges." For both John Cruz and Andrew Crockett, one can hear rhythm in music, see it in surfing, and in both cases feel its effect.

Jack Johnson uses rhythm to literally bring song into his surfing: "I always sing a song when I'm riding a wave. Especially somewhere where the wave's long enough to get going and forget the fact that you've taken off. Then you just start getting a song in your head and you kind of get this rhythm going sometimes. Somewhere like Rincon, where you can just get a rhythm going, and having a nice groove in your head kind of helps out."[12]

In chapter 5, I relayed how Tom Curren compared his surfing experiences to his rhythmic sense when drumming: he compared ending a fast drum fill on the beat correctly to landing a good surfing maneuver "in the pocket" of a wave. In either case, as a drummer or as a surfer, he actively collaborates with the other musicians or with the wave, respectively. Laura Enever, a professional surfer from Sydney, says of the similarities between music and surfing: "Some of the best advice I've been given is that, when you're riding a wave, imagine you are listening to music—surfing to the beat, feeling the rhythm."[13] I hear these discussions of rhythm and of waves as indigenous music theory on the one hand, and a worldview or cosmology on the other, as surfing musicians make sense of phenomenological experiences.

Making sense of experiences is key in a third type of homology, which in many instances is presented as a metanarrative: it brings surfing and musicking together in the ways that create similar affective and corporeal feelings. Not just any feeling, but the description of a certain quality of feeling that is special, transcendent, and sometimes described as out-of-body. As I explained in the introduction, this sort of experience or feeling is described by psychologist Mihaly Csikszentmihalyi as "flow"—a term and theory that shows up in recent ethnomusicological and sports studies.[14] By "flow" Csikszentmihalyi means a range of optimal, pleasurable, and desirable experiences. They are moments or extended periods of intense focus and concentration where distractions disappear and time passes unnoticed.[15] I believe that this is exactly what surfers are describing when they talk about making music and surfing using terms such as "the groove," "timelessness," "the zone," "in sync," "in the moment," "state of harmony," "heart," "instinctive," "nonthinking," "unconscious," and a "mindless, timeless experience."[16]

In one of several projects that treat surfing as an art form, Andrew Crockett sets out specifically to understand what he calls "the unconscious side of surfing and music, the feeling of timelessness experienced with some art forms."[17] This is exactly how Australian surfing musician Shannon Carroll compared musicking and surfing: "The key similarity between surfing and jamming is the sense of timelessness you experience when you're fully immersed in the moment. When you're playing a melody or a solo you are the surfer, drawing whichever lines the waves allow. . . . Good sound connections usually make for good sound waves."[18] Surfing blues musician Ash Gruwald also talks about timelessness, while adding "zone" and "in sync": "The 'Zone' that the surfer or musician experiences is a fleeting feeling at first, a moment where everything is in sync and a moment where time does indeed stand still, or perhaps just becomes irrelevant."[19]

Timelessness or time standing still is a sensation commonly reported by surfers as being experienced when they are "in the tube," meaning riding inside the hollow, cylindrical tube of spinning water sometimes created by waves in certain rarefied conditions. Getting "tubed" or "barreled," as surfers refer to it, is an extremely difficult thing to achieve, often terminating in a violent wipeout. The maneuver requires skill, timing, and a willingness to place oneself in the most dangerous part of a wave; thus it requires focused commitment. It is exactly this sort of intense focus that leads to a mental state of flow, according to Csikszentmihalyi.[20]

Surfers also talk about getting tubed using terms such as "timeless" and "mindless." Dave Rastovich drew connections between playing music and surfing in the tube this way: describing a good music jam session, he said, "I have no idea what I'm doing. But, I'm playing music." He then compared that to surfing: "When I get inside a tube, I'm not thinking at all, there's no thinking going on." Then, after an almost phenomenological explanation of bodily instinct, he concluded: "Surfing and music seem to be such good analogies, and such good examples of the way it works. You go into that mindless, timeless experience—timeless and mindless but so intelligent, so loaded, and so fuckin' fun."[21]

Al Hicks, also from Australia, is a drummer and surfer who emphasizes the necessity of finding flow in both endeavors. When I asked him what he thinks about when playing drums, he replied: "I actually think about flow on a wave and connecting things together, because on the drums it's really similar. You've gotta keep the flow going. If you get caught up, you're going to let the beat drop or it's not going to fit right."[22] Here flow seems to be synonymous with a steady rhythm and an ability to get locked in, get in the groove, with either sound or water rhythms. Will Conner, who splits his time between Australia and Florida, connects his own musicking and surfing through an essentially unconscious attachment to rhythm and breathing:

> For me it all kind of comes back to rhythm and after that it comes back to, really recently, to breathing. The Byron Bay in me is coming out, which is, you know, the hippie place. . . . . Obviously the music's no good unless the rhythm's right, and exactly the same with surfing. You have to have a rhythm. If you're off, you go down real quick. . . . It's all become kind of second nature now and it's just a natural thing, so you don't actually think. And maybe that's the key, you want to be like that. . . . Apparently that's the mental state you're supposed to be in, this state of nonthinking.[23]

Kelli Heath from Hawai'i, profiled in chapter 5, described her experiences surfing very similarly. She spoke about how her mind almost switches off once she is standing on her board surfing, and then switches back on the instant she "kicks out," or finishes her ride: "I can't ever remember what I'm thinking when I was on the wave, when I was riding the wave. I can never remember. It's like I left the world for a minute while I was on the wave."[24] She described her experience as "being in a moment" where she is focused on what she is doing, not what she is thinking. This, she said, is the state of focus that she seeks when she is performing music.

Surfing Is Selfish; Music You Share

In all of these homologies and analogies there remains a key distinction between the experience of watery waves and musical waves. The experience of "flow" when surfing is created when a lone surfer interacts with the ocean. However, when musicking, musicians have greater opportunity to interact with other people.[25] One is play with the ocean; the other, play with other people. A number of musicking surfers also note this distinction: free surfer and popular musician Donavon Frankenreiter put it this way: "Surfing's more of an individual sport, while you can share your tunes with people."[26] Australian Jim Banks draws the line sharply: "To me jamming is completely different from surfing, because surfing to me is a completely individual thing."[27]

I don't want to overplay this distinction; there are many exceptions. Musicking can be a very private and even isolating practice: the musician alone with his or her instrument for hours at time. Or, in my mind's eye, I see Duke Kahanamoku alone with his ukulele or guitar, calming his nerves before an important swimming race (see fig. 29).[28] Yet none of the surfing musicians I interviewed dwelled on the solitary aspects of musicking. Instead, they emphasized either performing for others or making music with others—two types of sharing. By the same token, while it is possible for two or more surfers to share the same wave, as explained in chapter 1, the dynamic and fairly intricate rules of surfing in a crowd and negotiating the lineup begin with this basic tenet of modern surfing: one surfer per wave.[29] Some surfers try to actively mediate this tension in crowded surfing lineups with grace and mutual support, as we saw with Mike Goodin, Al Lee, and Gene Lyon from Manhattan Beach in chapter 6. Yet the experience of the ride is often profoundly individual. Thus, the affinity group *surfers* is predicated upon the collectively shared but individually articulated experience of wave riding. Even when you're surfing with your friends, what you share is an understanding and appreciation of each other's individual experience riding waves; you don't share the actual experience. Musicking together, I propose, allows for a level of shared experience not possible in the water.

Perhaps for this reason, improvisation was highlighted by a number of the individuals featured in this study, and musical genres that facilitate both inclusivity and some level of improvisation are favored in some surfing groups. For example, Dave Rastovich and Andrew Crockett's *Life Like Liquid* project, which deliberately brought together a group of surfers to play music, emphasized two favorite jam formats of rock musicians since at least the 1970s: blues and reggae. A third musical form heard on the *Life Like Liquid* soundtrack is a bass ostinato- and percussion-grounded extended improvisation that contributing musician-surfer Ash Grunwald called "ambient" music. Examples from the soundtrack include "The Fold" and "Golden Orb Weaver" (audio example 9). Another example, also from Australia and also from a film with a soundtrack created by surfing musicians, is "Rain," played by the Val Dusty Experiment for Andrew Kidman's film *Litmus* (see video example 7). Kidman, who wrote and performed "Rain" with the Val Dusty Experiment, told me they wanted the song to sound like rain, like a storm.[30] Indeed, it starts with what sounds like rain falling on water, which fades into an acoustic guitar playing a three-chord pattern—E minor (four beats), D (four beats), C (eight beats)—that persists throughout. Over this, a singer and instrumentalists realize different melodic ideas, punctuated by percussion, including a gong that mimics wind or splashing water. Thus, part of the work is mimetic—sounds like rain, sounds like the crash of a wave—yet the sonic basis is a harmonic and rhythmic repetition, a cycle that never ends . . . until it does when the musicians seem to intuitively agree that all are ready to stop. When I listen, "Rain" conjures the sense of a long winter morning of surfing: some rain, some wind, a few nice lines drawn (or sung) across a wave face, and always more waves coming. The session seems timeless . . . until something inside me tells me it is time for my last wave for the day.

As we have seen, however, other pockets of musical activity among surfers emphasize participation over improvisation. The Bamboo Room Philharmonic in San Onofre emphasizes certain repertoires, especially hapa haole songs and jazz standards. There are excellent musicians in that circle who take full advantage of the opportunities for improvisation provided in the jazz pieces they play, but just as valued is knowledge of their core repertoire. The professional musicians who surf, profiled in chapter 5, present a similar situation. Though some are no doubt skilled improvisers, their forte is writing and performing (sharing) their own songs.

WHY SURFERS NEED MUSIC

In the spring of 2010 I interviewed Will Conner when we were both on Oʻahu, Hawaiʻi. Embodying the global—or at lease cosmopolitan—quality of some aspects of the surfing community, Will Conner calls both Florida and Byron Bay, Australia, home, but I've bumped into him in Hawai'i and California. One of Will's very first statements during our interview was that my book topic "sounds like it's really boring." He hastened to add that he did not intend to be offensive, but that for him surfing and musicking are "just like breathing. Everyone I know surfs and plays music. I've been doing it since I can remember."[31]

Maybe it would be a good thing if the question of music and surfing were a boring topic—if the assumption were that one naturally considered musicking part and parcel of being a surfer. After all, all humans are musical, ethnomusicologists will claim. Therefore, wouldn't a completely nonmusical surfer be the exception, the interesting question, the "man bites shark" headline that sells newspapers? I did not find that surfer, though there were more than a few who did not think that there is any particular connection between music and surfing. Fair enough. But most of those same individuals deeply engaged both musicking and surfing.

I began this book by stating that, as an ethnographer, I am compelled to consider seriously the claims by many surfers that surfing is somehow musical—that surfing and musicking go hand in hand. Such claims need not be heard as claims of exclusivity. Basic ethnomusicological tenets challenge any such claims to exclusive musicality: we find that to be human is to be musical, and that any significant and enduring community of people will create and adopt musical practices that are expressive and constitutive of that community.[32] I am not even sure that surfing is any more musical than other sporting activities. The percentage of baseball players who also cultivate musical skills is probably not that dissimilar to that of surfers, and there are musical practices that are explicitly associated with baseball. Since the mid–twentieth century, many baseball stadiums contained elaborate pipe or electronic organs, for example. Such stadium instruments are often found in basketball auditoriums as well. American football has a tradition of marching bands associated with it, and the NFL engenders substantial new music compositions for its television broadcasts. The Olympic Games' musical opening and closing ceremonies and the playing of gold medalists' national anthems are additional examples of music meeting sports. There are any number of books about music and sports yet to be written. Of course baseball, basketball, and football, as well as most of the sports featured in the Olympic Games, are what sports scholars call *achievement sports,* and can be considered as categorically different from lifestyle sports, surfing being primary among the latter.[33] And then there are surfers who do not consider surfing to be a sport at all, but a lifestyle or an art form. But this is not a comparative study about the musical ways and mores of different sporting tribes or lifestyles. It is enough that some surfers find significant links between their surfing and their musicking.

Thus, in the preceding pages are examples and cases studies of some of the many ways that individual surfers and groups of surfers express their musicality, and how they may or may not relate their music to their surfing. The goal has been to learn something about the affinity group *surfers*. What I have learned is that many surfers seek connections between their musicking and their surfing, and that they find the one cultural practice helps them make sense of the other. They also may use music to express some of the ways that surfing is meaningful for them. But not all surfers. Other surfers, wherever they are in the world, do not make strong connections between musicking and surfing. None of my research findings result in a rule that applies to all individuals or to any individual all the time. Even the surfer who does seek dry-land expressive outlets for the surfing experience may not turn to music. As Tom Curren noted (chap. 5), other surfers express themselves with painting or photography; it is not always music.

Yet there is the participatory potential in musicking that provides expressive and community-building possibilities that some surfers find significant. With both music and surfing, many of my research subjects emphasized participation and experience (as opposed to achievement). This, of course, is at the heart of Christopher Small's concept of musicking: the emphasis is on human activity and experience, not on music as a sound object or work of art.[34] This trend is consistent in my survey of musician-surfers. Just as I have not heard surfers talk about achieving a sense of timelessness or flow while *watching* others surf, they also do not often talk about flow when they *listen* to others play music. Perhaps one quality of many surfers of this New Surfing era is that the individual self desires to actively engage, to get in the water and paddle for the wave, to join the band and get in rhythm, in the groove, in the zone. This is what Thomas Turino calls "participatory performance."[35] As he explains, active musical participation increases the likelihood of social synchrony, bodily mirroring through musicking, intense focus on subtle changes in the group dynamic marked by improvised melodic riffs, and shifts in rhythmic subtleties. This attentive focus shields the musicking participant from distractions, be they external or internal, sometimes creating a sensation described as "thoughtless" or, as surfer Dave Rastovich put it, "timeless and mindless but so intelligent."

Being part of a surfing affinity group assumes some surfing competency, though, as with musicking, what that competency might be varies greatly. Turino wrote of the knowledge and ability to appropriately perform in a given musical style as an "index of belonging and social identity, because performance competence *is both sign and simultaneously a product of* shared musical knowledge and experience."[36] The same may apply to surfing competency. Surfing is the cultural practice that forms the index of belonging to the affinity group of surfers. Obtaining the intellectual and bodily knowledge to ride ocean waves is a performance that becomes an index of belonging in the surfing community. The challenge becomes how to experience this individual pleasure as a group. Perhaps this is why surfing is the prototypical lifestyle sport: the sport of surfing demands a lifestyle that gives cultural expression to the solitary practice of wave riding. This cultural expression of the surfing experience must be cultivated out of the water, since sharing the experience in the water is difficult at best. Musicking, like surfing, requires active involvement—play—that communicates directly, without symbolic or linguistic mediation. Thus musicking together is an especially effective expression of surfing alone. And musicking may be necessary for sustaining the very affinity group *surfers,* for without complementary ways of sharing something of the experience of surfing, each surfer remains alone, in self-selected solitude, at sea.

Notes

1. The term *musicking* I adopt from Christopher Small, *Musicking: The Meanings of Performing and Listening* (Hanover, NH: Wesleyan/University Press of New England, 1998), 9. Small's coinage encourages us to think of music as an activity in which we must engage rather than as an object of wonder left in the hands of a few specialists.

2. Brendon Thomas, "Music to the Ears: Improving Your Surfing through the Power of Song," *Surfer* 46, no. 6 (June 2005): 188; Louise Searle, "Go Your Own Way," *Surfgirl Magazine*, no. 28 (August 2010): 11.

3. John Blair, *The Illustrated Discography of Surf Music, 1961–1965*, 3rd ed. (Ann Arbor, MI: Popular Culture Ink, 1995), vi.

4. A fifth film, *Sound of the Surf*, produced by Thomas Duncan, is being made but was not yet released at the time of writing. Prerelease information indicates that the film will focus on the instrumental-rock genre of surf music discussed below. See www.soundofthesurf.com/.

5. The August 2010 issue of U.K.-based *Surfgirl Magazine* carries several profiles of female DJs, recommendations for surfing-related music events, and a feature called "Feel the Rhythm" (pp. 40–41), in which top female surfers comment on how they relate the feeling of surfing to music. *HUCK*, another U.K. magazine that appeals to surfers, skateboarders, and snowboarders, is as much about music and visual arts as about these three board-sports.

6. Belinda Wheaton, "Introduction: Mapping the Lifestyle Sport-scape," in *Understanding Lifestyle Sports: Consumption, Identity and Difference*, ed. Belinda Wheaton (London: Routledge, 2004), 1–28.

7. Examples of the term *tribe* used by and applied to surfers abound. Notable recent manifestations are Roger Mansfield's book *The Surfing Tribe: A*

History of Surfing in Britain (Newquay, UK: Orca Publications, 2009) and Ignacio Félix Cota's book *Tribe of the Waves: Memories of Mexican Surfing* (2011).

8. Jean-Étienne Poirier, *Dancing the Wave: Audacity, Equilibrium, and Other Mysteries of Surfing,* trans. Michael H. Kohn (Boston: Shambhala, 2003), 6.

9. In the mid–twentieth century the search for empty waves most typically led to a surfing safari in tropical climates. Bruce Brown's 1964 film *The Endless Summer* captures this search well. In the first decade of the twenty-first century, the new frontier was cold-water surfing. For popular accounts of cold-water surfing, see Shawn Malone, "The Grand Sable Experiment," *Surfer's Journal* 18, no. 4 (2009): 36–45; Brian Nevins, "Ramblings in Vacationland," *Surfer's Journal* 18, no. 5 (2009): 70–79; and Noah Cohen, "North of Nowhere," *Surfer* 54, no. 6 (2013): 96–103.

10. This critique builds on my previous work. See *Making Music in the Polish Tatras: Tourists, Ethnographers, and Mountain Musicians* (Bloomington: Indiana University Press, 2005), where I trace the relatively recent emergence of an ethnic community within Poland's borderlands. In this present book I hope to show that, like ethnic groups, affinity groups are meaningful cultural constructions but are neither natural nor inherent. We can think of an affinity group of surfers in this way, using similar terms more commonly used to describe ethnic groups or other social groupings traditionally given political significance.

11. Mark Slobin used the term *affinity groups* in his book *Subcultural Sounds: Micromusics of the West* (Hanover, NH: Wesleyan University Press, 1993), 56, 68–69, 104–6. I adopt this term even though my concept of the community of surfers has more in common with Thomas Turino's *cultural cohorts* concept as described in his book *Music as Social Life: The Politics of Participation* (Chicago: University of Chicago Press, 2008), 111. Contrasting cultural cohorts with Benedict Anderson's "imagined communities" (*Imagined Communities: Reflections on the Origin and Spread of Nationalism,* rev. ed. [London: Verso, 1991]), Turino defines a cultural cohort as "an intentional interest group that forms around particular activities, a particular style complex, as well as a particular discourse about the style" (p. 161). I fully embrace Turino's claim that these communities are actual, not just imagined, though I would add that imagination is an important part of the creation of these communities. *Affinity group* suggests a community that is more loosely bound than a *cultural cohort.* Affinity may require a greater leap of imagination, while a cohort requires active agreement. Belinda Wheaton summarizes recent approaches to *lifestyle sports* in the introduction to her edited volume *Understanding Lifestyle Sports: Consumption, Identity and Difference* (London: Routledge, 2004), 1–28. Douglas Booth has published a book and several articles that are very helpful in interpreting surfing lifestyles: *Australian Beach Cultures: The History of Sun, Sand and Surf* (London: Frank Cass Publishers, 2001); "Expressions Sessions: Surfing, Style and Prestige," in *To the Extreme: Alternative Sports, Inside and Out,* edited by R. Rinehart and S. Sydor (Albany: State University of New York Press, 2003), 315–34; and "Surfing: From One (Cultural) Extreme to Another," in *Understanding Lifestyle Sports: Consumption, Identity and Difference,* edited by Belinda Wheaton (London: Routledge, 2004), 94–109

12. "New sports" is the designation preferred by Pierre Bourdieu in his book *Distinction: A Social Critique of the Judgement of Taste,* trans. Richard Nice (Cambridge, MA: Harvard University Press, 1984). Bourdieu associated new sports particularly with California in the 1960s. See also Wheaton, "Introduction," 3.

13. Robert E. Rinehart, "Arriving Sport: Alternatives to Formal Sports," in *Handbook of Sports Studies,* ed. Jay Oakley and Eric Dunning (London: Sage, 2000), 505. See also Wheaton, "Introduction," 2–3.

14. Wheaton, "Introduction," 4 (italics in the original).

15. Quoted in Tim Donnelly, "Sound Waves," *Surfers Path* 52 (December 2005/January 2006): 91.

16. This is consistent with most recent theories of identity from various fields including sociology, psychology, and ethnomusicology. An individual has multiple identities or selves, which are taken to be positions occupied and roles taken in any of the potentially many networks of relationships in which that individual engages; see Sheldon Stryker and Peter J. Burke, "The Past, Present, and Future of an Identity Theory," *Social Psychology Quarterly* 63, no. 4 (2000): 284–97. Turino, in *Music as Social Life,* distinguishes between *self,* which "is the composite of the total number of habits that determine the tendencies for everything we think, feel, experience, and do" (p. 101), and *identity,* which is "the *partial* and *variable* selection of habits and attributes that we use to represent ourselves to ourselves and to others" (p. 102). Different situations and social contexts require a different set of those variables. Thus, my identity varies: American, Irish, male, husband, teacher, musician, cyclist, surfer, and so on. In some social networks, some of these aspects of my various identities are revealed and relevant, and others are not.

17. Billabong's advertisements remind us that even experience can be commodified and used to sell products.

18. Steven Kotler, *West of Jesus: Surfing, Science and the Origins of Belief* (New York: Bloomsbury, 2006).

19. Mihaly Csikszentmihalyi, *Flow: The Psychology of Optimal Experience* (New York: Harper and Row, 1990). See also Wheaton, "Introduction," 11; and Kotler, *West of Jesus,* 139. Csikszentmihalyi's theory of flow is also used by ethnomusicologist Thomas Turino (*Music as Social Life,* 30).

20. Poirier, *Dancing the Wave,* 96.

21. Surfing readers will note that wave-forecasting services have been in place for decades, and that today ocean swells can be tracked and predicted at any given beach with some accuracy. Yet the variables are great, and the only way to know surfing conditions for certain is to go to the beach and look for oneself. Sometimes the predicted swell arrives on schedule; sometimes it never arrives; at other times it is adversely affected by local winds, tides, and currents.

22. Paul Strauch, lecture, University of San Diego, 22 February 2007, San Diego, CA.

23. Examples include the documentary film *Dogtown and Z-Boys,* by Stacy Peralta, wherein youths in a depressed urban area find discipline and direction through surfing and skateboarding for the Zephyr team (Sony Pictures, 2001); *On a Wave,* a surfing memoir by Thad Ziolkowski, who, as an adolescent in a

broken family, finds solace in surfing (New York: Grove Press, 2002); and pioneering pro surfer Mike Doyle's similar tale of growing up an awkward boy in a single-parent California home who then goes on to win the 1969 Duke Invitational at Sunset Beach, O'ahu, Hawai'i (Mike Doyle and Steve Sorensen, *Morning Glass: The Adventures of Legendary Waterman Mike Doyle* [Lake Forest, CA: Mike Doyle, 2004]).

24. Examples include Steven Kotler's *West of Jesus* (2006), a mix of anthropology, neuroscience, and spirituality; Jaimal Yogis's *Saltwater Buddha: A Surfer's Quest to Find Zen on the Sea* (Boston: Wisdom Publications, 2009); Jeremy V. Jones's *Walking on Water: The Spirituality of the World's Top Surfers* (Ventura, CA: Regal, 2006), which promotes a specifically Christian belief system; and Jeff Divine and Ben Marcus's collection of photo essays *Surfing and the Meaning of Life* (St. Paul, MN: Voyageur Press 2006). Christian philosopher and surfer Peter Kreeft has written several books on surfing and philosophy (*I Surf, Therefore I Am: A Philosophy of Surfing* [South Bend, IN: St. Augustine's Press, 2008]; *If Einstein Had Been a Surfer: A Surfer, a Scientist, and a Philosopher Discuss a "Universal Wave Theory" or "Theory of Everything"* [South Bend, IN: St. Augustine's Press, 2009]).

25. Brad Melekian, "Is God a Goofyfoot? If So, Surfing May Be the Next World Religion," *Surfer* 46, no. 3 (2005): 110–15. Another example is Greg Martin's cheeky report "A Mind Full of Surfing: Twenty Four Hours at a Buddhist Surf Retreat," which appeared in the British surf magazine *Wavelength* (no. 203 [June 2011]: 53–56).

CHAPTER 1

1. Excerpt from Mary Kawena Pukui, trans., "He inoa no Naihe (Name Chant for Naihe," Hawaiian Ethnological Notes, Bishop Museum Archives, Honolulu, Hawai'i, n.d., 3:87, 108.

2. Mary Kawena Pukui, "Songs (Meles) of Old Ka'u, Hawaii." *Journal of American Folklore* 62, no. 245 (July-September 1949): 255–56. See p. 255 for an explanation of how a chant composed for one person could come to be adapted for another.

3. Pukui, "He inoa no Naihe," 3:92, 113.

4. Many of the earliest accounts of surfing by non-Hawaiians and Hawaiians are collected and translated in John R.K. Clark, *Hawaiian Surfing: Traditions from the Past* (Honolulu: University of Hawai'i Press, 2011). See pp. 9–12 for accounts of nearly everyone surfing.

5. Patrick Moser, "The Rumors of Surfing's Demise Have Been Greatly Exaggerated," *Bamboo Ridge: Journal of Hawai'i Literature and Arts,* no. 98 (2011): 195–204; Moser, "Revival," *Kurungabaa: A Journal of Literature, History and Ideas from the Sea* 3, no. 1 (2010): 46–69.

6. These are the opening lines from the first part of "Name Chant for Naihe" as they appear in Mary Kawena Pukui and Alfons L. Korn, eds. and trans., *The Echo of Our Songs: Chants and Poems of the Hawaiians* (Honolulu: University Press of Hawai'i, 1973), 38–40. A more extensive portion of this mele is reprinted in Patrick Moser, ed., *Pacific Passages: An Anthology of Surf Writing*

(Honolulu: University of Hawai'i Press, 2008), 35. An earlier version of this mele was published by Nathaniel B. Emerson in *Unwritten Literature of Hawaii: The Sacred Songs of the Hula,* originally published in 1909 by the Bureau of American Ethnology and republished in 1965 (Rutland, VT: Tuttle), pp. 36–37.

7. The oldest known iconography depicting people riding waves, in this case on reed fishing boats, is from Peru and dates back over forty-five hundred years. See Matt Warshaw, *The History of Surfing* (San Francisco: Chronicle Books, 2010), 18–22.

8. Ben Finney and James D. Houston wrote the most detailed and authoritative history of surfing, first published in 1966 and then revised and published as *Surfing: A History of the Ancient Hawaiian Sport* in 1996 (San Francisco: Pomegranate Artbooks). See in particular pp. 23–25.

9. Warshaw, *History of Surfing,* 23. See also Mark Stranger, *Surfing Life: Surface, Substructure and the Commodification of the Sublime* (Burlington, VT: Ashgate Publishing Company, 2011), 18.

10. Emerson translates *Kahiki* as "Tahiti, or any foreign country: a term of grandiloquence" (*Unwritten Literature of Hawaii,* 36). Patrick Moser translates it more broadly as "foreign lands; often more particularly, the Society Islands, including Tahiti" (*Pacific Passages,* 40). C.D. Ka'ala Carmack, who read an early version of this chapter, reminds me that Hawaiians of this mele's era certainly knew that the best swells came from the north, the opposite of where Tahiti lay.

11. Warshaw, *History of Surfing,* 12.

12. Moser, *Pacific Passages,* 35.

13. Kirk Lee Aeder, "Epicenters of the Ali'i," *Surfer's Journal* 19, no. 1 (2010): 31–41.

14. Krista Comer, in her book *Surfer Girls in the New World Order* (Durham, NC: Duke University Press, 2010), offers an optimistic and highly nuanced study of women's growing place in New Surfing.

15. Fragment from "He nalu no Emmalani (Surf Chant for Queen Emma)," Hawaiian Ethnological Notes, collected by Mary Kawena Pukui, Bishop Museum Archives, Honolulu, Hawai'i, n.d., 3:458. English translation adapted from Mary Pukui.

16. For more on *hōlua,* see Paul Holmes, "The Transformation of Tom Stone," *Surfer's Journal* 18, no. 5 (2009): 28–39.

17. Though surfing is not as integrated into mainland North American and European culture today, we still use surfing as a metaphor for certain activities, usually those perceived as fluid and possibly a bit edgy, as when we speak of "surfing the Web" and "couch surfing." For provocative riffs on surfing as a metaphor in postmodern society, see Comer, *Surfer Girls,* 5, 12–13.

18. Mary Kawena Pukui, Samuel H. Elbert, and Esther T. Mookini, *Place Names of Hawaii,* rev. ed. (Honolulu: University Press of Hawai'i, 1974), 227.

19. Pukui, Elbert, and Mookini, *Place Names of Hawaii,* 188.

20. Finney and Houston, *Surfing,* 32.

21. Fragment from Pukui, "He nalu no Emmalani," 3:461. English translation adapted from Mary Pukui.

22. Earlier versions of this sentence read that all were surf destinations except Russia, but the January 2013 edition of *Surfer* magazine carried a feature article, "Russia's Forbidden Peninsula," by Ben Weiland (vol. 54, no. 1: 62–75). The cold-water surfing frontier has reached Russia. Two readers with close ties to Hawai'i—Professor Ricardo D. Trimillos and C.D. Ka'ala Carmack—pointed out that all of these nations also had colonial designs on Hawai'i.

23. Pukui, "He inoa no Naihe," 3:83, 104.

24. Clark, *Hawaiian Surfing*, 22.

25. Clark, *Hawaiian Surfing*, 7.

26. Moser, "Rumors of Surfing's Demise," 195. G.W. Bates, *Sandwich Island Notes. By a Häole* (New York: Harper & Brothers, 1854).

27. Isaiah Helekunihi Walker, *Waves of Resistance: Surfing and History in Twentieth-Century Hawai'i* (Honolulu: University of Hawai'i Press, 2011), 26–31.

28. The concern with *inutility* was almost a religious doctrine with the predominantly Calvinist missionaries, who placed great value on productive utilitarian activities. This of course played in to the United States' vision of Hawai'i as a natural resource to be exploited. Missionary William Ellis (1794–1872), who spent many years in the Society Islands and Hawai'i, provided enthusiastic descriptions of surfing while also expressing approval of the reduction of traditional Hawaiian pleasures: "When we consider the debasing tendency of many, and the inutility of others, we shall rather rejoice that much of the time of the adults is passed in more rational and beneficial pursuits" (quoted in Moser, *Pacific Passages*, 92–93; the text was originally published in 1829).

29. I thank Ricardo Trimillos for reminding me of the social impact on Hawaiian commoners of the plantations, and the parallel changes among Hawaiian royalty as they began to interact with Europeans.

30. Walker, *Waves of Resistance*, 26.

31. Finney and Houston, *Surfing*, 53.

32. Samuel S. Hill, *Travels* (London: Chapman and Hall, 1856). The segment on surfing from Hill's publication is reprinted in Moser, *Pacific Passages*, 108–11. See also Moser, "Rumors of Surfing's Demise," 200–201, for an interpretation of Hill's account.

33. Walker, *Waves of Resistance*, 52–55.

34. Walker, *Waves of Resistance*, 12–13, 125, 38–39.

35. Moser, "Revival," 47.

36. Jack London, from "Riding the South Seas Surf," *Women's Home Companion* 34, no. 10, October 1907. Reprinted in Moser, *Pacific Passages*, 138

37. London, "Riding the South Seas Surf." Reprinted in Moser, *Pacific Passages*, 139.

38. Moser, "Revival," 47.

39. Walker, *Waves of Resistance*, 89. See also Jane C. Desmond, *Staging Tourism: Bodies on Display from Waikiki to Sea World* (Chicago: University of Chicago Press, 1999), 48.

40. George S. Kanahele, ed., *Hawaiian Music and Musicians: An Illustrated History* (Honolulu: University of Hawai'i Press, 1979), 106–7; Elizabeth Tatar,

Strains of Change: The Impact of Tourism on Hawaiian Music (Honolulu: Bishop Museum Press, 1987), 1–13.

41. Elizabeth Buck, *Paradise Remade: The Politics of Culture and History in Hawai'i* (Philadelphia: Temple University Press, 1993), 174–75.

42. Warshaw, *History of Surfing*, 48; Walker, *Waves of Resistance,* 30.

43. Warshaw, *History of Surfing,* 48–52. See also Joel Conroy's film *Waveriders.* Written by Conroy and Lauren Davies, the film traces the life of Freeth and his influence of on modern surfing, and retraces Freeth's father's migration from Ireland to Hawai'i (produced by Margo Harkin; UK and Ireland, 2008).

44. Grandy Timmons, *Waikīkī Beachboy* (Honolulu: Editions Limited, 1989).

45. E. J. Oshier, recorded interviews with the author, 4 November 2006 and 1 December 2006, San Clemente, CA.

46. Here I used the term *icon* as suggested by ethnomusicologist Thomas Turino, building on the semiotic theories of Charles Sander Peirce. See Turino, *Music as Social Life: The Politics of Participation* (Chicago: University of Chicago Press, 2008), 6–8; and Turino, "Signs of Imagination, Identity, and Experience: A Peircian Semiotic Theory for Music," *Ethnomusicology* 43, no. 2: 234. Hapa haole music evokes Hawai'i in the minds of some listeners and performers; thus it becomes an iconic sign for Hawai'i and things Hawaiian. It stands for Hawai'i in some sense.

47. *Hapa Haole Songs: Lyrics to Hawaiian Songs Written in English, 1916–1978,* www.squareone.org/Hapa/.

48. Tatar, *Strains of Change,* 7–9.

49. The Hawaiian-language songs, however, provide glimpses of the islands of Maui and Kaua'i, for example, in the hula song "Na Pua" from Noble's collection. We are reminded that all three songbooks, while seeking an audience beyond Hawai'i, also serve the local, Hawaiian audience.

50. Amy Ku'uleialoha Stillman, "Hawaiian Music for Listening Pleasure," accessed 15 April 2012, http://amykstillman.wordpress.com.

51. Kanahele, *Hawaiian Music and Musicians,* 214.

52. Kanahele, *Hawaiian Music and Musicians,* 215–17.

53. Kanahele, *Hawaiian Music and Musicians,* 217, dates the original publication of *King's Book of Hawaiian Melodies* at 1920, but the earliest edition appeared in 1916.

54. Kanahele, *Hawaiian Music and Musicians,* 216. Kanahele agrees that "Honolulu Maids" "comes close to being *hapa haole.*"

55. Charles E. King, *King's Book of Hawaiian Melodies* (Honolulu: Charles E. King, 1948), 101.

56. See Kanahele, *Hawaiian Music and Musicians,* for entries on Hawaiian music in England (74–85) and Japan (178–89).

CHAPTER 2

1. David P. Szatmary, "Surfboards and Hot Rods: California, Here We Come." in *A Time to Rock: A Social History of Rock-and-Roll* (New York:

Schirmer Books, 1996), 82; George O. Carney, "Cowabunga! Surfer Rock and the Five Themes of Geography," *Popular Music and Society* 23, no. 4 (1999): 5.

2. I have Gaston Georis to thank for pointing out the impact of the transistor radio on California beach life. Georis was one of the founding members of the Sandals, the band that created the music for the surfing movie *The Endless Summer,* discussed in chapter 3.

3. Jack London, from "Riding the South Seas Surf," 1907. Reprinted in Patrick Moser, *Pacific Passages: An Anthology of Surf Writings* (Honolulu: University of Hawai'i Press, 2008), 139.

4. For example, in my hometown of Santa Barbara, California, an island in the Goleta Slough that was the site of a Chumash Indian village was leveled during World War II to create an airfield in the Goleta wetlands. This is now the site of the Santa Barbara Municipal Airport.

5. The landscape of urban areas of Hawaii's coast has not fared much better (Honolulu and Waikīkī are the obvious examples), but there the erasure of native peoples is not as complete as it is in California. While there are some Native Americans surfing in California's waters, there presence is strongest in place names: Malibu is an English corruption of "Hamalius"—the Chumash Indian name for this famous Southern California point break. Still, I can rattle off many more surfing beaches bearing Spanish names.

6. Tom Wolfe, "The Pump House Gang," in the collection of essays by the same name (New York: Farrar, Straus & Giroux, 1968), 17–39.

7. Cecilia Rasmussen, "In 'Whites Only' Era, an Oasis for L.A.'s Blacks," *Los Angeles Times,* 3 July 2005.

8. Juan Onésimo Sandoval, Hans P. Johnson, and Sonya M. Tafoya, "Who's Your Neighbor? Residential Segregation and Diversity in California," *California Counts: Population Trends and Profiles* 4, no. 1 (San Francisco: Public Policy Institute of California, 2002): 1, 16, accessed 3 September 2012, www.ppic.org/content/pubs/cacounts/CC_802JSCC.pdf.

9. Paul Johnson, recorded interview with the author, San Clemente, CA, 20 November 2010.

10. This interpretation of 1960s surf music as being a precursor to North American punk is supported by John Blair in *The Illustrated Discography of Surf Music, 1961–1965* (3rd ed., Ann Arbor, MI: Popular Culture Ink.) and in his notes for the CD *Cowabunga! The Surf Box* (Los Angeles: Rhino Records, 1996), 6–7; and by Bill Osgerby in "'Chewing Out a Rhythm on My Bubble-Gum': The Teenage Aesthetic and Genealogies of American Punk," in *Punk Rock: So What? The Cultural Legacy of Punk,* ed. Roger Sabin (London: Routledge, 1999), 155–59.

11. Robert J. Dalley, *Surfin' Guitars: Instrumental Surf Bands of the Sixties,* 2nd ed. (Ann Arbor, MI: Popular Culture Ink. 1996), 104; Blair, *Cowabunga! The Surf Box,* 6–7, 13–14.

12. Unless otherwise indicated, early and usually original recordings of the music mentioned in this chapter can be heard on *Cowabunga! The Surf Box* (Los Angeles: Rhino Records, 1996).

13. Versions of this oral history by Johnson can be found in several places, including the booklet that accompanies the 1996 Rhino Records CD box set

Cowabunga! The Surf Box; notes to *The Bel Airs: The Origins of Surf Music* (GEE-DEE music CD 270156-2, 2000); on film in *Pounding Surf! A Drummer's Guide to Surf Music* (Costa Mesa, CA: E.G.O. Productions, 2008), DVD, track 3; and repeated to me personally in my 2010 interview with Johnson.

14. Quoted in Dalley, *Surfin' Guitars,* 103.

15. Surfer Admin, "King of Surf Guitar: Dick Dale" *Surfer* online (posted 19 May 2010), www.surfermag.com/features/king-of-surf-guitar-dick-dale-%e2% 80%9cyou%e2%80%99ll-never-hear-surf-music-again-that%e2%80%99s -a-big-lie%e2%80%9d-%e2%80%93-jimi-hendrix/.

16. Johnson, interview.

17. Developing the semiotic theories of Charles Sanders Peirce, this relationship is what Thomas Turino calls an "indexical" relationship between the sign (music) and surfing (the object). To the extent that the music is directly affected by surfing, such as the relationship that Dick Dale claims, it is a "dicent index," meaning that the object (surfing) directly affects the sign representing surfing (Surf Music). See Thomas Turino, *Music as Social Life: The Politics of Participation* (Chicago: University of Chicago Press, 2008), 9, 42.

18. Again applying Peirce's theories to music, Turino would call this an indexical relationship between a sign (instrumental rock, in this case) and the thing it stands for (surfing). Turino, *Music as Social Life,* 8.

19. Dick Dale in John Blair, *The Illustrated Discography of Surf Music, 1961–1965* (Ann Arbor, MI: Popular Culture Ink. 1995), i.

20. I have seen Dick Dale play at the Gene Autry Museum of Western Heritage, Los Angeles, 22 June 2003, and at the Fender Center, Corona, CA, 19 June 2004.

21. Dalley, *Surfin' Guitars,* 103.

22. Blair, *Illustrated Discography of Surf Music;* Dalley, *Surfin' Guitars.*

23. Blair, *Cowabunga!,* 14–15.

24. For more on the roots of barbershop singing in African-American traditions, see Gage Averill's book *Four Parts, No Waiting: A Social History of American Barbershop Harmony* (New York: Oxford University Press, 2003), especially pp. 179–80. The Beach Boys themselves acknowledge their links to barbershop harmony traditions. In 2012, I had the pleasure of seeing the Beach Boys' Fiftieth Anniversary Tour performance in Santa Barbara, California. Introducing one of their early hits, one of the original band members (I think it was Mike Love) commented: "Listen . . . it's barbershop."

25. Blair, *Cowabunga! The Surf Box,* 20.

26. For such claims, see George O. Carney, "Cowabunga! Surfer Rock and the Five Themes of Geography," *Popular Music and Society* 23, no. 4 (1999): 10; and Blair, *Illustrated Discography of Surf Music,* vi.

27. Claims of originality in this early-1960s intersection of rock 'n' roll and surfing are best understood in the context of the colonization and globalization of surfing itself, as discussed in the previous chapter.

28. Carney, "Cowabunga!" 9, 12.

29. Transcribed from David Parsa's 2008 film *Live: A Music and Surfing Experience* (David Parsa Films), DVD, track 6. See Warshaw, *Encyclopedia of Surfing,* 194, for a similar quote by Noll.

30. Transcribed from Parsa, *Live,* track 6.

31. Mike Doyle and Steve Sorensen, *Morning Glass: The Adventures of Legendary Waterman Mike Doyle* (Lake Forest, CA: Mike Doyle, 2004), 96.

32. Bill Pitts, recorded interview, 2 January 2004, Santa Cruz, CA.

33. See also Roger Manisfield's book *The Surfing Tribe: A History of Surfing in Britain* (Newquay, UK: Orca Publications, 2009), 56, for a similar statement about the stimulation of "Surf Music from California." There he writes that guitar bands came first, such as the Ventures and the Chantays, followed by the Beach Boys and Jan and Dean. Note that the Ventures were not from California and were a surf band only by association.

34. Jack Williams, notes on the jacket cover of *Waikiki Surf Battle,* vol. 1, *Sounds of Hawaii,* SH5014, 1963. (I would like to thank Gary Dunn, who first told me about the Waikīkī Surf Battle events and who gave me his copy of this LP.)

35. Descriptions of Surf Music as white are found in John Blair's *The Illustrated Discography of Surf Music,* iii; Carney's article "Cowabunga!" (10); and in my interview with guitarist Paul Johnson (20 November 2010, San Clemente, CA).

36. George Lipsitz introduced me to the contributions of the Vegas brothers to Surf Music.

37. The interpretation of Surf Music revivals as "waves" is canonized in the Rhino Records four-CD box set *Cowabunga! The Surf Box* (1996).

CHAPTER 3

1. Surf movies contrast with skateboarding films, in which the sounds of the wheels and shoes on pavement are an important part of the soundtrack.

2. Filmmaker Andrew Kidman told me that he sometimes finds the sound recorded when filming useable and even perfect for the filmic motion, but that most of the time it is not used (e-mail message to the author, 12 March 2013). One notable attempt to record the sonic experience of a surfer can be seen in Jim Freeman and Greg MacGillivray's 1972 film *Five Summer Stories,* for which surfer Corky Carroll was wired with a waterproof microphone and sent out to surf waves at Pipeline, Hawai'i—arguably the most famous and one of the most dangerous waves in the world. The results are amusing, but not worth repeating.

3. Dana Brown, recorded telephone interview with the author, 12 April 2011.

4. This use of *index* is drawn from Thomas Turino's theory of music and signs that attempts to provide a model for understanding the affective power of music. See Thomas Turino, "Signs of Imagination, Identity, and Experience: A Peircian Semiotic Theory for Music," *Ethnomusicology* 43, no. 2 (1999): 221–55; and Turino, *Music as Social Life: The Politics of Participation* (Chicago: University of Chicago Press, 2008). A *sign* is something that stands for something else—the *object.* In this case, the music is the sign and surfing is the object. There are various ways a sign can come to represent an object, one of which Turino (after Peirce) calls an *index,* meaning the sign and object come to be associated by co-occurrence, which is exactly what happens when one views

a surf movie: filmic images of surfing and the music selected by the filmmaker are encountered by the viewer-listener simultaneously. The effect (or the *interpretant* in Turino's system) can be powerful.

5. Mark Slobin, *Global Soundtracks: Worlds of Film Music* (Middletown, Conn.: Wesleyan University Press, 2008), 3–4.

6. For a recent expression of surfers' suspicion of popular-culture treatments of surfing, see Samuel Lewis, "Of Movies and Mavericks," *Surfer* 53, no. 6 (June 2012): 40–46, which asks some tough questions about Hollywood's attempts to put big waves on the big screen.

7. Matt Warshaw, *Surf Movie Tonight! Surf Movie Poster Art, 1957–2004* (San Francisco: Chronicle Books, 2005), 7.

8. One of the most common complaints in New Surfing communities is that there are too many surfers these days and that the surfing lineups are overly crowded. This attitude was captured well on a wry bumper sticker that I saw in Santa Barbara, California, recently on a truck stacked high with surfboards: "Don't try surfing. It's not that fun." *Gidget* is frequently blamed for overpopularizing the sport. For example, prominent surfing historian and publisher of the *Surfer's Journal* Steve Pezman blames the movie with starting a surfing fad that swelled the number of surfers in the United States to the millions (in Timothy T. DeLa Vega, ed., *200 Years of Surfing Literature: An Annotated Bibliography*, [Hanapepe, Kaua'i, HI: Timothy T. DeLa Vega, 2004], 5). *Gidget* the movie was preceded by a best-selling novel of the same title written by Frederick Kohner and based on the experiences of his daughter, Kathy Kohner, as she learned to surf at Malibu. See Frederick Kohner, *Gidget* (New York: Berkley Books, 2001). Frederick Kohner also wrote the script for the movie.

9. The Hollywood-produced *Blue Crush* was preceded and inspired by a surf movie of the same title released in 1998. I discuss the original *Blue Crush* later in this chapter.

10. Candy Johnson was a dancing front woman for a lounge band, the Exciters. Her high-energy gyrating dancing was featured in four American International Pictures beach-party films.

11. As with Surf Music, beach-party films played differently in California than in other parts of the world. Stephen John McParland is a Sydney, Australia, surfer and surfboard shaper who was inspired by Surf Music. He became an influential record collector and has written several books about Surf Music as well as a book on the music in beach party films, *It's Party Time: A Musical Appreciation of the Beach Party Film Genre* (North Strathfield, NSW, Australia: PTB Productions, 1992). However, his interest in these films seems to be driven by the music used in the films, not the surfing action.

12. Matt Warshaw, *The Encyclopedia of Surfing* (Orlando: Harcourt, 2003), 582. See also Warshaw, *The History of Surfing* (San Francisco: Chronicle Books, 2010), 137–38.

13. Warshaw, *Surf Movie Tonight*, 8. See also Drew Kampion, *Stoked! A History of Surf Culture*, rev. ed. (Layton, UT: Gibbs Smith, 2003). The *Surfer's Journal* and other magazines have also published interviews with many leading surf-movie makers.

14. Warshaw, *Surf Movie Tonight*, 7.

15. Brad Barrett, "Odds & Ends: Confessions of an Unrehabilitated Gremmie, or, A San Diego-centric Analog History of '60s Surf Fun," *Surfer's Journal* 20, no. 2 (April–May 2011): 60–71.

16. Sam George, conversation with the author, 11 May 2006, Arlington Theater, Santa Barbara, CA.

17. Jazz Profiles, "Bud Shank – Part 1," accessed 5 June 2011, http:// jazzprofiles.blogspot.com/2009/01/bud-shank-part-1.html.

18. Turino, *Music as Social Life,* 42. See note 4 above.

19. Brad Barrett, "Bud Shank: The Pacific Jazz Bud Shank Studio Sessions (1956–61)," *Surfer's Journal* 9, no. 1 (Early Spring 2000), 6.

20. "Ala Moana" is named after a place and a particular surfing spot on the south shore of Oʻahu, Hawaiʻi.

21. Barrett, "Bud Shank," 6.

22. John Blair, "Cowabunga! The Surf Box" notes accompanying CD box set (Los Angeles: Rhino Records, Inc., 1996), 5.

23. Though Bruce Brown's films are always playful, he also wanted surfing to gain some respect in the sporting world. In an interview, he told me that in the 1950s surfers were generally misunderstood and that they unjustly received the blame for antisocial behavior on some beaches. Countering this image is one of the accomplishments he is most proud of with his later movie *The Endless Summer*. He believes this movie helped show the general public that surfing was "all-American" and something to be proud of (recorded telephone interview with the author, 30 April 2011).

24. Brown, telephone interview.

25. Brown, telephone interview. Also, during a guest visit to one of my classes at the University of California, Santa Barbara, Gaston Georis, one of the original members of the Sandals, recalled meeting Brown at a party where the band was playing, and offering to create music for his film there (recorded class visit, 29 October 2003). Though some of the details of their accounts differ, the essence is the same: they were a band of very young men with only a modest local following. They offered their music for his next film, and he liked what he heard.

26. Three original members of the Sandals—Walter Georis, Gaston Georis, and John Blakely—rerecorded the soundtrack for *The Endless Summer* in 1992, released on a CD by Tri-Surf Records in 2000. These performances employ a sound that has a bit more edge than the more mellow original performances; they are more like Surf Music. Gaston Georis, the oldest member of the Sandals, has explained to me that at least his musical tastes were formed in Europe, and that this contributes to the sound of the band. He and his brother were born in Belgium and moved to the United States when he was about fourteen. During a summer trip back to Europe, he acquired records by Cliff Richard and the Shadows, and these became an important influence in his own music.

27. Steve Barilotti, "Celluloid Sacrament: Reviving the Surf Film Ritual in the New Millennium," *Surfer* 45, no. 7 (July 2004): 115.

28. Barilotti, "Celluloid Sacrament," 123.

29. This band is not to be confused with the 1980s British band the Farm. In addition to the group of five musicians who formed the core of Farm, Roger

Heath and Adrienne Miller played on some of the pieces, adding vocals, recorder, and occasionally guitar. Also on the soundtrack for the film is one piece, "Wind n Sea," by Doug Dragon, performed by Doug (piano), Daryl Dragon (vibraphone and melodica), Hale Blaine (drums), and Eddie Carter (bass).

30. Dennis Dragon first told me about the recording of the "Coming of the Dawn" portion of the soundtrack live at the Lobero Theatre during an interview in Santa Barbara, California, 27 June 2004. He later clarified in e-mail messages, sent to me on 16 and 17 June 2011, that the music was recorded at the Lobero during a screening for the band, not when the public was present. That recording was ultimately edited and added to soundtrack for the "Coming of the Dawn" portion of the film. This accounts for the audible edits, including a cross-fade, that one can hear on the soundtrack.

31. Denny Aaberg, recorded interview with the author, 23 April 2005, Pacific Palisades, CA.

32. Using the semiotic theory of signs developed by Charles Sanders Peirce (*Philosophical Writings of Peirce*, ed. Justus Buchler [New York: Dover, 1955]) and refined by Turino for interpreting music, we can see these examples of music as dicent indices of surfing, or at least of filmic images of surfing and waves. A dicent index is directly affected by the object for which it stands—in this case, surfing and waves. See Turino, *Music as Social Life*, 42–44.

33. Wikipedia, s.v. "Crystal Voyager," accessed 18 April 2011, http://en.wikipedia.org/wiki/Crystal_Voyager. See also the bonus feature interview with David Elfick on the DVD release of *Crystal Voyager*.

34. Alexander Walker, quoted on the back of the Umbrella Entertainment DVD release of *Crystal Voyager*.

35. *Pacific Vibrations* was remastered and screened at the kickoff of the 2010 U.S. Open of Surfing, at Huntington Beach, California, and was broadcast by MGM HD on August 7, yet the movie is still not available for purchase because of the unlicensed soundtrack.

36. Greg MacGillivray, prescreening roundtable for *Five Summer Stories*, Surfing Heritage Museum, San Clemente, CA, 15 September 2007.

37. Warshaw, *Encyclopedia of Surfing*, 584.

38. Warshaw, *Encyclopedia of Surfing*, 562.

39. Jack Johnson, recorded interview with the author, 28 April 2010, O'ahu, HI.

40. Johnson, interview.

41. One or the other version of *Blue Crush* is credited in insider surf literature with increasing the numbers of female surfers. See, for example, Michael Scott Moore, *Sweetness and Blood: How Surfing Spread from Hawaii and California to the Rest of the World, with Some Unexpected Results* (New York: Rodale, 2010), 187. Usually these references appear to be to the Hollywood feature film. On the other hand, Janna Irons's article "Womentum" (a play on Steele's film *Momentum*) in *Surfer* magazine (vol. 56, no. 6 [June 2011], 114) calls Ballard's original surf-movie version "the film that launched the biggest surge in women's surfing history." Yet she notes in the same sentence that that film spawned the Hollywood version. An informal poll of students at my

oceanside university suggests that young women are much more likely to have seen the Hollywood-produced *Blue Crush*.

42. Warshaw, *Encyclopedia of Surfing*, 552.

43. Andrew Kidman, e-mail communication to the author, 27 April 2013. See also the trailer for the film posted on Kidman's Web site at www.andrewkidman.com/film/litmus-1996/.

44. Andrew Kidman, recorded interview with the author, 13 May 2005, Santa Barbara, CA.

45. The concept of *social synchrony* is explained in Edward Hall's book *Beyond Culture* (Garden City, NY: Anchor, 1977). Thomas Turino applies this concept specifically to music and dance in his book *Music as Social Life*, 41–43.

CHAPTER 4

1. Thomas Turino, "Signs of Imagination, Identity, and Experience: A Peircian Semiotic Theory for Music," *Ethnomusicology* 43, no. 2 (1999): 221–55; Thomas Turino, *Music as Social Life: The Politics of Participation* (Chicago: University of Chicago Press, 2008), 8–10.

2. Lorenzo Valdambrini, e-mail message to the author, 16 September 2009.

3. Gian Maria Vaglietti, personal communication with the author, 24 July 2009, Calafuria, Italy.

4. Pollo Del Mar Web site, accessed 18 September 2009, http://pollodelmar.com/frame.html.

5. Quoted from Dobronyi's blog: http://pdmeurope2009.blogspot.com/2009/07/saturday-july-25-livorno.html.

6. Gian Maria Vaglietti, personal communication with the author, 24 July 2009, Calafuria, Italy.

7. Vaglietti, personal communication.

8. Nick Ford and David Brown, *Surfing and Social Theory: Experience, Embodiment and Narrative of the Dream Glide* (London: Routledge, 2006), 70–71.

9. Andrea Lo Coco, informal conversation with the author, 24 July 2009, Calafuria, Italy.

10. Roger Mansfield, *The Surfing Tribe: A History of Surfing in Britain* (Newquay, UK: Orca Publications, 2009), 62.

11. James Rodd, recorded interview with the author, 6 August 2009, Newquay, UK.

12. Rodd, interview.

13. I converted the prices from British pounds sterling to U.S. dollars using the exchange rates current at the time of the festivals: $1.77 to the British pound in August 2005 and $1.69 to the pound in 2009.

14. Sam George, *The Perfect Day: The Music from 40 Years of* Surfer *Magazine* (Hollywood, CA: The Right Stuff/Capitol Records, 2001), CD liner notes.

15. Daphna Oyserman, "Self-Concept and Identity," in *Self and Social Identity*, ed. Marilynn B. Brewer and Miles Hewstone (Malden, MA: Blackwell Publishing, 2004), 5ff.

16. Rodd, interview.

17. I used the online crowd-sourced encyclopedia Wikipedia to check genre and style descriptions for these bands. Since popular-music style and genre designations change quickly, Wikipedia is more likely than paper publications to contain up-to-date terms.

18. Ben Howard and Owain Davies, recorded interview with the author, 6 August 2009, Newquay, UK.

19. Phil Dirt quoted in Parke Puterbaugh, "Shooting the Curl," *US Airlines Magazine*, (May 1997): 69–70.

20. John Blair, *The Illustrated Discography of Surf Music, 1961–1965*, 3rd ed. (Ann Arbor, MI: Popular Culture Ink); and notes for *Cowabunga! The Surf Box* (Los Angeles: Rhino Records, 1996), 6–7.

21. Bill Osgerby, "'Chewing Out a Rhythm on My Bubble-Gum': The Teenage Aesthetic and Genealogies of American Punk," in *Punk Rock: So What? The Cultural Legacy of Punk*, ed. Roger Sabin (London: Routledge, 1999), 155–59.

22. Paul Johnson, personal communication with the author, 3 March 2006, San Diego, CA.

23. Sam Bolle, personal communication with the author, 22 June 2003, Los Angeles.

CHAPTER 5

1. This legend is presented in several sources, e.g., Mary Kawena Pukui, "Songs (Meles) of Old Ka'u, Hawaii," *Journal of American Folklore* 62, no. 245 (July–September 1949): 255–56; and repeated in Ben Finney and James D. Houston, *Surfing: A History of the Ancient Hawaiian Sport*, rev. ed. (San Francisco: Pomegranate Artbooks, 1996), 40–41.

2. Isaiah Helekunihi Walker, *Waves of Resistance: Surfing and History in Twentieth-Century Hawai'i* (Honolulu: University of Hawai'i Press, 2011), 70–79.

3. Matt Warshaw, *The History of Surfing* (San Francisco: Chronicle Books, 2010), 52–53; and Warshaw, *The Encyclopedia of Surfing* (Orlando, FL: Harcourt, 2003), 48–49. The most thorough account of the Waikīkī Beachboys is Grady Timmons' book *Waikiki Beachboy* (Honolulu: Editions Limited, 1989); see in particular chap. 4, "A Beachboy Party," for accounts of their musical activities (83–101).

4. Sandra Kimberley Hall, *Duke: A Great Hawaiian* (Honolulu: Bess Press, 2004), 35.

5. Timmons, *Waikiki Beachboy*, 75–76; Warshaw, *Encyclopedia of Surfing*, 309.

6. Toby Miller, *Sportsex* (Philadelphia: Temple University Press, 2001), 11, 134.

7. Mark Anders, "Bar Chords and Single Blades: Donavon Frankenreiter's Canyon Life," *Surfer's Journal* 14, no. 2 (2005): 58.

8. Anders, "Bar Chords and Single Blades," 63.

9. David Lee Scales provides insight into the pro surfer's need for image and media attention in his article "Intermission," *Surfer* 53, no. 9 (September 2012): 74–83.

10. Much of this information and all of the quotes come from a recorded telephone interview by the author with Kelli Heath, 2 May 2010.

11. Heath, interview.

12. Mihaly Csikszentmihalyi, *Flow: The Psychology of Optimal Experience* (New York: Harper and Row, 1990), 40–41.

13. Alex Wade, "Surfer Immortal," *Huck* 2, no. 10 (May 2008): 50–51.

14. Unless otherwise noted, quotes of Tom Curren are transcribed from a recorded interview with the author made in Goleta, California, 1 April 2007.

15. Curren was later quoted making very similar comparisons between drumming and surfing, including being "in the pocket" in Alex Wade's 2008 profile of Curren (Wade, "Surfer Immortal," 52).

16. Jay DiMartino, "Sound Waves," About.com, posted 26 July 26 2012, accessed 30 July 2012, http://surfing.about.com/b/2012/07/26/sound-waves-2.htm.

17. This and other quotes of are transcribed from a recorded interview by the author with Jack Johnson, 28 April 2010, Oʻahu, HI.

18. Mikael Wood, review of *To the Sea, Entertainment Weekly*, 26 May 26 2010, accessed 27 July 2012, www.ew.com/ew/article/0,,20388607,00.html.

19. Pointing up the fact that instrumental Surf Music from the 1960s was often related to surfing only nominally, the Chantays' biggest hit was first called "Liberty's Whip" and then "44 Magnum" before they settled on the title "Pipeline." See Robert J. Dalley, *Surfin' Guitars: Instrumental Surf Bands of the Sixties*, 2nd ed. (Ann Arbor, MI: Popular Culture Ink), 69.

CHAPTER 6

1. This is a key point in Toby Miller's *Sportsex* (Philadelphia: Temple University Press, 2001).

2. Thomas Turino, *Music as Social Life: The Politics of Participation* (Chicago: University of Chicago Press, 2008), 26.

3. Turino, *Music as Social Life*, 24. Listening is not always passive and can be very active. However, the ubiquity of recorded-music playback in public spaces (stores, airports, restaurants), while driving in cars, and so forth does allow for passive listening, or even a need to actively block out the music so that one can concentrate on the road, a conversation, or a transaction.

4. Isaiah Helekunihi Walker, *Waves of Resistance: Surfing and History in Twentieth-Century Hawaiʻi* (Honolulu: University of Hawaiʻi Press, 2011), 79; see also pp. 70–79.

5. Donald H. James, *Surfing San Onofre to Point Dume, 1936–1942: Photographs by Don James* (San Francisco: Chronicle Books, 1998), 14–15.

6. E.J. Oshier, "The Bamboo Room Philharmonic: A History," in *The San Onofre Surfing Club, 1952–2002, 50th Anniversary Commemorative Album* (San Clemente, CA: San Onofre Surfing Club, 2002), 205.

7. Stories of surfing, musicking, and camping on the beach at San Onofre abound, but I am especially grateful to E.J. Oshier (recorded interviews 4 September and 1 December 2006, San Clemente, CA), Robert (Bob or "Jake") Jacobs (recorded interview, 1 December 2006, San Onofre), and Gwen

"Honeybaby" Waters (recorded interview, 15 September 2007, San Clemente, CA) for oral histories of early San Onofre surfing and partying. I also owe a great debt of gratitude to David Weisenthal, who provided me with introductions to many of my San Onofre contacts.

8. Glenn Alapag, recorded interview with the author, 26 June 2006, San Clemente, CA.

9. Alapag, interview.

10. Mike Goodin, e-mail correspondence with the author, 29 January 2010. The following two block quotations of Goodin are also from this e-mail exchange.

11. For an example of significant cultural differences in seemingly universal human social needs, see my article "Theorizing Fieldwork Impact: Malinowski, Peasant-Love, and Friendship," *British Journal of Ethnomusicology* 12, no 1: (2003): 1–17

12. The Beach Boys also engaged in the lyrical mapping of California's surfing spots, plus Hawaii's Waimea and Australia's Narrabeen, in their song "Surfin' U.S.A." The inspiration, however, was Chubby Checker's "Twistin' U.S.A." and not Hawaiian mele. See John Blair's notes to *Cowabunga! The Surf Box* (Los Angeles: Rhino Records, 1996), 20.

13. The popularity of Jawaiian music was linked in the 1980s with a political connection some felt between oppressed island peoples of Jamaica and Hawai'i. Though the term "Jawaiian" is still used by some, others object to the suggestion of Rastafarianism and the implication that the music is not essentially Hawaiian. I thank Ricardo Trimillos, emeritus professor of Asian studies and ethnomusicology at the University of Hawai'i at Manoa, for insight into the changing implications of the term *Jawaiian*.

14. Ernie Cruz Jr., conversation with the author, Hau'ula, Hawai'i, 24 April 2010.

15. Ernie Cruz Jr., phone conversation with the author, 15 October 2012.

16. The song "Ua Mau" is by William Ka'imi. The three verses are in English and speak of wrongs done to Hawai'i in the past and ongoing. The chorus is a Hawaiian phrase, "Ua mau ke ea o ka 'āina i ka pono," which was proclaimed by King Kamehameha III in 1843 when sovereignty was restored after Hawai'i was briefly occupied by the British. The phrase is now the Hawaiian state motto and is usually translated as "The life of the land is perpetuated in righteousness," but as Hawaiian musician and scholar Ka'ala Carmack expressed it to me, the translation might better be understood as "To honor and preserve our land and way of life, we must all do the right thing" (e-mail correspondence, 23 August 2012). In the context of Ka'imi's "Ua Mau," I interpret the phrase as a call for a return to Hawaiian sovereignty.

17. Malissa Kealiihokulani Tongg's surfing and water-woman roots are deep. Her father, Michael Tongg, was at one time the president of the Polynesian Voyaging Society, which built and sailed a replica model of an ancient Polynesian long-distance voyaging canoe.

18. Malissa Kealiihokulani Tongg and Mike Kaawa, recorded interview with the author, 17 January 2008, Elks Club, Diamond Head, Waikīkī, O'ahu, Hawai'i.

19. Walker, *Waves of Resistance*, 105.

20. Walker, *Waves of Resistance*, 10–13, 57–58, 168.

21. See James D. Houston with Eddie Kamae, *Hawaiian Son: The Life and Music of Eddie Kamae* (Honolulu: 'Ai Pōhaku Press, 2004). On p. 125, Kamae claims that it was musicians who were the voices of the early Hawaiian Renaissance, not writers, politicians, or campus activists.

22. Neil Halstead, recorded interview with the author, 19 August 2010, Newquay, UK.

23. E. J. Oshier, recorded interview with the author, 4 November 2006, San Clemente, CA.

CHAPTER 7

1. Stephanie Gilmore, quoted in "Feel the Rhythm," *Surfgirl Magazine*, no. 28 (August 2010): 41. Gilmore is an Australian professional surfer and has won the Associated Surfing Professionals' Women's World Tour five times. Jamiroquai is a London-based acid jazz band.

2. Author's field notes, 14 November 2006, Kaua'i, HI.

3. Tim Donnelly, "Sound Waves," *Surfers Path* 52 (December 2005/January 2006): 76.

4. Jack Johnson, recorded interview with the author, 28 April 2010, O'ahu, HI.

5. See Gavin Pretor-Pinney, *The Wave Watcher's Companion: Ocean Waves, Stadium Waves, and All the Rest of Life's Undulations* (New York: Penguin, 2010), 28–30.

6. Dave Rastovich, in the booklets accompanying both the *Life Like Liquid* DVD and the album release of the soundtrack (both published in Byron Bay, Australia, by Low Pressure Productions, 2006).

7. Pretor-Pinney, *Wave Watcher's Companion*.

8. Peter Kreeft, interview by Marvin Olasky, *World* 25, no. 14 (17 July 2010): 28–29.

9. Bob L. Sturm, *Music from the Ocean* CD (published by the composer under the label Composerscientistrecordings, 2002).

10. John Cruz, quoted in Donnelly, "Sound Waves," 93.

11. Andrew Crockett, Internet video interview with the author, 28 September 2011, Burringbar, NSW, Australia; and Santa Barbara, CA.

12. Transcribed from the David Parsa film *Live*, chap. 14. Rincon, a surf break south of Santa Barbara, California, offers notoriously long rides on good days.

13. Laura Enever, quoted in "Feel the Rhythm," *Surfgirl Magazine*, no. 28 (August 2010): 40.

14. Mihaly Csikszentmihalyi's best-selling 1990 book *Flow: The Psychology of Optimal Experience* (New York: Harper and Row) helped popularize the concept of flow, but I do not believe it is the source of the frequent use of the term by surfers. However, ethnomusicologist Thomas Turino, in *Music as Social Life: The Politics of Participation* (Chicago: University of Chicago Press, 2008), 4–5, 30, and sports-studies pioneer Belinda Wheaton in the introduction to her edited

book *Understanding Lifestyle Sports: Consumption, Identity and Difference* (London: Routledge, 2004), 11, both draw directly from Csikszentmihalyi for their applications of the theory of flow to musicking and to sports, respectively.

15. Csikszentmihalyi, *Flow,* 40–42.

16. All of these terms and phrases are taken from my own and published interviews with surfer-musicians, and are cited elsewhere in this book.

17. Andrew Crockett, *Switch-foot: Surfing, Art, Music* (Byron Bay, NSW, Australia: Billabong, 2005), 53.

18. Shannon Carroll, quoted in Crockett, *Switch-foot,* 57.

19. Ash Gruwald, quoted in Crockett, *Switch-foot,* 61.

20. Csikszentmihalyi, *Flow,* 40.

21. Dave Rastovich, quoted in Josh Kimball, "The Rasta: The Fish, Freedom and Philosophy of Dave Rastovich," *Surfer's Path* 61 (June/July 2007): 85.

22. Al Hicks, recorded interview with the author, 1 October 2011, Gaviota State Beach, Santa Barbara County, CA.

23. Will Conner, interview with the author, 27 April 2012, North Shore, Oʻahu, HI.

24. Kelli Heath, telephone interview with the author, 2 May 2010.

25. Of course, musicians do practice alone, and soloists perform alone. But in both cases, the objective is usually, though not always, to perform with others or for others. Thus the solo performer still interacts with her or his audience. Rare is the musician who never performs in the presence of others.

26. Donavon Frankenreiter, quoted in Brendon Thomas, "Music to the Ears: Improving Your Surfing through the Power of Song," *Surfer* 46, no. 6 (June 2005): 190.

27. Jim Banks, quoted in Crockett, *Switch-foot,* 61.

28. Sandra Kimberley Hall, *Duke: A Great Hawaiian* (Honolulu: Bess Press, 2004), 34–35.

29. As already noted, most surfers enjoy having at least a friend with them in the water to share the pleasure of surfing (and to keep an eye out for each other), but generally they do not share waves. There are exceptions. For example, I have a few friends with whom I enjoy sharing the same wave. Mike Goodin's metaphor of surfers surfing alone yet together in an orchestra where each surfer is both individually expressive while sharing a collective moment (see chapter 6), stands as a counterpoint to most other descriptions of surfing that I documented. Generally the "one wave, one surfer" rule prevails.

30. Andrew Kidman, recorded interview with the author, 13 May 2005, Santa Barbara, CA.

31. Conner, interview.

32. John Blacking's classic statement on ethnomusicology, *How Musical Is Man* (Seattle: University of Washington Press, 1973), and Christopher Small's challenging book *Musicking: The Meanings of Performing and Listening* (Hanover, NH: Wesleyan University Press, 1998) both show how humans are innately musical, though societies that emphasize specialization often unintentionally discourage musical behavior among many.

33. Belinda Wheaton, referenced in the introduction, proposes certain distinctions between achievement sports and lifestyle sports. See Wheaton,

Understanding Lifestyle Sports: Consumption, Identity and Difference (London: Routledge, 2004), 2.

34. Christopher Small, *Musicking: The Meanings of Performing and Listening* (Hanover, NH: Wesleyan/University Press of New England, 1998), 2, 8–9.

35. Turino, *Music as Social Life,* 42–43.

36. Turino, *Music as Social Life,* 43 (italics in the original).

Bibliography

Aeder, Kirk Lee. 2010. "Epicenters of the Aliʻi." *Surfer's Journal* 19, no. 1: 31–41.

Anders, Mark. 2005. "Bar Chords and Single Blades: Donavon Frankenreiter's Canyon Life." *Surfer's Journal* 14, no. 2: 56–65.

Anderson, Benedict. 1991. *Imagined Communities: Reflections on the Origin and Spread of Nationalism*. Rev. ed. London: Verso. First published in 1983.

Averill, Gage. 2003. *Four Parts, No Waiting: A Social History of American Barbershop Harmony*. New York: Oxford University Press.

Barilotti, Steve. 2004. "Celluloid Sacrament: Reviving the Surf Film Ritual in the New Millennium." *Surfer* 45, no. 7 (July): 110–27.

Barrett, Brad. 2000. "Bud Shank: The Pacific Jazz Bud Shank Studio Sessions (1956–61)." *Surfer's Journal* 9, no. 1 (Early Spring): 5–6, 9.

———. 2011. "Odds & Ends: Confessions of an Unrehabilitated Gremmie; or, A San Diego-centric Analog History of '60s Surf Fun." *Surfer's Journal* 20, no. 2 (April–May): 60–71.

Bates, G. W. 1854. *Sandwich Island Notes. By a Häole*. New York: Harper & Brothers.

Blacking, John. 1973. *How Musical Is Man?* Seattle: University of Washington Press.

Blair, John. 1995. *The Illustrated Discography of Surf Music, 1961–1965*. 3rd ed. Ann Arbor, MI: Popular Culture Ink.

———. 1996. Liner notes for *Cowabunga! The Surf Box*. Compact disc. Los Angeles: Rhino Records.

Booth, Douglas. 2001. *Australian Beach Cultures: The History of Sun, Sand and Surf*. London: Frank Cass Publishers.

———. 2003. "Expressions Sessions: Surfing, Style and Prestige." In *To the Extreme: Alternative Sports, Inside and Out*, edited by R. Rinehart and S. Sydor, 315–36. Albany: State University of New York Press.

———. 2004. "Surfing: From One (Cultural) Extreme to Another." In *Understanding Lifestyle Sports: Consumption, Identity and Difference*, edited by Belinda Wheaton, 94–109. London: Routledge.

Bourdieu, Pierre. 1984. *Distinction: A Social Critique of the Judgement of Taste*. Translated by Richard Nice. Cambridge, MA: Harvard University Press.

Buck, Elizabeth. 1993. *Paradise Remade: The Politics of Culture and History in Hawai'i*. Philadelphia: Temple University Press.

Carney, George O. 1999. "Cowabunga! Surfer Rock and the Five Themes of Geography." *Popular Music and Society* 23, no. 4: 3–29.

Clark, John R.K. 2011. *Hawaiian Surfing: Traditions from the Past*. Honolulu: University of Hawai'i Press.

Cohen, Noah. 2013. "North of Nowhere." *Surfer* 54, no. 6: 96–103.

Comer, Krista. 2010. *Surfer Girls in the New World Order*. Durham, NC: Duke University Press.

Cooley, Timothy J. 2003. "Theorizing Fieldwork Impact: Malinowski, Peasant-Love, and Friendship." *British Journal of Ethnomusicology* 12, no. 1: 1–17.

———. 2005. *Making Music in the Polish Tatras: Tourists, Ethnographers, and Mountain Musicians*. Bloomington: Indiana University Press.

Cota, Ignacio Félix. *Tribe of the Waves: Memories of Mexican Surfing*. N.p., 2011.

Crockett, Andrew. 2005. *Switch-foot: Surfing, Art, Music*. Illustrated by Harry Daily. Byron Bay, NSW, Australia: Billabong.

Csikszentmihalyi, Mihaly. 1990. *Flow: The Psychology of Optimal Experience*. New York: Harper and Row.

Dalley, Robert J. 1996. *Surfin' Guitars: Instrumental Surf Bands of the Sixties*. 2nd ed. Ann Arbor, MI: Popular Culture Ink.

DeLa Vega, Timothy T., ed. 2004. *200 Years of Surfing Literature: An Annotated Bibliography*. Hanapepe, Kaua'i, HI: Timothy T. DeLa Vega.

Desmond, Jane C. 1999. *Staging Tourism: Bodies on Display from Waikiki to Sea World*. Chicago: University of Chicago Press.

DiMartino, Jay. "Sound Waves." About.com. Posted 26 July 2012. Accessed 27 May 2013. http://surfing.about.com/b/2012/07/26/sound-waves-2.htm.

Dirt, Phil. n.d. Reverbcentral.com. Accessed 17 November 2009. www.reverbcentral.com.

Divine, Jeff, and Ben Marcus. 2006. *Surfing and the Meaning of Life*. St. Paul, MN: Voyageur Press.

Donnelly, Tim. 2005. "Sound Waves." *Surfers Path* 52 (December 2005/January 2006): 76–101.

Doyle, Mike, and Steve Sorensen. 2004. *Morning Glass: The Adventures of Legendary Waterman Mike Doyle*. Lake Forest, CA: Mike Doyle. First published in 1993.

Emerson, Nathaniel B. 1965. *Unwritten Literature of Hawaii: The Sacred Songs of the Hula*. Rutland, VT: Tuttle. First published in 1909 by the Bureau of American Ethnology.

"Feel the Rhythm." 2010. *Surfgirl Magazine*, no. 38 (August): 40–41.

Finney, Ben, and James D. Houston. 1996. *Surfing: A History of the Ancient Hawaiian Sport.* Rev. ed. San Francisco: Pomegranate Artbooks. First published in 1966.

Ford, Nick, and David Brown. 2006. *Surfing and Social Theory: Experience, Embodiment and Narrative of the Dream Glide.* London: Routledge.

George, Sam. 2001. *The Perfect Day: The Music from 40 Years of Surfer Magazine.* CD liner notes. Hollywood, CA: The Right Stuff/Capitol Records.

Hall, Edward. 1977. *Beyond Culture.* Garden City, NY: Anchor.

Hall, Sandra Kimberley. 2004. *Duke: A Great Hawaiian.* Honolulu: Bess Press.

Hapa Haole Songs: Lyrics to Hawaiian Songs Written in English, 1916–1978. www.squareone.org/Hapa/.

Hill, Samuel S. 1856. *Travels.* London: Chapman and Hall. Hill's segment on surfing is reprinted in Moser, *Pacific Passages,* 108–11.

Holmes, Paul. 2009. "The Transformation of Tom Stone." *Surfer's Journal* 18, no. 5: 28–39.

Houston, James D., with Eddie Kamae. 2004. *Hawaiian Son: The Life and Music of Eddie Kamae.* Honolulu: 'Ai Pōhaku Press.

Irons, Janna. 2011. "Womentum." *Surfer* 52, no. 6 (June): 110–16.

James, Donald H. 1998. *Surfing San Onofre to Point Dume, 1936–1942: Photographs by Don James.* San Francisco: Chronicle Books. First published in 1996.

Jones, Jeremy V. 2006. *Walking on Water: The Spirituality of the World's Top Surfers.* Ventura, CA: Regal.

Kampion, Drew. 2003. *Stoked! A History of Surf Culture.* Rev. ed. Layton, UT: Gibbs Smith.

Kanahele, George S., ed. 1979. *Hawaiian Music and Musicians: An Illustrated History.* Honolulu: University of Hawai'i Press.

Kimball, Josh. 2007. "The Rasta: The Fish, Freedom and Philosophy of Dave Rastovich." *Surfer's Path* 61 (June/July): 74–85.

King, Charles E. 1948. *King's Book of Hawaiian Melodies.* Honolulu: Charles E. King.

Kohner, Frederick. 2001. *Gidget.* New York: Berkley Books. First published in 1957. (The 2001 edition includes a foreword.)

Kotler, Steven. 2006. *West of Jesus: Surfing, Science and the Origins of Belief.* New York: Bloomsbury.

Kreeft, Peter. 2008. *I Surf, Therefore I Am: A Philosophy of Surfing.* South Bend, IN: St. Augustine's Press.

———. 2009. *If Einstein Had Been a Surfer: A Surfer, a Scientist, and a Philosopher Discuss a "Universal Wave Theory" or "Theory of Everything."* South Bend, IN: St. Augustine's Press.

———. 2010. Interview by Marvin Olasky. *World* 25, no. 14 (July 17): 28–29.

Lewis, Samuel. 2012. "Of Movies and Mavericks." *Surfer* 53, no. 6 (June): 40–46.

London, Jack. 1907. "Riding the South Seas Surf." *Women's Home Companion* 34, no. 10 (October): 9–10. Reprinted in Moser, *Pacific Passages,* 137–46.

Malone, Shawn. 2009. "The Grand Sable Experiment." *Surfer's Journal* 18, no. 4: 36–45.

Mansfield, Roger. 2009. *The Surfing Tribe: A History of Surfing in Britain.* Newquay, UK: Orca Publications.

Martin, Greg. 2011. "A Mind Full of Surfing: Twenty Four Hours at a Buddhist Surf Retreat." *Wave Length,* no. 203 (June): 53–56.

McParland, Stephen J. 1992. *It's Party Time: A Musical Appreciation of the Beach Party Film Genre.* North Strathfield, NSW, Australia: PTB Productions.

Melekian, Brad. 2005. "Is God a Goofyfoot? If So, Surfing May Be the Next World Religion." *Surfer* 46, no. 3: 110–15.

Miller, Toby. 2001. *Sportsex.* Philadelphia: Temple University Press.

Moore, Michael Scott. 2010. *Sweetness and Blood: How Surfing Spread from Hawaii and California to the Rest of the World, with Some Unexpected Results.* New York: Rodale.

Moser, Patrick, ed. 2008. *Pacific Passages: An Anthology of Surf Writings.* Honolulu: University of Hawai'i Press.

———. 2010. "Revival." *Kurungabaa: A Journal of Literature, History and Ideas from the Sea* 3, no. 1: 46–69.

———. 2011. "The Rumors of Surfing's Demise Have Been Greatly Exaggerated." *Bamboo Ridge: Journal of Hawai'i Literature and Arts,* no. 98: 195–204.

Nevins, Brian. 2009. "Ramblings in Vacationland." *Surfer's Journal* 18 no. 5: 70–79.

Noble, Johnny. 1935. *Johnny Noble's Book of Famous Hawaiian Melodies: Including Hulas and Popular Hawaiian Standards.* New York: Miller Music.

Osgerby, Bill. 1999. "'Chewing Out a Rhythm on My Bubble-Gum': The Teenage Aesthetic and Genealogies of American Punk." In *Punk Rock: So What? The Cultural Legacy of Punk,* edited by Roger Sabin, 154–69. London: Routledge.

Oshier, E. J. 2002. "The Bamboo Room Philharmonic: A History." In *The San Onofre Surfing Club, 1952–2002, 50th Anniversary Commemorative Album,* 204–11. San Clemente, CA: San Onofre Surfing Club.

Oyserman, Daphna. 2004. "Self-Concept and Identity." In *Self and Social Identity,* edited by Marilynn B. Brewer and Miles Hewstone, 5–24. Malden, MA: Blackwell Publishing.

Peirce, Charles Sanders. 1955. *Philosophical Writings of Peirce.* Edited by Justus Buchler. New York: Dover.

Poirier, Jean-Étienne, 2003. *Dancing the Wave: Audacity, Equilibrium, and Other Mysteries of Surfing.* Translated by Michael H. Kohn. Boston: Shambhala. Originally published in French under the title *Hopupu* (Sillery, QC, Canada: Les Editions du Septentrion, 2000).

Pretor-Pinney, Gavin. 2010. *The Wave Watcher's Companion: Ocean Waves, Stadium Waves, and All the Rest of Life's Undulations.* New York: Penguin.

Pukui, Mary Kawena, trans. N.d. "He inoa no Naihe (Name Chant for Naihe)" [also known as "Deification of Canoe for Naihe"]. Hawaiian Ethnological Notes. Bishop Museum, Honolulu, HI.

———. trans. N.d. "He nalu no Emmalani" (Surf chant for Queen Emma). Hawaiian Ethnological Notes. Bishop Museum, Honolulu, HI.

———. 1949. "Songs (Meles) of Old Ka'u, Hawaii." *Journal of American Folklore* 62, no. 245 (July–September): 247–58.

Pukui, Mary Kawena, Samuel H. Elbert, and Esther T. Mookini. 1974. *Place Names of Hawaii*. Rev. ed. Honolulu: University Press of Hawai'i.

Pukui, Mary Kawena, and Alfons L. Korn, eds. and trans. 1973. *The Echo of Our Songs: Chants and Poems of the Hawaiians*. Honolulu: University Press of Hawai'i.

Puterbaugh, Parke. 1997. "Shooting the Curl." *US Airlines Magazine*, May, 67–73.

Rasmussen, Cecilia. 2005. "In 'Whites Only' Era, an Oasis for L.A.'s Blacks." *Los Angeles Times*, 3 July.

Rinehart, Robert E. 2000. "Arriving Sport: Alternatives to Formal Sports." In *Handbook of Sports Studies*, edited by Jay Oakley and Eric Dunning, 504–19. London: Sage.

Sandoval, Juan Onésimo, Hans P. Johnson, and Sonya M. Tafoya. 2002. "Who's Your Neighbor? Residential Segregation and Diversity in California." *California Counts: Population Trends and Profiles* 4, no. 1 (San Francisco: Public Policy Institute of California, 2002), 1, 16. Accessed 3 September 2012. www.ppic.org/content/pubs/cacounts/CC_802JSCC.pdf.

Scales, David Lee. 2012. "Intermission." *Surfer* 53, no. 9: 74–83.

Searle, Louise. 2010. "Go Your Own Way." *Surfgirl Magazine*, no. 28 (August): 10–11.

Slobin, Mark. 1993. *Subcultural Sounds: Micromusics of the West*. Hanover, NH: Wesleyan University Press.

———. 2008. *Global Soundtracks: Worlds of Film Music*. Middletown, CT: Wesleyan University Press.

Small, Christopher. 1998. *Musicking: The Meanings of Performing and Listening*. Hanover, NH: Wesleyan/University Press of New England.

Stedman, Leanne. 1997. "From Gidget to Gonad Man: Surfers, Feminists and Postmodernisation." *Journal of Sociology* 33, no. 1: 75–90.

Stillman, Amy Ku'uleialoha. "Hawaiian Music for Listening Pleasure." Accessed 15 April 2012. http://amykstillman.wordpress.com.

Stokes, Martin, ed. 1994. *Ethnicity, Identity, and Music: The Musical Construction of Place*. New York: Berg.

Stranger, Mark. 2011. *Surfing Life: Surface, Substructure and the Commodification of the Sublime*. Burlington, VT: Ashgate Publishing Company.

Stryker, Sheldon, and Peter J. Burke. 2000. "The Past, Present, and Future of an Identity Theory." *Social Psychology Quarterly* 63, no. 4: 284–97.

Surfer Admin. "King of Surf Guitar: Dick Dale." *Surfer* online. Posted 19 May 2010. Accessed 25 February 2013. www.surfermag.com/features/king-of-surf-guitar-dick-dale-%e2%80%9cyou%e2%80%99ll-never-hear-surf-music-again-that%e2%80%99s-a-big-lie%e2%80%9d-%e2%80%93-jimi-hendrix/.

Swoboda, Gunter. 2000. "Tribal Pissings." In *Surf Rage*, compiled by Nat Young, 74–84. Angourie, NSW, Australia: Nymboida Press.

Szatmary, David P. 1996. "Surfboards and Hot Rods: California, Here We Come." In *A Time to Rock: A Social History of Rock 'n' Roll*, 81–90. New York: Schirmer Books. First published in 1987.

Tatar, Elizabeth. 1987. *Strains of Change: The Impact of Tourism on Hawaiian Music*. Honolulu: Bishop Museum Press.

Thomas, Brendon. 2005. "Music to the Ears: Improving Your Surfing through the Power of Song." *Surfer* 46, no. 6 (June): 188, 190.

Timmons, Grady. 1989. *Waikiki Beachboy*. Honolulu: Editions Limited.

Turino, Thomas. 1999. "Signs of Imagination, Identity, and Experience: A Peircian Semiotic Theory for Music." *Ethnomusicology* 43, no. 2: 221–55.

———. 2008. *Music as Social Life: The Politics of Participation*. Chicago: University of Chicago Press.

Wade, Alex. 2008. "Surfer Immortal." Photographs by Sam Christmas. *Huck* 2, no. 10 (May): 48–55.

Walker, Isaiah Helekunihi. 2011. *Waves of Resistance: Surfing and History in Twentieth-Century Hawai'i*. Honolulu: University of Hawai'i Press.

Warshaw, Matt. 2003. *The Encyclopedia of Surfing*. Orlando, FL: Harcourt.

———, ed. 2004. *Zero Break: An Illustrated Collection of Surf Writing, 1777–2004*. Orlando, FL: Harcourt.

———. 2005. *Surf Movie Tonight! Surf Movie Poster Art, 1957–2004*. San Francisco: Chronicle Books.

———. 2010. *The History of Surfing*. San Francisco: Chronicle Books.

Weiland, Ben. 2013. "Russia's Forbidden Peninsula." Photographs by Chris Buckard. *Surfer* 54, no. 1: 62–75.

Wheaton, Belinda. 2004a. "Introduction: Mapping the Lifestyle Sport-scape." In *Understanding Lifestyle Sports: Consumption, Identity and Difference*, edited by Belinda Wheaton, 1–28. London: Routledge.

———. 2004b. "'New Lads'? Competing Masculinities in the Windsurfing Culture." In *Understanding Lifestyle Sports: Consumption, Identity and Difference*, edited by Belinda Wheaton, 113–30. London: Routledge.

Wolfe, Tom. 1968. "The Pump House Gang." In *The Pump House Gang*, 17–39. New York: Farrar, Straus & Giroux.

Wood, Mikael. 2010. Review of *To the Sea*. *Entertainment Weekly*, May 26. Accessed 27 July 2012. www.ew.com/ew/article/0,,20388607,00.html.

Yogis, Jaimal. 2009. *Saltwater Buddha: A Surfer's Quest to Find Zen on the Sea*. Boston: Wisdom Publications.

Ziolkowski, Thad. 2002. *On a Wave*. New York: Grove Press.

Discography

The Beach Boys. 1966. *Pet Sounds*. Capitol Records DT 2458, LP.
———. 2006. "Good Vibrations." On *Good Vibrations*. Capitol Records 09463 44962 2 3, CD. First recorded in 1966.
The Bel-Airs. 2000. *The Bel Airs: The Origins of Surf Music*. GEE-DEE music 270156–2, CD.
Carroll, Charles "Corky." 2011. *Laid Back*. EM Records EM1093LP, LP. First recorded in 1971.
———. 1979. *A Surfer for President*. N.p., LP.
Cowabunga! The Surf Box. 1996. Rhino Records R2 72418, 4 CDs.
Cruz, Ernie, Jr. 2001. *Portraits*. Pi'inalu Music PM 1052, CD.
Cunha, Sonny. 1916. "My Honolulu Hula Girl." Recorded by Horace Wright and Rene Dietrich with accompaniment by Louise and Ferera on Hawaiian guitars and ukulele. Victor Record 18159-B, 78 rpm record.
Curren, Tom. 1995. *Ocean Surfaces*. Surfside, CD.
———. 2003. *Tom Curren*. Wedge Entertainment WE5TC1203, CD.
Ex Presidenti. 2005. *Pirati*. Surfer Girl Records 002 SGR 05, CD.
Farm. 2007. *The Innermost Limits of Pure Fun: Original Soundtrack Recording*. N.p., CD. First recorded in 1969.
Frankenreiter, Donavon. 2004. *Donavon Frankenreiter*. Brushfire Records B0002438–02, CD.
G. Love & Special Sauce. 1999. *Philadelphonic*. 550 Music BK 69746, CD.
The Girlas. 2006. *Now or Never*. Kototama Productions KOTO 02, CD.
Howard, Ben. 2009. *These Waters*. Dualtone, EP electronic download and CD.
The Ink Spots. 2001. "Do I Worry?" On *Rare Air: 1937–1944*. Interstate Music Ltd.: Frlyright FLY CD 67, CD.
James Michener's Favorite Music of the South Sea Islands. 1965. RCA Victor LPM-2995, LP.

Johnson, Jack. 2000. *Brushfire Fairytales*. Everloving Records 22 860 994–2, CD.

———. 2003. *Thicker than Water: Music from a Film by Jack Johnson and the Malloys*. Brushfire Records Boo01674–02, CD.

———. 2010. *To the Sea*. Brushfire Records Boo14266–01, CD.

Kaʻau Crater Boys. 1996. *Making Waves*. Roy Sakuma Productions RSCD 4535, CD.

———. 1998. *The Best of Kaʻau Crater Boys*. Roy Sakuma Productions RSCD 2278, CD.

Kaawa, Mike. 1999. *Hwn Boy*. Mountain Apple Company MACD 2058, CD.

———. 2003. *Hwn Groove*. Hwn Boy Records & Entertainment HBRCD 9001, CD.

Low Pressure Sound System. 2006. *Life Like Liquid Soundtrack*. Low Pressure Productions, 2 CDs. www.lifelikeliquid.com.

Machado, Rob. 2010. *Melali: The Drifter Sessions* (Soundtrack). Jon Swift Music, CD.

Pink Floyd. 1971. *Meddle*. Harvest Records SHVL 795, LP.

The Platters. 1955. "Only You (and You Alone)," on *The Platters*. Mercury Record Corporation TW11548, 45 rpm record.

The Sandals. 1966. *The Endless Summer*, original soundtrack. World-Pacific Records LP 1832, LP.

———. 2000 [1992]. *The Endless Summer*, soundtrack, rerecorded. Tri-Surf Records TR101CD, CD.

Smith, Johnny. 1954. "Walk, Don't Run!" on *In a Sentimental Mood*. Royal Roost RLP 424, LP.

Sturm, Bob L. 2002. *Music From the Ocean*. Composerscientistrecordings, CD.

The Surfers. 1998. *Songs from the Pipe*. Epic EPC 491499 2, CD.

The Val Dusty Experiment. 2002. *Music from Litmus*. CD.

The Ventures. 1960. *Walk Don't Run*. Dolton Records BST 8003, LP.

Williams, Jack. 1963. *Waikiki Surf Battle*. Vol. 1. Sounds of Hawaii SH5014, LP.

Filmography

Barefoot Adventure. 1960. Directed by Bruce Brown. Bruce Brown Films. DVD release, 1990 (ID8789OTDVD).

Beach Party. 1963. Directed by William Asher. American International Pictures. DVD release, 2004, MGM (1006939.1.A); packaged with *Bikini Beach*.

Big Wednesday. 1978. Directed by John Milius. Warner Bros. DVD release, 2002, Warner Home Video (11182).

Blue Crush. 1998. DVD. Directed by Bill Ballard. Billygoat Productions.

Blue Crush. 2002. DVD. Directed by John Stockwell. Universal Pictures.

Chasing the Lotus. 2006. DVD. Directed by Gregory Schell and Chris Bell. Schell/Bell Productions.

Crystal Voyager. 1973. Directed by David Elfick. DVD release, 2003, Umbrella Entertainment Pty Ltd. (DAVID0179).

Dogtown and Z-Boys. DVD. 2001. Directed by Stacy Peralta. Sony Pictures (07903).

The Drifter. 2009. DVD. Directed by Taylor Steele. Hurley International (2–520698).

The Endless Summer. 1964. Directed by Bruce Brown. Aviva International. DVD release, 1990, Bruce Brown Films (ID8790OTDVD).

First Love. 2010. DVD. Directed by Clare Gorman. Rip Curl.

Five Summer Stories. 1972. Directed by Greg MacGillivray and Jim Freeman. MacGillivray-Freeman Films. DVD release, 1994 (ASIN: B002IFKQCW).

Gidget. 1959. Directed by Paul Wendkos. Columbia Pictures. DVD rerelease, 2004, Columbia Pictures (04807).

Glass Love. 2005. DVD. Directed by Andrew Kidman. Andrew Kidman. www.andrewdixman.com.

Heart of the Sea: Kapolioka'ehukai. 2002. DVD. Directed by Lisa Denker and Charlotte Lagarde. Women Make Movies.

The Innermost Limits of Pure Fun. 1969. Directed by George Greenough. DVD release, 2007, Surfvideo.com (ASIN: B002IAPWGC).

Leave a Message. 2011. Streaming video. Directed by Jason Kenworthy and Aaron Lieber. Nike. www.youtube.com/watch?v=igUy2DvlVtw.

Life Like Liquid. 2006. DVD. Directed by Dave Rastovich. Byron Bay, Australia: Low Pressure Productions. www.lifelikeliquid.com.

Litmus: A Surfing Odyssey. 1996. DVD. Directed by Andrew Kidman, Jon Fran, and Mark Sutherland. Val Dusty Experiment. www.andrewkidman.com.

Live: A Music and Surfing Experience. 2008. DVD. Directed by David Parsa. David Parsa Films.

Lost in the Ether. 2010. DVD. Directed by Andrew Kidman. Andrew Kidman. www.andrewkidman.com.

Momentum. 1992. VHS. Directed by Taylor Steele. Poor Specimen. DVD release, 2002; packaged with *Momentum II*.

Morning of the Earth. 1972. Directed by Alby Falzon. DVD release, 2003. www.morningoftheearth.net.

Muscle Beach Party. 1964. Directed by William Asher. American International Pictures. DVD release, 2003, MGM (1004484.1.A); packaged with *Ski Party*.

Musica Surfica. 2008. Mick Sowry. Melbourne: UsPhoques. DVD.

Pacific Vibrations. 1970. Directed by John Severson. (No VHS or DVD release.)

The Performers. 1984. VHS. Directed by Jack McCoy and Harry Hodge. Quiksilver.

Point Break. 1991. Directed by Kathryn Bigelow. Largo Entertainment. DVD release, 2006, Twentieth Century-Fox.

Pounding Surf! A Drummer's Guide to Surf Music. 2008. DVD. Directed by Bob Caldwell, Tracy Longstreth, Dusty Watson, Paul Johnson, and Matt Quilter. E.G.O. Productions.

Rainbow Bridge. 1972. Directed by Chuck Wein. DVD release, 2008.

Ride the Wild Surf. 1964. Directed by Don Taylor. Columbia Pictures. DVD release, 2004, Columbia Pictures (07802).

Riding Giants. 2004. DVD. Directed by Stacy Peralta. Sony Pictures Classics (06006).

Searching for Tom Curren. 1997. VHS. Directed by Sonny Miller. Rip Curl.

September Sessions. 2000. DVD. Directed by Jack Johnson. Moonshine Conspiracy (440 060 091–9).

Ski Party. 1965. Directed by Alan Rafkin. American International Pictures. DVD release, 2003, MGM (1004484.1.B); packaged with *Muscle Beach Party*.

Slippery When Wet. 1958. Directed by Bruce Brown. Bruce Brown Films. DVD release, 1990 (ID8791OTDVD).

Sound of the Surf. Forthcoming. Directed by Thomas Duncan. www.sound-ofthesurf.com.

Soul Surfer. DVD. 2011. Directed by Sean McNamara. Sony Pictures Entertainment.

Storm Riders. 1981. Directed by David Lourie, Dick Hoole, and Jack McCoy. McCoy Films. DVD release, 2006.

Surfing for Life. DVD. 1999. Directed by David L. Brown.

Thicker Than Water. 2000. DVD. Directed by Jack Johnson, Chris Malloy, and Emmett Malloy. Poor Specimen.

Waveriders. 2008. Produced by Margo Harkin. Inís Films (UK and Ireland). DVD release, 2009, Element Pictures Distribution (EPDDVD09).

The Women and the Waves. 2009. Directed by Heather Hudson. Film Works Entertainment. DVD release, 2011.

Woodstock: 3 Days of Peace and Music. 1970. Directed by Michael Wadleigh. Warner Bros. DVD release, 1977, Warner Home Video.